Regent Motor Services, Church Gresley,

The Viking Coaches &
  Viking Motors (Burton) Ltd.
  Woodville and Burton upon Trent,

    &*

Victoria Motorways,
  Netherseal & Burton upon Trent,
 & Victoria Motorways Ltd.
  Woodville and Burton upon Trent

1919 - 1987

By H. N. Twells OBE

Designed & Published by H. N. Twells OBE

First Published 2005
© 2005 Harold Nelson Twells OBE

ISBN 978 0 9551963 0 0
ISBN 0 9551963 0 2

Note: Unless stated otherwise, all photographs in this book are either by the author,
or from his private collection where the source is unknown.
All other pictures are credited to the best extent possible, but should any mistakes have been made,
sincere apologies are tendered in advance and corrections should be sent to the author.

Printed in England by The Amadeus Press, Cleckheaton, West Yorkshire BD19 4TQ

Text set in 10pt Times by Highlight Type Bureau Ltd, Bradford, West Yorkshire BD8 7BY

Published by Harold Nelson Twells OBE
2 Chartwell Rise, Wingerworth, Chesterfield S42 6SU

Index of Contents:

Author's Introduction

The completion of this book fulfils a long held ambition which has its origins in the late 1940's and early 50's.

My personal interest in Viking Coaches dates from soon after the end of the 2nd World War, when my mother began organising coach trips to various seaside resorts at weekends during the summer months, and to shows at the Coventry Hippodrome, and Theatres Royal in Birmingham and Nottingham.. Whilst trips by train from Swadlincote were regularly available to a variety of destinations, they could not match the comfort and 'door-to-door' convenience provided by the private coach trip. Such was the travel attraction after the austere war years, that two and often three coaches were needed to transport the entourage to the popular destinations. A 6am start and we were soon reeling off the miles, and whichever destination was in sight, it was ..rollin.. rollin ! With Knutsford appearing to be half-way to virtually everywhere, the excitement started to build once the second stage of the journey was underway.

Inevitably, Blackpool was the most popular resort in the immediate post-war years, particularly when the Illuminations resumed, and past Kirkham RAF station, eyes were peeled to see who would be the first to spot Blackpool Tower - and inevitably there were many splurious sightings ! The exertions and enjoyment of the seaside and a 5pm or soon thereafter departure from wherever, saw us on the long and winding road home. Once in local territory, the half-awake last goodbyes were rolled out as the drivers did their best to drop people off as near to home as possible. Destinations added to the list included Sandringham and Hunstanton, Windsor, London, Rhyl, and New Brighton via the Mersey Tunnel.

In addition to mother's private hire, we also used Viking's weekly Blackpool service for the annual one-week holiday in the early 1950's, and for several years from 1962, also used the overnight service to Torquay.

A further involvement with Viking came after I became Hon.Secretary of The South Derbyshire Camera Club in 1961, with the organisation of photographic outings one of the responsibilities. Viking coaches provided the transport for photographic weekends in the 'English Lake District', with the Yorkshire Moors, Hereford and Wye Valley, amongst the other interesting destinations visited. The coaches were always full.

My interest in Viking therefore, is a very long standing and personal one with memories galore, and over the years I have taken and collected photographs of the coaches and other artefacts whenever the opportunity arose, in the hope that one day, a book such as this might be possible. My earnest wish is that this volume will help revive happy memories of two highly regarded local companies, Viking Motors and Victoria Motorways, which both contributed a great deal to the transport infrastructure and the people in South Derbyshire, Burton and Derby areas. The book also presents an opportunity to provide information on the first company with which, almost by chance, Mr. W. J. Lloyd became involved, namely 'Regent Motor Services', prior to him starting Viking Coaches.

I would like to take this opportunity to express my warmest thanks to Mr. John G. Lloyd, former Managing Director of Viking Motors and Victoria Motorways, who, when approached by me in 2001, readily agreed to assist in whatever way he could. I have enjoyed the meetings we have had and without his support, this volume would not have been possible.

May I also thank those who have supplied photographs, all of which have been acknowledged where origin is known. In addition to my own pictures, other un-attributed photographs have been purchased over a period of time from a number of sources including the superb Photobus collection, stall holders at various bus, tram and railway centres, and loaned by friends.

However, it would be re-miss of me not to mention a number of individuals and organisations who have been particularly helpful. My thanks are therefore extended to The PSV Circle, The Omnibus Society, The Kithead Trust, R.B.Hall Ltd., John Bennett and John Dixon, for their support in identifying vehicle and archive information; former Viking & Victoria employees, Roland King, the late Eric Nicholls, Ron Coleman, Stan Parkes, Arthur Prince, Malcolm Price, Brenda Veitch, Jane Musto, for their interest and assistance; former General Manager John Holmes, for his unique and immensely interesting hands-on account of the time he spent with Viking; to Keith West, Derek Wilkinson, David Stanier, Roy Marshall, Thomas Knowles, Philip Thomas, Peter Yeomans, the Magic Attic, and T.W.W.Moore, who have loaned or provided copies of photographs from their own collections; to Alan Condie for the loan of Victoria tickets; to former school colleagues Kath McLoughlin, Derek Kinsey and Geoff Topliss; and to long standing friends Rita Walton, Pat Warren, Noreen Jones, and Peter White. I greatly appreciate the support you have all extended to me. I hope you all enjoy this book.

Harold Nelson Twells OBE. October 2005

PLATE 1

The combined *'Viking Motors'* **&** *'Victoria Motorways'* **fleet assembled at the Company's Old Brewery Yard, High Street, Woodville in 1948, with the blossom on trees suggesting an early April date, and a Sunday morning, before any of the vehicles had departed.   Vehicle No. FA 8961** (No.7 in line-up) **had arrived new from Burlingham body builders in Blackpool, in March 1948.   However, three vehicles, two Viking coaches (VO 4066 & BR 8228), and one Victoria bus (FS 1762), are not in the line-up, and they may well have been the only vehicles on hire or on service on the day of the photograph.   The three vehicles were not disposed of by Viking or Victoria until after 1948.**

Note: the 1-21 numbers below indicate position of the vehicle from the LEFT – they are NOT vehicle fleet numbers.

1.	**FA 8883**	**AEC coach**		12.	FA 8791	Daimler bus
2.	FA 8167	AEC bus		13.	ADG 742	Albion PK115
3.	FA 8792	Daimler bus		**14.**	**GG 4946**	**Albion coach***
4.	**FA 7205**	**Albion coach**		15.	OV 9147	Maudsley bus
5.	**FA 5740**	**Albion coach**		16.	FA 8224	AEC bus
6.	ATE 79	Leyland bus		17.	ATE 78	Leyland bus
7.	**FA 8961**	**AEC coach**		18.	ARA 172	Leyland bus
8.	**FA 8882**	**AEC coach**		19.	VT 7065	T.S.M. bus
9.	**FA 6199**	**AEC coach**		20.	TF 3172	Leyland bus
10.	**FA 4960**	**Leyland coach**		21.	ATE 77	Leyland bus
11.	FA 8822	Daimler bus				

Viking vehicles in heavy type, the remainder Victoria.   ADG 742 has cream or white lower panels, which may have been the former owner's livery, with 'VICTORIA' added beneath the driver's window.

* GG 4946 transferred to Viking Motors fleet from Victoria Motorways in 1944.

Viking/Victoria Structure Chart

Records show that in 1919, three South Derbyshire businesses were either formed, or were already operating in one or more forms of transportation.   Mr. E. M. Sales, trading as Victoria Motorways, operated a taxi & bus service from the village of Netherseal, whilst Messrs. Clamp & Bailey, Church Gresley garage proprietors, also operated a taxi and a charabanc coach, which was used for tours and holiday trips.   The third business was started by a Mr. G. V. Dennis, who invited his brother-in-law, a Mr. W. J. Lloyd, to join him as a partner in the business of carrying goods around the area.   It is not known when Dennis and Lloyd started to operate as 'Regent Motor Services', but an LMS Railway Report in 1926, states that a Regent bus service between Church Gresley and Burton, via Swadlincote, commenced on 4 December 1924.

Whilst the primary purpose of this structure chart is to identify the significant dates in the history of each of the three companies from 1919 onwards, it is also intended to show how Mr. W. J. Lloyd's partnership with Mr. Dennis from 1919, was the start of a very successful involvement in helping to develop the bus and coach services in the South Derbyshire and Burton upon Trent areas, which eventually extended over 58 years.

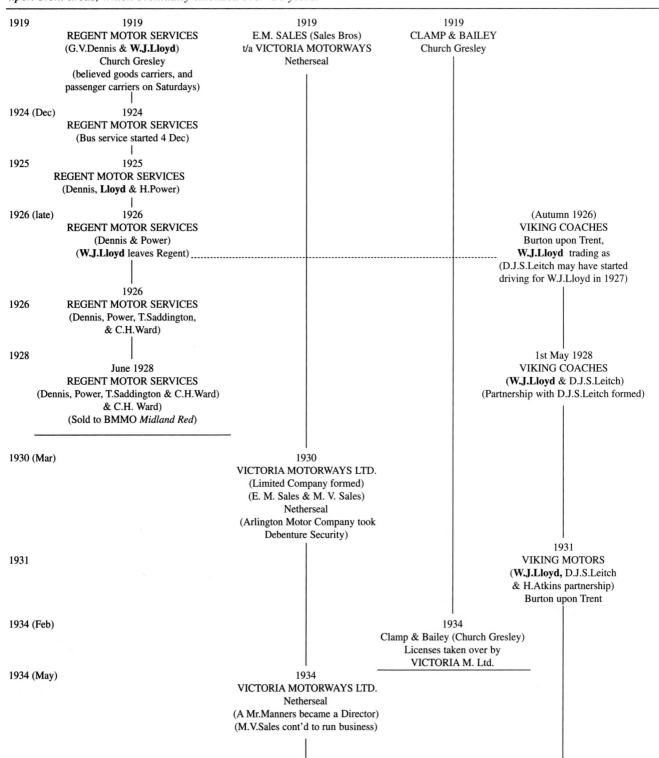

1919	1919 REGENT MOTOR SERVICES (G.V.Dennis & **W.J.Lloyd**) Church Gresley (believed goods carriers, and passenger carriers on Saturdays)	1919 E.M. SALES (Sales Bros) t/a VICTORIA MOTORWAYS Netherseal	1919 CLAMP & BAILEY Church Gresley	
1924 (Dec)	1924 REGENT MOTOR SERVICES (Bus service started 4 Dec)			
1925	1925 REGENT MOTOR SERVICES (Dennis, **Lloyd** & H.Power)			
1926 (late)	1926 REGENT MOTOR SERVICES (Dennis & Power) (**W.J.Lloyd** leaves Regent)			(Autumn 1926) VIKING COACHES Burton upon Trent, **W.J.Lloyd** trading as (D.J.S.Leitch may have started driving for W.J.Lloyd in 1927)
1926	1926 REGENT MOTOR SERVICES (Dennis, Power, T.Saddington, & C.H.Ward)			
1928	June 1928 REGENT MOTOR SERVICES (Dennis, Power, T.Saddington & C.H.Ward) & C.H. Ward) (Sold to BMMO *Midland Red*)			1st May 1928 VIKING COACHES (**W.J.Lloyd** & D.J.S.Leitch) (Partnership with D.J.S.Leitch formed)
1930 (Mar)		1930 VICTORIA MOTORWAYS LTD. (Limited Company formed) (E. M. Sales & M. V. Sales) Netherseal (Arlington Motor Company took Debenture Security)		
1931				1931 VIKING MOTORS (**W.J.Lloyd**, D.J.S.Leitch & H.Atkins partnership) Burton upon Trent
1934 (Feb)			1934 Clamp & Bailey (Church Gresley) Licenses taken over by VICTORIA M. Ltd.	
1934 (May)		1934 VICTORIA MOTORWAYS LTD. Netherseal (A Mr.Manners became a Director) (M.V.Sales cont'd to run business)		

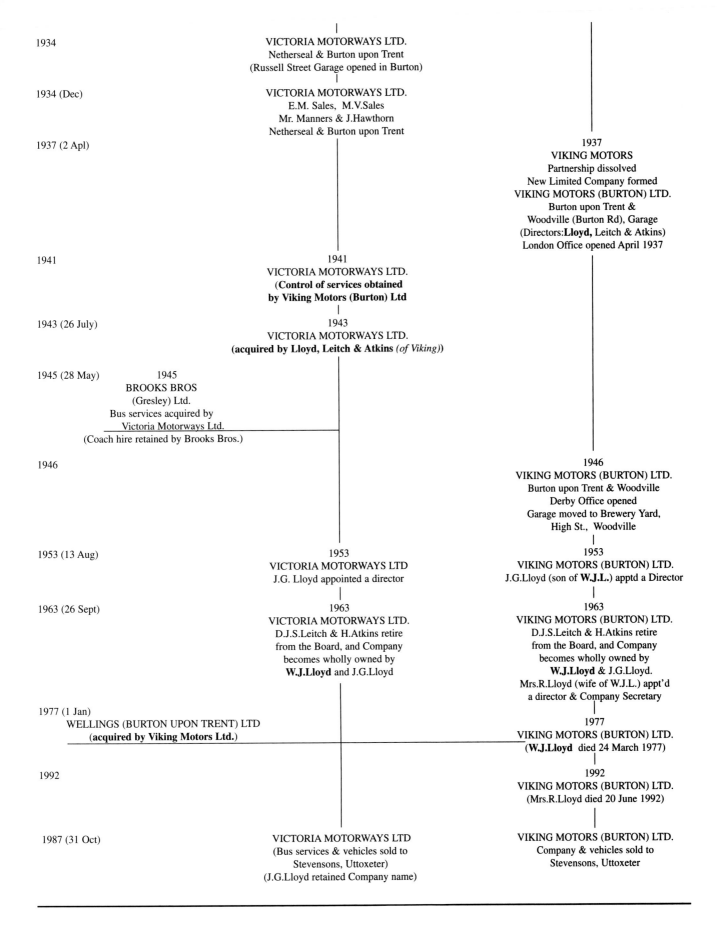

1934

VICTORIA MOTORWAYS LTD.
Netherseal & Burton upon Trent
(Russell Street Garage opened in Burton)

1934 (Dec)

VICTORIA MOTORWAYS LTD.
E.M. Sales, M.V.Sales
Mr. Manners & J.Hawthorn
Netherseal & Burton upon Trent

1937 (2 Apl)

1937
VIKING MOTORS
Partnership dissolved
New Limited Company formed
VIKING MOTORS (BURTON) LTD.
Burton upon Trent &
Woodville (Burton Rd), Garage
(Directors:**Lloyd,** Leitch & Atkins)
London Office opened April 1937

1941

1941
VICTORIA MOTORWAYS LTD.
**(Control of services obtained
by Viking Motors (Burton) Ltd**

1943 (26 July)

1943
VICTORIA MOTORWAYS LTD.
(acquired by Lloyd, Leitch & Atkins *(of Viking)***)**

1945 (28 May)

1945
BROOKS BROS
(Gresley) Ltd.
Bus services acquired by
Victoria Motorways Ltd.
(Coach hire retained by Brooks Bros.)

1946

1946
VIKING MOTORS (BURTON) LTD.
Burton upon Trent & Woodville
Derby Office opened
Garage moved to Brewery Yard,
High St., Woodville

1953 (13 Aug)

1953
VICTORIA MOTORWAYS LTD
J.G. Lloyd appointed a director

1953
VIKING MOTORS (BURTON) LTD.
J.G.Lloyd (son of **W.J.L.**) apptd a Director

1963 (26 Sept)

1963
VICTORIA MOTORWAYS LTD.
D.J.S.Leitch & H.Atkins retire
from the Board, and Company
becomes wholly owned by
W.J.Lloyd and J.G.Lloyd

1963
VIKING MOTORS (BURTON) LTD.
D.J.S.Leitch & H.Atkins retire
from the Board, and Company
becomes wholly owned by
W.J.Lloyd & J.G.Lloyd.
Mrs.R.Lloyd (wife of W.J.L.) appt'd
a director & Company Secretary

1977 (1 Jan)

WELLINGS (BURTON UPON TRENT) LTD
(acquired by Viking Motors Ltd.)

1977
VIKING MOTORS (BURTON) LTD.
(W.J.Lloyd died 24 March 1977)

1992

1992
VIKING MOTORS (BURTON) LTD.
(Mrs.R.Lloyd died 20 June 1992)

1987 (31 Oct)

VICTORIA MOTORWAYS LTD
(Bus services & vehicles sold to
Stevensons, Uttoxeter)
(J.G.Lloyd retained Company name)

VIKING MOTORS (BURTON) LTD.
Company & vehicles sold to
Stevensons, Uttoxeter

PLATE 2. *The first three directors of Viking Motors (Burton) Ltd. about to enjoy dinner. Mr. W. J. Lloyd, founder of 'The Viking Coaches', which later became 'Viking Motors (Burton) Ltd., is seen with Mrs. Lloyd and fellow directors, Mr. Horace Atkins (on right), and Mr. Don Leitch (on left) with Mrs. Leitch. The photograph is not dated, but the Christmas Greetings poster on the door behind Mr. Lloyd suggests the directors may have been hosting an employee Christmas dinner c.1950's.*

PLATE 3 (left)
A later photograph of Mr. W. J. (Bill) Lloyd. He remained a director until his passing on 24 March 1977.

PLATE 4 (right)
Mr. John Graham Lloyd, son of W.J.L., became an engineering apprentice with Daimler Motors Ltd., Coventry, and after a period of Army service, joined Altrincham Coachways, coach operators and dealers, gaining experience on both sides of the business. He moved from Altrincham to Birmingham Corporation Transport for further experience before joining Tudor Transport of Woodville, a lorry company with six vehicles, owned jointly by Mr. W.J. Lloyd and Mr. L. Insley. He joined the Viking and Victoria companies as a Director in 1953, and on the death of his father in 1977, became Managing Director of each company. He retained these appointments until 31st October, 1987, when the vehicles and business of Victoria Motorways, but not the company itself, together with the vehicles and the Viking Motors (Burton) Ltd. company name and business were sold.

Regent Motor Services 1919-1928

Mr. William J. Lloyd's involvement with motor transport began sometime after 1919, when he was invited to join Mr. G. V. Dennis as a partner in Regent Motor Services, at that time a goods carrier operating a Ford T with flat truck body. This early entry into the transport industry was the start of a long career in the lorry, bus and motor coach industries in the South Derbyshire and Burton upon Trent areas, which eventually covered a period of 58 years, until he passed away on 24th July 1977.

Mr. G. V. Dennis started his own transport business in 1919 with a Ford T lorry, which he used for delivering ice blocks from the Burton Pure Ice & Cold Storage Co. Ltd., factory at Bond End, Burton, to shops and pubs in the Burton and the South Derbyshire area, which required ice on a daily basis. He also carried other goods as opportunities arose around the area. Every Saturday, the Ford T was fitted with bench seats down both sides of the vehicle, so that it could be used as a bus to transport passengers from South Derbyshire to Burton and return. As this business became busier, Mr. Dennis was keen to buy another vehicle and expand, and he invited his brother-in-law, Mr. William J. Lloyd, to join him as a partner in running Regent Motor Services.

Mr. Lloyd lived in Moira and worked at nearby Donisthorpe Colliery as a 'Deputy', the mining term for the head of a group of miners working underground. He was taking his Under-Manager's Certificate when Mr. Dennis's invitation came, and was also considering emigrating to Australia on a £10. assisted passage scheme. Whilst it had appeared he and his wife were seriously considering a new life on the other side of the world, they decided to forgo that opportunity, and accepted Mr. Dennis's invitation to help

expand his transport activities, which it is believed was trading under the 'Regent' name. Mr. Lloyd contributed £100. to become a partner, and this allowed the purchase of a second vehicle.

Mr. Vic Dennis's home was at No. 106 Regent Street, Church Gresley, and the 'Regent' in the name of the company came from Regent Street, and not as has been suggested in more recent times, from the 'Regent Cinema' in Church Gresley. An open area behind No.106 was suitable as hard-standing for vehicles, and this became the 'Regent Garage' premises, with access gained through an archway above which was one of No.106's bedrooms.

The Ford T was fitted with a single forward gear and reverse, and when Ford produced a new gearbox with three forward gears and reverse, Mr. Dennis bought one to fit to the Ford T lorry. Mr. Lloyd recounted to his son, Mr. John G. Lloyd, that he and Vic Dennis worked all night to change the gearbox, taking great care to place the parts in a set order as they were removed from the vehicle, so that re-assembly would be relatively straight forward. However, after installing the new gearbox the vehicle was started up, and it quickly became apparent that it now had one forward and three reverse gears.

PLATE 5
The date of this photograph is not known, but the 'Regent' fleet name is flanked by the two words 'Safety Coach'. This may have been added to emphasise safe travel by bus, possibly resulting from the very unfortunate accident to one of the Burton-Ashby tramcars on 8th October 1919.

A 1926 LMS Railway report about the effect that bus competition in the South Derbyshire area was having on the LMS-owned Burton & Ashby Light Railways tram services, gives the 4 December 1923 as the date when Mr. V. Dennis (Regent) commenced running one bus between Woodville and Burton via Midway. The records of R. B. Hall Ltd., a Swadlincote printing firm, show that on the 17 December 1923, they supplied 25 printed timetable cards, size 14" x 11", headed 'Bus Service', with a second batch of 12 cards in March 1924, and a third batch of 20 in May that year. The report also records that a second Regent bus was in operation on the Woodville – Midway – Burton service from 24 April 1924, with increased service frequency from 4 December 1924.

On 11 August 1924, 50 timetable cards with eyelets for hanging, were printed for a 'Midway Bus Service', which it is believed ran between the Swadlincote Delph and Midway, to provide a connection with Regent's Woodville-Burton service.

Whilst the LMS Report records that Regent's service from the Boot Inn, Church Gresley, to Burton via Swadlincote and Newhall, commenced on 4 December 1924, the local printer's records for printed timetables supplied to G.V.Dennis (Regent), suggest this service may well have commenced in August 1924. An Order Book entry, No.40470 on the 25 August, indicates it was a first order for 1000 x 4page booklets printed 'Regent Bus Service', supplied at a cost of £1.15s.0d., with no previous order reference quoted in the order book. On the 29 October 1924, order No. 40647 was for a further 2000 x 4page timetable booklets, it being marked as a repeat of the earlier order No. 40470. The Regent timetable for the Gresley-Burton service (see Plate 7) shows Order No.40747 printed thereon, which identifies it as being one of 1000 printed on 9 December 1924, with a note in the order book indicating it was a repeat of the earlier 40647 order. The printed timetable order references therefore point very

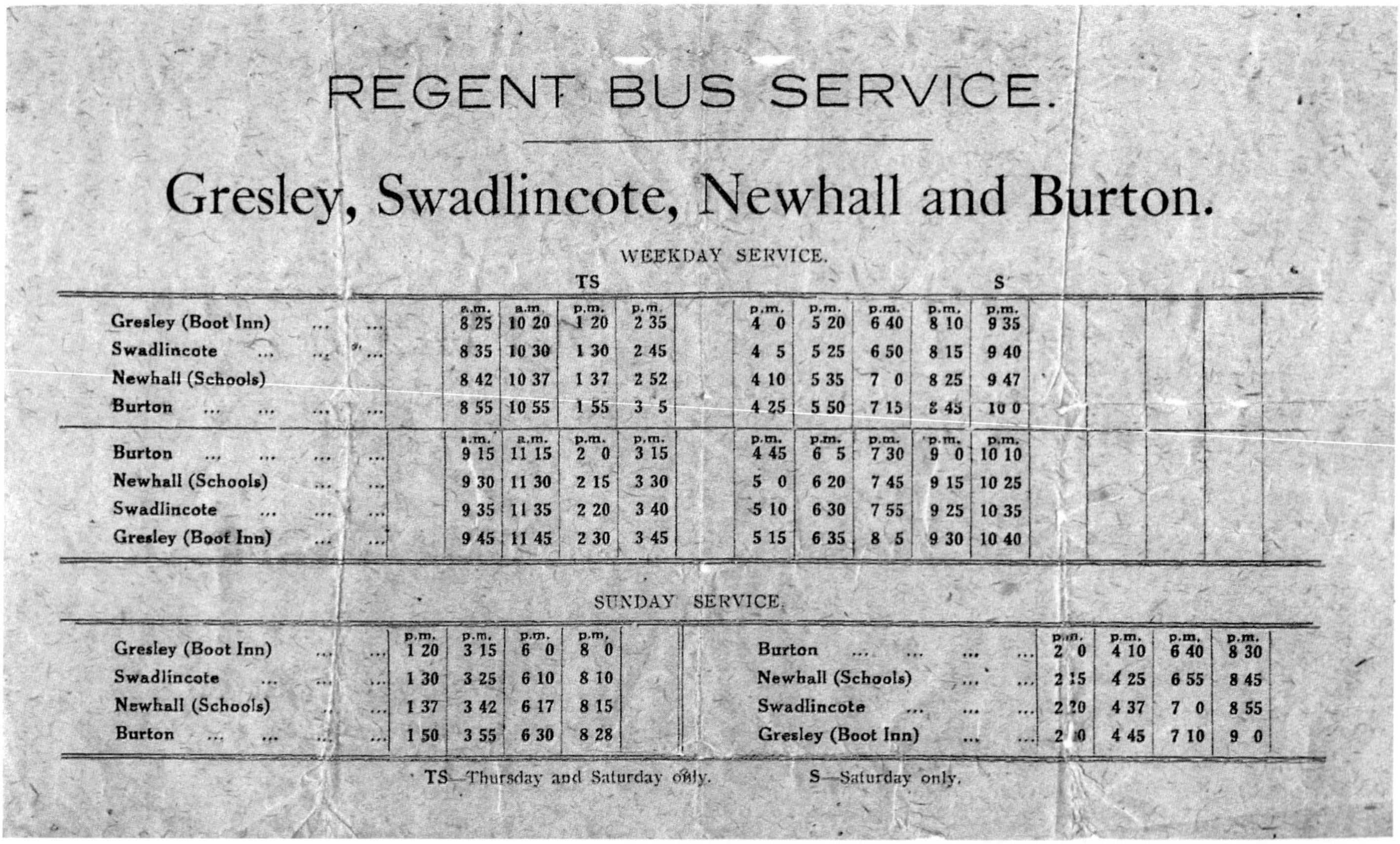

REGENT BUS SERVICE.

Gresley, Swadlincote, Newhall and Burton.

WEEKDAY SERVICE.

	TS				S				
	a.m.	a.m.	p.m.	p.m.	p.m.	p.m.	p.m.	p.m.	p.m.
Gresley (Boot Inn)	8 25	10 20	1 20	2 35	4 0	5 20	6 40	8 10	9 35
Swadlincote	8 35	10 30	1 30	2 45	4 5	5 25	6 50	8 15	9 40
Newhall (Schools)	8 42	10 37	1 37	2 52	4 10	5 35	7 0	8 25	9 47
Burton	8 55	10 55	1 55	3 5	4 25	5 50	7 15	8 45	10 0

	a.m.	a.m.	p.m.	p.m.	p.m.	p.m.	p.m.	p.m.	p.m.
Burton	9 15	11 15	2 0	3 15	4 45	6 5	7 30	9 0	10 10
Newhall (Schools)	9 30	11 30	2 15	3 30	5 0	6 20	7 45	9 15	10 25
Swadlincote	9 35	11 35	2 20	3 40	5 10	6 30	7 55	9 25	10 35
Gresley (Boot Inn)	9 45	11 45	2 30	3 45	5 15	6 35	8 5	9 30	10 40

SUNDAY SERVICE.

	p.m.	p.m.	p.m.	p.m.			p.m.	p.m.	p.m.	p.m.
Gresley (Boot Inn)	1 20	3 15	6 0	8 0	Burton		2 0	4 10	6 40	8 30
Swadlincote	1 30	3 25	6 10	8 10	Newhall (Schools)		2 15	4 25	6 55	8 45
Newhall (Schools)	1 37	3 42	6 17	8 15	Swadlincote		2 20	4 37	7 0	8 55
Burton	1 50	3 55	6 30	8 28	Gresley (Boot Inn)		2 30	4 45	7 10	9 0

TS—Thursday and Saturday only.   S—Saturday only.

PLATE 6

1000 copies of this original undated Regent timetable, described as a 4 page booklet (it was folded down the middle), were printed on 12 December 1924, at a cost of £1.8s.6d. (equiv. £1.42p). However, this was one of the third print run of this timetable. The first 1000 were printed on 25 August 1924, with a further 2000 copies on 29 October that year. The timings allow for one-vehicle in operation, and at morning and evening peak periods, it is probable one or more duplicate buses would be run to the timings shown.

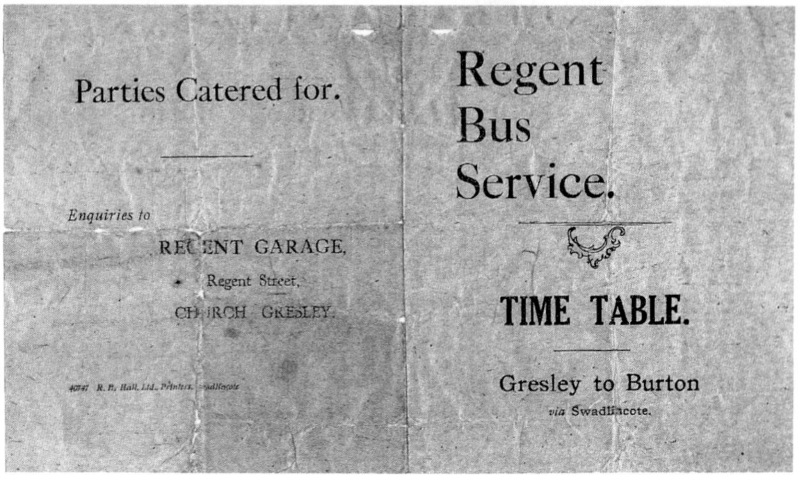

PLATE 7

The outside of the timetable, with the name of R.B.Hall Ltd., Printers, Swadlincote, with Order No. 40747.

Parties Catered for.

Enquiries to

RECENT GARAGE,
Regent Street,
CHURCH GRESLEY.

40747. R. B. Hall, Ltd., Printers, Swadlincote.

Regent Bus Service.

TIME TABLE.

Gresley to Burton
via Swadlincote.

markedly to a late August 1924 start date for Regent's Gresley-Burton service, it being extremely unlikely that Mr. Dennis would have wanted to have had the 1000 August and 2000 October batches of timetables printed months ahead of the service commencing.

The timetable schedule shown (Plate 6) was such that one vehicle could work the Gresley-Burton services throughout the day, including the additional services on Thursday and Saturdays. Similarly, one vehicle could operate the four Sunday services, commencing from Gresley at 1.20pm. Whilst this suggests only one vehicle was required, the vehicles could seat only 14 or 20 passengers, and it is probable that the convenience and attraction of the new bus services required one or more vehicles running as duplicates at peak times for each timetabled departure.

Unfortunately, despite extensive inquiries being made, there appears to be no record of buses purchased for the 20

December 1923 commencement of Regent's first service between Woodville and Burton, nor the second vehicle added in April 1924, nor for the start of the Gresley-Burton service in December 1924. Apart from the 1919 Ford T, the earliest vehicle data found to date is the May 1925 Reo Speed Wagon acquisition shown in the Regent Vehicle Listing (P14), and four more Reo buses added in 1925.

From the 9 April 1925, the Gresley – Burton service was extended from Burton Wetmore Park through to Union Street, Burton, and from 13 April 1925, the Gresley terminus was moved approximately one half mile beyond the Boot Inn on Market Street, to George Street, most probably to the wide area outside Gresley Colliery, which would have allowed vehicles to turn easily.

In 1925, a Mr. F. B. Power, who was married to Vic Dennis's sister, joined the Regent partnership, and he may well have bought his way into the partnership, particularly as five new Reo 14 seater buses joined the fleet during 1925 –

PLATE 8. *This vehicle is believed to be NU 7396, a Reo Speed Wagon model, new to Regent and first registered on 18 August 1925. The conductor (3rd from left) is Don Newbold.*

one each in May, June, August, October and November.

A sixth new bus joined the Regent fleet on 13 March 1926, all licensed by Swadlincote Urban District Council, and they are seen lined up in Plate 10.

Regent's route from the Gresley Colliery terminus was to the Boot Inn, then via Swadlincote Market Place, Swadlincote Railway Station, Newhall High Street, Wood Lane, Bretby Lane End, Burton Trent Bridge, Horninglow Street, Guild Street, and Union Street, Burton.

Printer's records in February 1928, indicate that 100 books of 12 tickets each, size 2¾" x 1⅜" , for 2d, 3d, 4d (pre-decimal pence) values, were produced as 'Discount tickets', suggesting that Regent were about to introduce such a ticketing scheme.   On 30 April 1928, a further 100 books of 'Discount tickets', for values of 1d, 1½d, 2d, 3d, 4d, 5d, were delivered.

From the commencement of Regent's first service between Woodville-Midway-Burton in December 1923, and the Church Gresley-Burton service from December 1924, Regent was a direct competitor of the Burton & Ashby Light Railways tram services between Burton, Newhall, Swadlincote, Woodville and Church Gresley.   The journey would have been faster by bus than by tramcar, and declining passenger loadings and inevitably revenues, was a major factor which led to tram service frequency being reduced.   In the years 1917-9 passenger journeys on the trams had exceeded 3 million per annum, yet the undertaking was still loss making, and such situation could not have continued without the substantial backing of the Midland Railway Company.   By 1922 tram passenger

numbers were down to around 2m. per annum, and by 1925, they had fallen to 1½m, with Regent and the Central buses operated by Parkes Garage (Swadlincote) Ltd., direct competitors to the trams.

The progressive loss of passengers from tram to bus operators from 1924 onwards, exacerbated by the trams being out of use during the 1926 General Strike, proved to be the decisive factor which resulted in closure of the tramway, the final day of operation being 19th February, 1927.   Records show that tram receipts for week 30 each year, reduced from £520.(1924), £338.(1925), to £88.(1926), and with increased competition from both Midland Red and Central buses on the Burton, Newhall, Swadlincote, Woodville, Ashby route, and from Regent between Gresley, Swadlincote & Burton, the tramway was left with no other option but to close.

Whilst Regent's journey time between Church Gresley and Burton can be seen in the accompanying timetable – 35mins – the tram journey time between Swadlincote and Burton was approximately 35 minutes, with a further ten minutes for the Gresley-Swadlincote section.

Train services between Swadlincote and Burton, operated by the Midland Railway (up to 31 Dec 1922) and by the LMS Railway (from 1 Jan 1923), were very poor, and no threat to the competition from Regent or the tram services, although the journey time by train was a much speedier 13 minutes between the two stations.   Castle Gresley railway station on the direct Burton to Ashby and Leicester route was the nearest to Church Gresley, approx ½ mile from Regent's George Street terminus.   The train

PLATE 9
This vehicle would appear to be the March 1926 arrival, NU 8612, when compared to the group of six in Plate 10. The conductor on the right is believed to be a Mr. Maurice Shuttleworth, whilst the driver's first name was Eric.....
Courtesy Burton Daily Mail Ltd., per 'The Magic Attic'

service was two trains to Burton before 9am, and one service from Burton to Castle Gresley at 5.43pm, again providing little or no competition for the more regular bus services despite the shorter journey times.

The Birmingham & Midland Motor Omnibus Co. Ltd., (Midland Red), with its activities spreading across the Midlands, had opened a garage in Tamworth on 1st February 1918, and when operators such as Regent introduced their services, the Midland Red were not long in providing competition. The exact date when they sent buses from the Tamworth garage to operate a new service between Ashby-de-la-Zouch and Burton upon Trent, via Woodville, Swadlincote and Newhall, in direct competition to the Burton–Ashby tramway, is not known, but it may well have been in response to the commencement of Regent's Woodville-Midway-Burton service from 20 December 1923. The Midland Red operational technique appears to have been to run their bus a minute or so ahead of the tram or other operator's bus, hoping to capture waiting passengers. Such practice, taken to its extreme, was no doubt intended to run competitors out of business.

Regent's strength lay in the fact that it operated the first bus service between Woodville-Midway-Burton, and the only bus service between Church Gresley and Swadlincote, and passengers derious of getting into and out of Burton, were unlikely to want to switch buses to or from Midland Red in Swadlincote in great numbers. It is suggested that Church Gresley 'locals' were more likely to support Regent, the local operator, rather than one from outside the area.

When Midland Red opened a garage in Coalville on 6th December 1925, operation of the Ashby-Burton service was transferred from Tamworth to the Coalville garage.

Mr. Lloyd decided to leave Regent in the second half of 1926, to set up his own transport business in Burton, operating from a rented garage at 30 Union Street, and after successfully starting the business, it is believed he was joined by a Mr. D.J.S.Leitch soon afterwards. A January 1928 entry in Mr. W. J. Lloyd's diary indicates that a new partnership with Mr. Leitch, trading as 'Lloyd & Leitch', would commence on 1 May 1928.

Some time after Mr. Lloyd's departure in 1926, Mr. Dennis brought two additional partners into Regent. A Mr. T. Saddington (Hay & Straw Merchant), and a Mr. C. H. Ward (Baker), both of Swadlincote, became partners in Regent, with their probable financial investment being used to finance the payment to Mr. Lloyd of his share of the value of the business, as well as ensuring Regent would be able to continue to operate.

Late spring in 1928 brought a proposal from The Birmingham & Midland Motor Omnibus Co. Ltd. (Midland Red) whose Registered Office was at 88, Kingsway, London, to purchase the Regent service. The proposal was obviously acceptable to the Regent partners, and the first of two legal documents to be signed was "An Agreement for the sale of Goodwill", dated 8th June, 1928. The second legal document, an Assignment concluded on the 30th June, 1928, was the document under which the BMMO completed the purchase of the *"....goodwill of 'The Regent Motor Service' including all motor omnibus services now operated or maintained by the Vendors (Regent)."* As with all legal documentation, the two agreements indicate that BMMO having..*"....investigated the title of the Vendors to the said goodwill hereby accepts the same".*

The standing of Regent Motor Services over the period 1919-1928, in establishing a good service between Church Gresley and Burton, can be gauged by the fact that the price paid by BMMO for the rights to the one service, was £1,800., a rather princely sum in 1928.

The legal documentation also included a Restrictive Covenant to prevent the Vendors (Regent Motor Service partners), *"...carrying on a business as motor omnibus proprietors or any similar business or to operate motor omnibus services or carry passengers in motor omnibuses or charabancs by private treaty or on advertised tours or trips in the said town of Church Gresley or within a distance of eighty miles from the Swadlincote Town Hall west and south and fifty miles north and east and also that the Vendors will not at any time either alone or jointly or in partnership with or as agent or manager for any other person or persons and either directly or indirectly carry on or be concerned or interested in or assist any other person or persons to carry on or be concerned or obtain any interest in the business of a motor omnibus proprietor in the said town of Church Gresley or within eighty miles........and fifty miles........direction."*

The 80 mile restriction effectively blanketed the greater part of the Midland Red company's established territory, which covered its Birmingham stronghold and permeation across the Midland counties, including Leicestershire, Warwickshire, Worcestershire, and Staffordshire.

However, the 50 mile restriction *'north and east'* was effectively ignored by Mr. G.V.Dennis when he moved from Church Gresley to West Bridgford – 25 miles away - and started up the Robin Hood coach business in Nottingham.

The two agreements also state that …*"Nothing herein contained shall prevent the Vendors either collectively or individually from carrying on a business either by themselves or in partnership with any other person or as members of any firm or Company as Garage Proprietors or dealers in motor cars or their accessories or from entering into the service of any person firm or Company carrying on any of the said businesses.*

The two 1928 agreements indicate that the Regent Motor Service was owned at that time by four partners: George Victor Dennis (Motor Engineer), Felix Brannock Power (Motor Engineer), Charles Henry Ward (Baker) and Tom Saddington (Hay and Straw Merchant). (C.H.Ward and T.Saddington both had businesses in Swadlincote).

Data published on the Regent fleet by 'The PSV Circle', suggests that the first Regent bus was a Ford T, purchased by Regent in 1919, and disposed of in 1928, and as indicated in the early part of this section, a Ford T was used as a lorry, with seats added at weekends for bus operation. The Ford T appears to have been purposely omitted from the 1926 line-up of Regent buses (Plate 10) perhaps because of its aged appearance.

An announcement in the Railway Gazette for 17th September 1926 provides a final epitaph to the success of Regent's bus services between Church Gresley and Burton. It states: *"The Burton & Ashby Light Railway is to be abandoned. The metals are shortly to be removed and the overhead wires taken down. This step is attributed to motor omnibus competition in the district."*

Exterior and interior views of a 24-seater low load-line Garner saloon bus.

The accompanying two illustrations appeared in the 2 November 1926 Commercial Motor magazine, and show one of two Garner bodied buses supplied to Regent Motor Services (No. OP700). The article states: *"The low load-line passenger vehicle has now won a large measure of public support, with the result that models of this type are now being produced in increasing numbers by almost all commercial vehicle makers"*. The two photographs show a bus *"... which incorporate this characteristic of low loading* (supplied by) *Henry Garner Ltd., Tyseley, Birmingham ... to Regent Motor Services of Church Gresley. The bus is a good example of modern bus construction which incorporates features which make for safe and comfortable travel"*. The chassis was a standard Garner low-loading model fitted with four-wheel brakes and shod with 20inch x 6inch Dunlop S.S. cord tyres, with twin rears. The bus could reach a speed of 40mph on the level, and is reported as *"... possessing highly efficient capabilities when hilly country is being negotiated"*. Externally, the vehicle was similar to Regent's standard saloon uses with fixed side windows, above which were long rectangular ventilators. *"This purchaser of the vehicle decided to dispense with the usual one-man-operated type door at the forward end on the near side, and instead to have a door in the partition between the driving cab and passenger compartment, thus separating the two sections"*. The passenger compartment was divided into two, the part at the rear being intended for smokers, and there was an emergency door in the back panel. The semi-bucket seats faced forward with the exception of two longitudinal seats fitted above the rear wheel arches, with all seats upholstered in good quality leather, and grab handles at the back of each transverse pair of seats. *"The interior ... is stained in light and dark shades of oak..."*. Two shallow steps lead to the platform level of the body. The second Garner (No. OP12788), was of similar general design and construction, but had drop side windows instead of the fixed glass with ventilators above.

Courtesy 'The Commercial Motor Magazine'.

PLATE 10
Six American Reo vehicles seen on waste ground alongside Market Street, Church Gresley, on land which was later landscaped and became Gresley Park – the Maurice Lea Memorial Park. The vehicles from the left are as follows: NU 8612, NU 7946, NU 7672, NU 6652, NU 7396, NU 6277. The registration date of NU 8612 suggests the photograph was taken after mid-March 1926. L-R – Mr.V.Dennis, Mr.W.J.Lloyd, Mr.H.Power, partners in Regent, are seen with other employees, including Don Newbold, a conductor, (2nd from right). Don later joined Viking. NU 8612 is in pristine condition, particularly the number plate, compared to the other five vehicles in 'used service condition', and with the personnel smartly attired, the picture was probably taken on the Sunday morning after NU 8612's arrival.

REGENT MOTOR SERVICES – List of Vehicles

This summary of vehicles known to have been owned by Regent Motor Services, has been compiled from research by PSV Circle members and the Circle's Fleet History publication PD18, one of a series detailing the bus and coach fleets of operators around the United Kingdom. The author wishes to thank The PSV Circle for their permission to include the information in this publication.

Regn No.	Type		Body by:	Seating	New in:	To Regent	Date W/drawn	Pre-Regent owners & disposal
1919								
?	Ford T		?	B14-	?/19	?/19	?/28	disposal not traced
1920-24								
The only vehicle known to have been operated between 1920-24 is the Ford T recorded above								
1925								
NU 6277	REO Speed wagon		?	B14	5/25	11/5/25	14/10/30	Reg'n Area t'fd Northants to Oxon
NU 6652	REO	"	?	B14	6/25	5/6/25	2/32	Brewin & Hudson, and Holmes & Hudson v.2/32
NU 7396	REO	"	Harrison	B14	8/25	18/8/25	29/1/32	Flint to Cheshire
NU 7672	REO	"	Harrison	B14	10/25	2/10/25	12/5/28	Northants to Bucks Reg. Void 1930's
NU 7946	REO Major		?	B20	11/25	23/11/25	3/12/28	to Warwicks. Reg. Void 11/38
1926								
NU 8612	REO Pullman		Harrison	B20	3/26	13/3/26	23/7/28	Crisp, Northwold. Reg. Void 2/40
OP 700	Garner LP		Garner	B24F	?/26	?/26	?	disposal not traced
OP 1278	Garner LP		Garner	B24F	9/26	?/26	?/28	New as Garner demonstrator vehicle To Green, Wymeswold
1928								
The following two vehicles are listed in PD18 as delivered to Regent Motor Services, but the individual registration records show both registered in Mr. W.J.Lloyd's name, not Regent Motor Services.								
UT 2176	Chevrolet LO		Willard	B14-	1/28	1/28	10/28	To unidentified Hertfordshire operator
HE 3701	REO Sprinter		?	B14-	1/28	?/28	?/28	New to Newton, Barnsley To Wileman & Hart, Donisthorpe ?/28, LL 6/31

Regent's services and goodwill were sold to The Birmingham & Midland Motor Omnibus Co.Ltd., on 30th June 1928, but the vehicles were not purchased by 'Midland Red'.

'The Viking Coaches';   The Lloyd-Leitch Partnership, & Viking Motors (Burton) Ltd.   1926-1987

The precise date when Mr. W. J. Lloyd left Regent Motor Services is not known, but in a speech to Swadlincote Rotary Club in the 1960's, he recalled that... "...in 1926 I decided to go on my own, so I bought an Albion coach with pneumatic tyres and four speed gear box, and started a Blackpool service, working night and day driving, cleaning, etc., operating as 'The Viking Coaches".   He also added that he had gone to the Birmingham office of Albion Motors, and knocked on the office door, and when it was answered and asked what he wanted – he said "I would like to buy a coach please ! ".   His original diary for the year 1927 suggests he was operating one coach and most probably one car as a taxi by January 1927.   However, given the level of activity recorded in January 1927, it is now evident his departure from Regent was in late summer 1926.   The Lloyd-Leitch partnership, trading as 'Viking Coaches', was formed on 1st May 1928, with registration of Viking Motors (Burton) Ltd., at Companies House on 2nd April 1937.

Section 1 – 1926 to 1966

The origin of the 'Viking' company name has intrigued many minds over the years, but Mr. W. J. Lloyd always stated he adopted it from the Albion 'Viking' chassis type which, with a body built by W.D.Smith of West Bromwich, was delivered in May 1927.   Mr. Lloyd's 1927 diary records an Albion chassis No. 5037F, and engine No. 25037F.   It has been established that these relate to the first coach No.RA 2838, and this vehicle is shown below, albeit with blank numberplate.

Mr. Lloyd started his business from a rented asbestos lock-up garage in Union Street, Burton, which he purchased c.1955.   The asbestos structure was replaced by a larger brick garage with office accommodation, which remained in company ownership as The Central Garage until November 1987.

After leaving Regent in 1926, the first vehicle purchased by Mr. Lloyd is believed to have been a lorry, used to collect ash and other waste materials from factories in the Birmingham area. Lorry cartage would have provided a regular cash flow in the early months following Mr. Lloyds departure from Regent, but it is not known whether any additional lorries were operated in the later 1920's. However, it is known that by the start of the Second World War, a fleet of 16 lorries carrying the name of Viking Motors, was operated by the Company.

Prior to the launch of Viking, a high proportion of the seasonal holiday traffic from the Burton area was to the various coastal resorts, particularly in Lancashire and North Wales, which had long been the preserve of the Midland Railway up to 1922, and from 1923 onwards, the LMS and LNE Railways.   In 1921, Messrs. 'G. W. Wellings', a firm of funeral directors who would have been well-known across the Burton area, commenced a charabanc coach business with two vehicles, and ran a regular summer service to Skegness, with tours and private hire to other locations.   They started to make inroads into holiday traffic from the town and this may well have been the catalyst which led Mr. Lloyd to leave Regent and start the Viking Coaches business.

PLATE 11. *Mr. W.J. Lloyd's first Viking coach, registration believed to be RA 2838, an Albion 'Viking' PN26 type chassis, with a W.D.Smith of West Bromwich body, photographed near the factory, prior to delivery in May 1927.   The Viking Motors name was adopted from the chassis type.*

PLATE 12. *This group of vehicles seen near Woodville Tollgate, was assembled to transport 90 members of the Woodville Womens Unionist Association to Buxton in July 1927. The first vehicle is Mr. Lloyd's first Viking coach RA 2838, the second is a Victoria bus, possibly REO No.UT 1173 (new 6/27), whilst the third bus is a Regent Safety Coach , believed to be NU 8612. An entry in Mr.Lloyd's 1927 diary for 74 passengers into Derbyshire, suggests the date may have been 26 July.*

1927

The 1927 diary provides a remarkable and quite unique insight into Mr. Lloyd's early business activities, and on the first day of 1927, Saturday, 1st January, there is reference to Alton Towers, with four customer names and a suggestion of up to ten passengers booked. Individual name entries may well refer to a taxi booking. Saturday, 15th January, records nine names and locations, some with 3 or 2 alongside, suggesting these were the number of seats booked. A destination is not recorded. On 19th January, two destinations are recorded – Alton (Towers) & Stratford – which suggests a requirement for either two vehicles, or possibly 6 ! Alongside '4 to Alton' the number 72 is shown – could this be four vehicles each carrying 18 passengers, perhaps using four hired vehicles, from say Regent ?

Thursday, 27th January suggests 26 passengers booked: 30th January suggests 19 passengers booked, with the same numbers also shown on 31st January, and inclusion of 'wk' (week) and 'fortnight' believed to relate to holiday bookings for Blackpool.

An entry on Wednesday 9th February refers to an 'AJS' HM 7720, with frame and engine number recorded, suggesting the purchase of a motor cycle.

On Friday 18th February there is a first reference to an Austin 'Essex', a limousine type vehicle, which the diary record suggests was in frequent use as a taxi.

Many of the early 1927 entries suggest bookings were being taken for a planned weekly Blackpool service during the summer season, and two diary entries provide an interesting insight into Mr. Lloyd's advance planning. The 10 March entry records the number of seats vacant on each of four Saturdays in July and August, whilst a 22 March entry, states *'See A.Hart re Blackpool'*. Mr. A. Hart operated one coach from a garage in Donisthorpe, and he also took bookings for Viking's Blackpool service, saving people the problem of walking from Measham, Donisthorpe, Moira to

Gresley to book their seats. Passenger numbers for Blackpool exceeded one 26 seat coach load on the following dates – 23 July *(44 + 9x^1/$_2$)*, 6 Aug *(45 + 6x^1/$_2$)*, 13 Aug *(44 + 4x^1/$_2$)*, 27 Aug *(40 + 4x^1/$_2$)* and 3 Sept *(40 + 2x^1/$_2$)*, and whilst it is not known who provided the vehicle for the excess load, it would not have been anyone in the immediate area.

Unfortunately, the diary is silent between 29th March and 20th May 1927, but thereafter, a wide range of bookings have been recorded. The weekly summer season Blackpool service commenced on Saturday 2nd July and ran through to 10th September. After this date, coaching activity appears to have been much reduced to the end of 1927.

Unfortunately, whilst the diary does not record the cumulative value of fares taken for the inaugural Blackpool seasonal service, the fare was 11/- return. The first season's passenger numbers suggest it would have been considered a very successful introduction. Analysis of the ten week Blackpool service bookings shows the following passenger figures:

Day passengers	*327*
marked 'wk'	*16*
'fort'	*40*
'3 wks'	*1*
Total passengers	*384*

1928

The opening entry on 1st Jan 1928 lists several towns between Glasgow and Preston, with a fare of 33/- per person, this probably being a quotation rather than a booking.

The diary entry for Thursday 5th January, 1928 is very interesting, inasmuch as it refers to Lewis & Crabtree, Heywood, Manchester (name also in the back pages of the 1927 diary) and 'Built for Fieldsends Salford', with OX 4006, a 1927 Birmingham registration number recorded. This may have been a vehicle which was offered to Viking, and the reason for Mr. Lloyd's diary entry, but there is no record of it being purchased by him.

Some further interesting information identified from official vehicle registration records, indicates that two buses originally recorded as delivered to Regent Motor Services in early 1928, were in fact registered in the personal name of Mr. W. J. Lloyd, and not Regent. These were a Chevrolet with 14 seat Willard bus body, Reg. UT 2176, delivered new in January 1928, whilst the second, Reg. HE 3701, was a second-hand Reo Sprinter with 14 seater bus body, new to Newton of Barnsley in January 1928, and transferred to Mr. W. J. Lloyd later in 1928. Little else is known about these two vehicles, and as there is no reference to either in Mr. Lloyd's diaries, could it be that Mr. Lloyd loaned funds for the purchase of the two vehicles, for Regent to operate ? The Chevrolet is recorded as sold in October 1928 to Wileman & Hart of Donisthorpe and was last licensed in June 1931, whilst ownership of the Reo Sprinter was transferred to an Hertfordshire operator during 1928.

A significant diary entry on Sunday 8 January, 1928 states - *"Partnership to commence May 1st 1928"* - and whilst this indicates the date when Mr. Donald J. S. Leitch would join Mr. Lloyd to officially form the new *"Lloyd-Leitch partnership, trading as 'Viking Coaches',* it is

believed he worked for Mr. Lloyd in early 1927 as an employee. Mr. Leitch was married to the sister of Mr. E. M. Sales, operator of the *'Victoria Motorways'* country bus service from a garage in Netherseal, Leicestershire.

Bookings recorded for the first four months of the 1928 diary suggest that only one coach was being operated. However, on Saturday 19 May, bookings for two coaches are recorded: one coach plus a car for a trip to Dale Abbey, and another coach for a trip to Long Eaton. This suggests that by 19 May Viking had taken delivery of their new six cylinder Albion PK26 coach, No. FA 3271, recorded as delivered in May 1928. (Plate 13)

This coach had a substantially-constructed 26 seat coach body by Dixons, West Bromwich, with a ³/₄ length canvas hood fitted over the roof framework, and whilst the body was fully weather proof, when good weather conditions permitted, the canvas could be removed and the windows wound down converting it into a virtual open-top charabanc. The name *'The Viking Coaches'* was carried within a garter circle on the coach sides and most probably on the rear panel also, with ownership lettered on both sides as *'Lloyd & Leitch, Central Garage, Burton upon Trent'*. A top speed of 12 mph was lettered on the coach sides, but

PLATE 13
FA 3271 was new to Viking in May 1928. The garter circle has 'The Viking Coaches' within, and 'Lloyd & Leitch, Central Garage, Burton on Trent' lettering on the lower side panel. The livery is not known, but it may have been red or dark red with cream waist band. The significance of the (6) lettered on the print is not known. Mr. Leitch is in the driving seat. This substantially constructed chara-banc was on a bus chassis with straight frame at the rear, with no space for a boot. The lack of luggage space may have been the reason for its disposal after only 10 months with Viking.

observing such speed would have required between 7 and 8 hours for the 100 mile journey to Blackpool, including convenience stops. In practice, the journey was nearer six hours, suggesting 'speeding' on the open road was unavoidable ! Tours to other coastal resorts and notable centres were also run, and on one occasion when Mr. Lloyd was driving the coach in the Lincoln area, he was stopped by police for speeding, and prosecuted, resulting in a 'fifty shillings' fine (equiv. £2.50p) !

Vehicle registration records indicate that FA 3271 was sold by Viking in February 1929, and it was purchased by the Sandwell Motor Company, Birmingham during March that year.

The 1928 Birmingham pantomine season saw Viking providing the vehicle for several groups from the Burton area, as well as hirings by several public houses for visits to football matches at Derby County, Birmingham City, Aston Villa and Leicester City. Other groups were attracted to race meetings at Uttoxeter, Bromford Bridge (Birmingham) and Loughborough. The availability of more than one coach from May 1928 onwards attracted larger private hire assignments.

The 1928 diary does not record the same level of bookings as those recorded for 1927. Whilst there is no specific reference to there being a weekly summer season Blackpool service in 1928, continuing what appears to have been a very successful service in 1927, entries on 27 May 1928 refer on several occasions to 'wk' bookings, suggesting these may have been for Blackpool.

Bookings recorded on Saturdays 11 & 25 August and 1st September, are also believed to be for Blackpool, whilst those recorded on Saturdays, 8th 15th, 22nd of September, show one day, a week, and two week duration bookings for the Lancashire seaside resort.

Notes in the 1928 end-pages make reference to a 1924 Austin, and an Hillman All Weather vehicle, both of which were probably used as taxis, together with a list of contacts for local authorities in Leamington Spa, Skegness, Llandudno and Blackpool.

1929
A list of points recorded on 1 January 1929 relate to vehicle items, and include reference to faults. Later entries on 7

PLATE 14

This Albion PNC26 type chassis with 26 seat charabanc body by W.J.Smith, No.FA 3518, was delivered new in February 1929, most probably as replacement for the boot-less FA 3271 referred to in Plate 13. The smiling gentleman is Don Newbold, who was a very popular Viking driver until retirement. He also took on the conductor role when required.

March - *'coach to Dixons'* - and on 16 March -*'coach ready ? '* – suggest the coach being checked over by Dixons before being disposed of. PSV publication PD18 records disposal of a vehicle as *'Unidentified Albion 5/29'*, which suggests this was probably the 1928 Albion FA 3271.

Two Albion PNC26 type vehicles, one with 26 seat coach body by Smiths, were purchased new by 'Viking' in 1929, the first, No. FA 3518 (Plate 14) delivered in February, and the second FA 3760 by Dixon, in May that year. These two vehicles were operated by the Company for seven and five years respectively, with FA 3518 sold in April 1936 to a Cannock based operator, whilst the other vehicle was sold in October 1934.

The first of several large lorries was purchased in 1929, this being a ten ton vehicle with solid tyres, for carrying salt-glazed ware from Moira Pottery and other South Derbyshire manufacturers to the London area. Mr. Lloyd's 1960's Rotary Club speech included reference to a lorry ending up in the ditch, resulting in 10 tons of jam jars - not in crates – being scattered down the side of the road. On another occasion the driver found a runaway boy on the lorry when

it arrived in Derby. Overnight return loads, principally of fruit from London's Covent Garden wholesale market, were for Johnson Bros, wholesale fruit merchants in Derby, who stipulated delivery by 4.30am, to ensure supplies were in good time for the market opening at 6.00am. As the lorry fleet increased, clay ware from Moira pottery and other South Derbyshire manufacturers, was carried to many different parts of the country.

The 1929 diary is unfortunately silent for the period 5 Jan to 18 Feb, but after this date, a wide range of destinations and passenger information has been recorded. There appears to have been no shortage of passengers for the winter season pantomime shows, particularly as telephone numbers of four Birmingham theatres – *Empire* – *Prince of Wales* – *Theatre Royal* – *Hippodrome* - are recorded on 3 January 1929. Between 20 February and 6 March, there are seven 'Panto' trips recorded. One coach of 24 passengers to Llandudno on Good Friday, 29 March, a party of 26 on Saturday 30 March to an un-stated destination; and two coaches carrying 41 to Stourbridge & Worcester on Easter Monday, 1 April, made for a busy

PLATE 15
This vehicle is believed to have been the second new Albion PNC 26 type, with 26 seat charabanc body by Dixon of West Bromwich, delivered in May 1929. Registered FA 3760, it remained with Viking until October 1934. Mr.W. J.Lloyd is alongside Don Leitch, and a Mr. Bernard Whysart of the Dog & Partridge Hotel, Tutbury.

weekend. The Easter Monday booking was from the Rising Sun Inn in Woodville, and the fare of 13/- included dinner (lunch) in Worcester at 1pm, and tea taken in the Birmingham area at 5pm. A note of food items for the day is recorded.

On the 6 May, three coaches appear to have been booked for a trip to Stoke, but a 6/- fare and sum of £12.0.0. suggests there being forty passengers, which could be accommodated on two coaches. An entry on 7 May simply states 'Albions', and this appears to relate to a note on 9 May – 'Coach to Dixons 7th poss.', with various parts of a vehicle listed, presumably requiring attention.

Seventeen dates in 1929 are marked 'Blackpool', with 'wk' marked against passenger names on four further summer dates, suggesting these too were 'Blackpool' service dates. Analysis of passenger numbers show duration of journey:

Total (each ½ counted as 1)	465	marked 'wk'	177
		'Fort' (fortnight)	12
		'3 wks'	2
		unmarked (Day)	274
			465
		(incl. 37 half-fares)	

Amounts recorded as 'BT' (Blackpool Takings) totalled :

May	22.10.0.	)
June	74. 3.0.	)
July	123. 8.0.	)
August	285.14.0.	)
September	166.10.0.	)
October	166.15.0.	)
Total	£839. 0.0.	Average fare - £1.16.0d
		(£1.80 dec.)

Only 14 bookings were recorded for the final three months of 1929.

1930 onwards

Company records for 1930 and subsequent years have not been found, and therefore, detailed operational information is not available.

Mr. Lloyd told Rotarians that the Road Traffic Act came into force in 1930, and the general view was that operators could almost automatically carry on with operations as before, but no expansion could take place without the sanction of The Traffic Commissioners. He further commented that '...any application to do anything different brought forth a rush of objectors from British Railways and other operators'. 'It was essential to have legal representation for everything you did and it must have been a gold mine for the legal profession.' 'In spite of all this we still managed to keep the wolf from the door and really it was the best thing that ever happened to us, because it eliminated wasteful competition and we had a protected industry.'

Opposition to the Traffic Commissioner role came from local councils, who had been responsible for issuing hackney carriage plates to licence a vehicle for its area, and also licensing drivers and conductors to operate in their area.

The following information on 'backing' licences issued by the North Western Traffic Area, which were initially issued for a twelve month period, has been kindly supplied by John Dixon of Offerton, Stockport.

Licence codes applicable to Viking licences were as follows:
D - West Midlands Traffic Area:
C - North Western Traffic Area:
L - Lloyd (operator name):
E - East Midlands Traffic Area:
E – Express Service: **E&T** – Excursion & Tours

Lic. Appln	Granted	Lic. type	From:	Lic. surrendered
DCL13 William John Lloyd (t/a **Viking Coach Co.**),				
Central Garage, Union St., Burton				
17.6.31	6.2.32	E	Burton upon Trent	
			– Blackpool	2.10.37
17.6.31	6.2.32	E&T	from Burton upon Trent	2.10.37
22.7.33	21.10.33	E&T	from Burton upon Trent	
ECL170 W.J.Lloyd, D.Leitch, H.Atkins (t/a **Viking Motors**),				
(same address)				
7.9.35	9.11.35	E&T	from Woodville	
12.9.36	31.10.36	E&T	from Woodville	surrendered
			(re-submitted appln)	11.9.37
DCL521 Viking Motors (Burton) Ltd. (same address)				
29.5.37	25.9.37	E&T	from Burton upon Trent	

PLATE 16
The vehicle is believed to be FA 4960, a Leyland TS4 type chassis, with an H.V.Burlingham 30 seat half-cab coach body, delivered new to Viking in January 1933. A number of Viking coaches carried the 'Blackpool Service' lettering above the side windows, which were provided with the added luxury of curtains. This vehicle, seen in the 'antique red and tan' livery, remained in service with Viking until September 1953.

PLATE 17
FA 5740, an Albion PV70 with Burlingham 31 seat coach body, delivered new to Viking in April 1935, continuing in Viking service until disposal in July 1951. Unfortunately, the driver's name is not known.

PLATE 18 (below)
Another superb H.V. Burlingham bodied coach. FA6199, AEC Regal chassis with 32 seat body, remained with Viking until disposal in February 1952. The coach had luggage space beneath the rear seats, and the raised roof section provided some additonal space for cases. A row of retractable steps was provided at the rear end. Cases carried 'on top' were protected from the worst of the weather by a heavy duty waterproof tarpaulin sheet. This view was taken before the Viking's head transfer was added to the offside panel (see Plate 19).
Courtesy Acorn Photography

ECL181 Viking Motors (Burton) Ltd. (same address)
29.5.37   25.9.37   E   Woodville – Blackpool
19.6.37   14.8.37   E&T   from Woodville

An entry in the North West Traffic Area Notice & Proceedings (commonly known in the industry as N&P's) No.10 of 17 June 1931, details the DCL13 Licence Application as follows:

DCL13/1 to DCL13/2
Application has been made by **William John Lloyd, of the Viking Coach Company, Central Garage, Union Street,** **Burton-on-Trent,** for the backing of a road service licence to run a service of express carriages between Burton-on-Trent and Blackpool on the following route through this area:

DCL13/1 –   Blackpool – By road A.50 to Warrington, then by A.49 to Bamber Bridge, then by A.582 to Preston, then by A.583 to Blackpool.
The service is to be run every Friday, Saturday, Sunday and Monday from May 1st to October 30th . It is proposed to take up and set down

PLATE 19
Nearside of FA 6199, with transfer and the Viking name prominently displayed on the roof luggage frame. Viking driver, Stan Parkes, collected this coach from Burlingham's Blackpool factory, and it remained in his charge until disposal in February 1952. The author recalls riding on this coach a number of times in the post war period, with Stan Parkes the driver.

Courtesy R.Marshall
collection

passengers at Warrington, Wigan and Blackpool, in this Traffic area.

*Application has been made by **William John Lloyd, of the Viking Coach Company, Central Garage, Union Street, Burton-on-Trent,** for the backing of a road service licence to run a group of excursions and tours on the following routes through this Traffic area, starting from Burton-on-Trent.*

DCL13/2 – From West Midland Traffic area: By A.515 to Buxton, A.624 and A.625 to Hathersage, A.622 to Bakewell, A.6 into West Midland Traffic Area.
From West Midland Traffic Area: By A.52 into this area, by A.55, A.554 and A.5. into West Midland Traffic area.
Other excursions and tours on special occasions. All tours to be run from Easter to October. The maximum number of vehicles to be used on this group of tours on one day is three.

The system of licences was that if a service operated in one traffic area only, one Road Service Licence (RSL) was required. However, if a service operated in two or more Traffic Areas, then a 'Primary' and one or more 'Backing' licence(s) were required. Viking's Burton upon Trent to Blackpool service required a 'Primary' licence issued by the West Midlands Traffic Area, together with a 'Backing' licence issued by the North Western Traffic Area.

In 1931, a Mr. Horace Atkins became the third partner in 'Viking Motors', and became a director of Viking Motors (Burton) Ltd., from when the company was formed until his retirement in the 1970's.

In January 1933 a further new vehicle joined the fleet. It was FA 4960, a Leyland TS4 type chassis, with what in those days, was a high quality Burlingham (of Blackpool) 30 seat coach body. This became the longest serving vehicle in the Viking fleet, in use with the company for over 20 years until it was sold to 'Ada Coaches', a Leicester operator, in September 1953.

It was over two years before the next new vehicle arrived, an Albion PV70 type 31 seat coach, No. FA 5740, again with Burlingham body, which joined the fleet in April 1935. A year later, and yet another very stylish Burlingham bodied 32 seat coach on AEC Regal chassis, FA 6199, was purchased, arguably the best of the pre-war Burlingham's.

Viking purchased Burton Road garage, Woodville c.1933, after Bob Poynton, had closed his garage business in 1933.

Land which adjoined the old Brunt & Bucknall Brewery premises with access off Hartshorne Road, was also used for coach standing, and some years later, a further adjacent area of the same former brewery land with road access on to High Street, Woodville, was also purchased.

Viking continued to operate the well established regular weekly Saturday service to Blackpool between July and August and again

PLATE 20. *London Office stamp.*

PLATE 21. *The London Office was primarily for goods transportation between London and the north. The driver wages shown were a very modest sum. The star marks are those of the Company's auditors.*

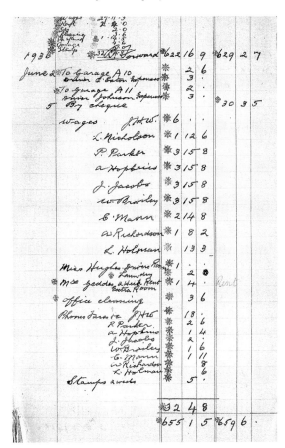

PLATE 22
FA7205, a Burlingham 32 seat coach on an Albion CX13 type chassis, delivered new to Viking in June 1938. Curtains were fitted to the side windows when the vehicle was new, whilst the roof panel above the side windows was originally lettered 'Viking Motors'. The lettering and curtains had been removed by the time this postwar photograph was taken.
Courtesy R.Marshall collection

throughout the illuminations period. Blackpool was the No. 1 destination for the company, with additional coaches used at weekends, for either Saturday to Saturday passengers, Friday to Sunday, or Saturday and Sunday day trips. When the lights and illuminated tableux were extended along the whole length of the promenade in 1926, they gave a big boost to the coach travel industry. Blackpool 'Lights' became an annual pilgrimage for many thousands from Viking's East Staffordshire and South Derbyshire catchment area.

Other resorts were also very popular for private hire groups and for day trips, with Southport, Rhyl, New Brighton, Scarborough, Skegness, Mablethorpe, Hunstanton and Great Yarmouth frequent destinations.

A London Office to handle the lorry cartage collections and deliveries, was open by April 1937, at 17 Bedford Chambers, Covent Garden, London WC2, with telephone number 'Temple Bar 3722', and this remained open until the start of the Second World War in September 1939. After closure, Alf Hopkins ran the London end of Viking's lorry cartage to and from the Capital, from his home in New Cross. In addition to London traffic, the cartage business had been expanded to include regular consignments of salt glazed pipes from South Derbyshire for delivery mostly in the London area, Liverpool and the Midlands. One of the lorry drivers, a Mr. Horace Parker, who commenced working for Viking in the mid-1930's, has remarkable recollections of long and relatively slow long distance journeys with the Albion lorries in use. He also recalls an eight-wheel Scammell with the long flatbed body, which was used for general haulage. During the early war years, several long haul journeys to Glasgow took around 15 hours each way, necessitating an overnight stay.

On the 2nd April, 1937, the partnership of W.J.Lloyd, D.J.S.Leitch and H.Atkins trading as Viking Motors, was dissolved, and the assets and liabilities transferred into a new company registered at Company's House on the same day under the name of **Viking Motors (Burton) Ltd.**

It is interesting to note, that some four days after the business became a Limited Company, the page of an Income & Expenditure book for the period commencing 6th April, 1937, has the new Company's rubber stamp, the names of the directors and the address of the London Office, stamped at the head of the page (Plate_21). However, the rubber stamp applied to the tops of all the pages for the period commencing some two weeks later, 20 April 1937, and right through to August 1940, shows only the Company and director names, with reference to the London Office having been removed from the rubber stamp.

By June 1938, a fourth Burlingham bodied coach, an Albion Valkrie CX13 type No.FA 7205, had been purchased, and this, together with the three earlier mentioned vehicles, remained with Viking throughout the war years, finally being retired between July 1951 and November 1953 - (Albion PV70 - FA 5740) July 1951; (AEC Regal - FA 6199) February 1952; (FA 4960 - Leyland TS4) September 1953; and (FA 7205 – Albion CX13) November 1953. All four saw service with other operators.

The declaration that Britain was at War came on 3rd September, 1939, and Blackpool Illuminations for that year were immediately cancelled, and severe restrictions were placed on all forms of transport, with only necessary journeys permitted.

On the outbreak of war normal coach operation was halted, and the Viking fleet of four vehicles, had to be used to carry people to Ordnance factories, aerodromes, and other military installations all over the Midlands. Mr. Lloyd and Viking were soon heavily involved in organising the movement of people across the Midlands to work places, and in the previously referred to speech to Rotarians in the 1960's, Mr. Lloyd commented that Viking had over 50 vehicles operating out of their Woodville premises. The wartime role required him to travel all over the Midlands and as far north as Lancashire, and he further commented that he was never stopped or questioned by the Police as to where he might be going, and he was heard to comment that he could get "all the fuel we wanted".

However, during WW2 the various Traffic Areas were replaced by Regional Traffic Commissioners (RTC), and all services were operated under RTC permits, instead of licences. The boundaries of the RTC were different to those of the Traffic Area, but no information has been found which defined the RTC areas. Fuel was rationed based upon the mileage authorised by the RTC and granted to the holder of the permit, who may not have been the provider of the vehicle or vehicles. It is highly probable therefore, that Viking was issued with the permit to operate more vehicles than they owned, and they would have been able to hire in vehicles up to the amount of mileage and fuel allowed by the RTC.

During the Second World War, four second-hand vehicles were added to the Viking fleet, the earliest being a 1929 AEC

PLATE 23
FA 8961 was the third of a batch of three new Burlingham 33 seat bodied AEC Regal III coaches delivered in 1948, and the first new coaches to be purchased after World War II. The body style had been developed by Burlingham from 1936 onwards and was the latest version of the body type fitted to FA 6199, but with a larger boot space in place of the roof luggage rack.

PLATE 24
The first of the batch of three postwar AEC Regal III coaches was FA 8882. The 'Viking' name beneath the driver's windscreen is in large block capitals, rather than the written style on FA 7205 (Plate 22), or smaller 'Viking Motors' on FA 6199 (Plate 18). This was the first coach to be named, with 'Valorous' seen on the engine cover. Courtesy P. White

Reliance (VT 2901) with Dixon 32 seat front entrance bus body which was acquired in 1940. This vehicle is recorded by the PSV Circle as being disposed of in December 1942, with no further operator or withdrawal recorded after this date. This is somewhat unusual, given that all available resources were pressed into service during the war period, thus suggesting therefore, that this vehicle may have been damaged beyond repair during December 1942, probably as a result of enemy action, and was scrapped.

By 1939, the company's road haulage business had been expanded into requiring a fleet 16 lorries, with a daily trunk service of earthenware and other goods from the Burton and Derby areas, and return loads of fruit and vegetables for Derby market from London's Covent Garden wholesale market. During the war the company also handled deliveries of munitions and other hardware to military locations and ports, as well as food commodities, including flour from Cooper's Mill at Acresford. The three directors of Viking purchased Victoria Motorways Ltd. as a going concern in 1943, and the additional work involved may have been the reason why Viking's lorries and the road haulage side of business were sold to another operator in the same year.

In 1941, Viking acquired operational control of Victoria Motorways Ltd. services, which ran into Burton upon Trent from Netherseal and Measham. The share capital of Victoria was acquired by the three Viking directors personally in June 1943, and they continued to operate the bus services under the separate identity of 'Victoria', with and extension of the service to Donisthorpe, until both operations were sold in November 1987.

Following the take-over of Victoria, the coach and bus fleets were maintained as one, from a workshop and garage premises on Burton Road, Woodville, some five miles east of Burton upon Trent, and a similar mileage from the Victoria service destinations in Measham and Donisthorpe. The Central Garage premises, Union Street, Burton

PLATE 25
FA 9326, the first of two new Daimler CVD6 type Burlingham coaches delivered in February 1949, and allotted the name 'Vampire'. The Viking head transfer on black triangle had 'Viking Motors' lettering along the bottom edge of the triangle.
Courtesy D.J.Stanier

PLATE 26
The new full fronted Burlingham 'Seagull' type centre entrance coach, delivered to Viking in June 1951. This was the first of six AEC Regal IV coaches purchased by Viking between 1951 and 1954. When delivered, the door was an internally sliding type, but this was soon replaced by an outside sliding type as seen in the next photograph. The livery is antique red and tan.

PLATE 27 (below)
The replacement outside sliding door is seen in this later view of AFA 499. The 'Road Liner' lettering is slightly different to that shown in Plate 26, whilst the name 'Vigilant' has been added. This was the first vehicle to receive the cut-out plastic Viking head, rather than the earlier transfer type.

continued as the Company's Registered Office, and there was sufficient space for several vehicles to be stabled in the garage and on secure land behind the garage. By 1948 the company's main workshops had been moved 300 yards from Burton Road to the larger Brewery Yard premises in High Street, Woodville, formerly Brunt & Bucknall's brewery, which had a much greater area for vehicle parking.

By the end of the War in 1945, the Viking fleet consisted of eight vehicles, the four pre-war bodied vehicles by Burlingham, plus one vehicle from each of the following body builders - Dixon, Charlesworth, Harrington and Cowieson. A considerable number of prisoners of war were carried by Viking between camp hostels and various farms where they were employed under supervision, and this work continued for a period before they were repatriated.

The gloom of the war years soon gave way to a more optimistic and self-supporting outlook, despite money remaining tight for most of the population after the cessation of hostilities. Theatre shows and the lure of the seaside soon returned to the thoughts and aspirations of the populace, and in many instances, what could be termed 'travel clubs' were set up, with 'members' paying in a few pence each week as savings, to be spent on a trip by coach at a later date, which of course, Viking strove to provide.

The Blackpool holiday season express service re-commenced in May 1946, and for the August bank holiday Monday, former Viking driver, Ron Coleman, recalls that the demand for tickets was collosal. All eight Viking coaches and several Victoria buses were quickly full, and such was the eventual demand, every one of Burton Corporation's single deck buses (possibly as many as twelve), together with several of Stevensons (of Uttoxeter) vehicles were required to cater for everyone booked, with the total of 27 vehicles used. Ron led the procession in his regular coach, the Albion Valiant FA 5740, and one of Stevenson's vehicles took the role as 'tail-end Charlie' bringing up the rear, to try to ensure all vehicles reached Blackpool, as many of the drivers that day did not know the route to take.

Geoff Topliss, who was at Hastings Road County

Secondary School with the author, recalls being on this mammoth outing. His family had always travelled to Blackpool for holidays by train from Swadlincote, but his father decided they would use the Viking weekly service as a change from the train. They walked from their home on Hearthcote Road and when they arrived at Swadlincote Delph, there were four Burton Corporation single deck buses on hire to Viking. Wooden slatted seats made for a less than comfortable journey, and as the buses were not fitted with the usual coach luggage boot, there was no alternative to the cases being stowed in the gangway.

The removal of wartime fuel restrictions in 1949, allowed bus and coach operators greater flexibility to re-commence tour, excursion and holiday express services for which they were licenced, and one of the major prewar attractions, Blackpool illuminations, were re-introduced in September 1949 for a six week period. Large numbers of coaches and excursion trains from all parts of the country, carried thousands of excited passengers to the Lancashire resort every week of the illuminations season. In addition to Viking's own coaches, additional vehicles were hired from other bus and coach operators to fulfill demand for Friday night-Sunday short breaks, as well as day trips, with the return journey following a tour of the lights.

The fifteen month period between January 1948 and March 1949, saw the largest influx of vehicles to the Viking

fleet, when seven new Burlingham bodied half-cab coaches were purchased to satisfy the boom in private hire operation and the increasing popularity of the regular weekly services to Blackpool, being experienced in the early post-war years. Four of these vehicles were on AEC Regal III chassis, and three on Daimler CVD6 chassis. They were splendid vehicles of their time arriving after the austere wartime years, and characterised by sweeping stainless steel beading between the brown and red panels, and they were the mainstay for all coach work until the arrival of the new generation of full-fronted coaches in the 1950's. The first of the 1948 batch of new vehicles, AEC Regal III No. FA 8882, (Plate 24) became the last of the batch to be withdrawn by Viking, and sold on in May 1958.

The arrival of the first two coaches in January 1948, heralded the introduction of fleet numbers, and in addition, names, all commencing with the letter 'V', were applied to the new 1948 batch of vehicles. Names appear to have been applied to vehicles until the mid-1960's, but not all new vehicles received a name. Only three names appear to have been used on more than one vehicle, and from the Company's own records, thirteen names were actually applied to vehicles, whilst a further thirteen were chosen but never applied. (see Plate 202) The last vehicle to have a name applied appears to have been LFA 153, a Bedford SB3 with Duple front entrance 41 seat coach body, new to Viking in May 1960, which was given the name *Valiant*, which had earlier been carried by FA 9354 which was sold in October 1954.

Another early post-war adornment, was the addition of a cast metal Viking Warrior's head to the radiator cap of the half cab vehicles with exposed radiators, but again, it does not appear this was fitted to all exposed radiator vehicles. (Plate 24)

In the immediate post-war years, there was evidence of major changes in bus and coach design, as a result of the development of chassis which would allow a vehicle engine to be accommodated within the chassis frame, or in a compartment on the off-side of the vehicle, rather than mounted on the chassis frame alongside the driving cab at the front of the vehicle.

Experiments with rear-engine and under-floor engine vehicles by Midland Red from 1935, and through the war period, and by Leyland with a centrally mounted side engine compartment on the offside, paved the way which led to a quite dramatic change in vehicle designs from c.1949/50 onwards. The full-fronted style with set back front axle, led directly to chassis manufacturers producing the underfloor engine configuration, with leading body builders soon offering their own full-fronted body types.

Viking's first 'new modern style' full-fronted coach, an AEC Regal IV chassis fitted with a 39 seat Burlingham Seagull *'Road Liner'* body, AFA 499, arrived in June 1951, and immediately the image of the 'half-cab' coach was that they were old-fashioned. Several operators took the short-term and less expensive option to 'modernise' their fleet

PLATE 30
One of two secondhand Alexander 41 seat Leyland PSUC1/2's purchased from Wigan based operators in September 1957. They were finished in a very smart and clean looking light buff and red style, and BJP 271, seen here at Cleethorpes, did not receive a name.

Courtesy K.West

PLATE 31
This was one of four Duple bodied Bedford SB type purchased by Viking, all receiving the light buff and red style. 833 ERR came second hand to Viking in March 1961, and remained in the fleet for ten years until sold in May 1971.

image, by having old chassis fitted with new full-front style bodies. AFA 499 was originally delivered with a nearside centrally placed entrance door, which slid backwards inside the outer body panel (Plate 26).

A second Burlingham Seagull Regal lV, No. AFA 953, (Plate 146) arrived in June 1952, and both vehicles were used on the Blackpool services, with private hire clients latching onto 'requesting' one of the new vehicles when they were available, for their own trip. The Seagull body with set-back front wheels, was very heavy at the front end, and the Viking experience was that tyre wear was heavier than tyres on the conventional half-cab style of vehicle.

Whilst three of the 1948 Burlingham half-cab coaches remained in use until early 1958, all coach purchases were to the full-fronted under-floor engine configuration. In addition to the two Seagulls already referred to, four AEC Regal IV's with Plaxton bodywork arrived, two were new – BFA 565 (April) and BFA 566 (May) (Plate 28) in 1953 – with two secondhand examples RMB 159 (Plate 150) and RMB 240, both registered in July 1953, being purchased from Altrincham Coachways Ltd., in July 1954. The Plaxton bodies had the appearance of being larger than the Burlingham Seagull type, but unlike the Seagulls, they did not suffer the overweight problem at the front-end, despite two passenger seats being ahead of the front wheels.

The six under-floor engine coaches each with centre passenger entrance, purchased by Viking between 1951 and 1953, set a new standard for coach travel in the Burton and South Derbyshire area throughout the 1950's.

Licensing regulations required the Company's services

and vehicles to be licensed by both the West and East Midlands Traffic Areas, by virtue of the Company having a garage location in each of the legally-defined traffic areas. Operations from the company's Central Garage, Union Street, Burton upon Trent were licensed by the West Midlands Traffic Area in Birmingham, but when the Viking garage at Woodville opened, this location came within the jurisdiction of the East Midlands Traffic Area based in Nottingham. Vehicle examinations would normally have been carried out by the respective Traffic Area vehicle inspectors, but under an agreed arrangement, inspectors from the West Midlands Traffic Area carried out all examinations of the Viking and Victoria fleets.

In 1955, the company approached Willowbrook of Loughborough for the supply of front entrance bodies for two further AEC Reliance chassis. They were intended as dual purpose vehicles, built to coaching standards with headrest type seats, with the entrance immediately behind the front panel, ahead of the front axle. This door configuration would allow the vehicles to be used on coaching duties, as well as being available for use on Victoria stage carriage services when required, thus being designated a

PLATE 32
PFA 438. This Plaxton Panorama body was fitted to a Leyland L2 chassis, and delivered in Viking's new two-tone grey livery in April 1962. It was slightly more spacious than the two 1961 type Plaxton Panorama coaches, NFA 316/7 purchased by Viking in 1961.

PLATE 33
AFA 134B, the last AEC to be purchased by Viking. New in May 1964, it remained with the company until sold in April 1972. The windows were deeper than those on PFA 438.

PLATE 34 (centre)
One of six Bedford VAL six wheel coaches purchased by Viking. EFA 494D, the third of three Duple bodied examples, was new to Viking in April 1966, and is seen here parked in Derby.   Courtesy P. Yeomans per. J. Bennett

PLATE 35 (bottom)
EFA 495D with the Plaxton 'revised Panorama' body, one of two delivered new in March 1966. Plaxton's official history, refers to this front end style as: 'The front upperworks of the body were, in effect, divorced from the remainder from a styling view-point by the arrangement of trim to accentuate the pillar behind the first main side window".

DP – dual-purpose – type. DFA 548 (Plate 29) and 550 were delivered with Viking lettering, and Viking badge on each side, these being removed when they were transferred to Victoria for bus use in 1961.

In September 1957 two secondhand Alexander front entrance coach bodied Leylands – BJP 271/387 - were purchased from Wigan operators, and in 1960 were transferred to sister company, Victoria Motorways, the entrance ahead of the front wheels being ideally suited for the Victoria stage carriage services.

In May 1958, HFA 3, a Leyland Tiger Cub chassis, was fitted with the first Willowbrook-designated 'Viking' body type. With the exception of four Duple bodied Bedfords - one SBG (1956) and three SB3's (1959/60) (Plate 31) – which had the entrance behind the front wheels, virtually all subsequent Viking coach purchases had the entrance door ahead of the front wheels, and even though they carried Viking lettering, they were also used on Victoria services when required.

Another design innovation suggested by Viking director Mr. John Lloyd to Plaxton's, coach builders of Scarborough, was to raise the interior floor level to cover the wheel arches, which were always a discomfort and annoyance on long distance travels. However, Plaxton's expressed concern that raising the floor level would raise the centre of gravity, but Mr. Lloyd, agreed he would pay for the first vehicle to be finished in this form, and if the vehicle failed the statutory tilt test, he would pay the cost of lowering the floor - the vehicle passed the test. A further Viking requirement was to fit a Norwegian 'Finrad' heating system, which provided a much enhanced circulation of warm air, and this became the standard heating fitment on all new Viking vehicles.

Operating costs in the bus and coach industry were increasing, and the arrival of vehicles with increased carrying capacities, promised improved financial benefits for operators, providing of course full or nearly full loadings could be maintained. Revenues received from higher seating capacities would reduce the direct operational cost percentage of each vehicle, and the following statistics show the 18% improved capacity per vehicle achieved between 1950-1955, and the more marked 55% higher capacity between 1950-1965:

Year	No. of coaches Operated	Cumulative seating	Ave Veh. seating
1950	13	398	31
1955	11	423	38
1965	15	713	48

From 1956, Viking increased the number of licensed services they could operate, with summer season services to Norwich and Great Yarmouth, Scarborough, and Torquay, services which continued through to 1987. The boundary between the West & East Midlands Traffic Areas, was the Black Horse Inn, Stanton. The Licence Application for the Norwich & Yarmouth service to start from Burton was declined by the West Midland Traffic Area, but a licence was issued by the East Midlands Traffic Area. Viking overcame the difficulty by hiring the vehicle for the Yarmouth run, to run as a Victoria service bus between Wetmore Park, Burton and the Black Horse Inn, thereafter the coach running under the East Midlands licence for the remainder of the journeys to and from Yarmouth.

High utilisation of vehicles every day was of course the prime objective, and Viking's popularity in the Burton and South Derbyshire areas was reflected in the increasing number of day trip destinations for which licences were obtained. With multiple pick-up points en-route, heavy loadings were generally the order of the day, with many regular customers re-visiting destinations they had visited previously. Many destinations were fully booked weeks ahead of the date. Theatre trips to the major shows were popular, and one particular lady is recorded as having used Viking on 40 occasions to see the same 'Sound of Music' film at the Nottingham Odeon.

The easing of traffic levels during the Winter months allowed a preventive maintenance programme to be followed. Heavy overhauls were carried out during the winter period, and two coaches were de-licensed each year to allow such in-depth work to be carried out. A programme of minimum but necessary maintenance, was adopted during the coaching season, with the aim of minimising the interruption to vehicle availability during the rest of the year, and this proved to be a very effective way of maximising use of every vehicle.

Vehicle maintenance training was a priority for the Company, and from 1969 when the fleet was predominantly Ford based, all workshop staff were required to attend Ford equipment up-dating courses every 18 months. In addition, they were also required to pass the Ministry of Transport "Certifying Officers Course".

A general four year fleet replacement programme was instituted, but vehicle records show that some were retained for as little as two years, and others for as long as ten years.

John Lloyd believes that the coach industry became more price conscious in the late 1950's early 60's, and his own philosophy based on creating an aura of 'value conscious' travel was reflected in the high passenger loadings and repeat business that came to Viking right through to the mid-1980's.

Whilst the livery of vehicles is covered on pages 98-9, it is interesting to note that the final livery of two shades of grey applied to both Viking and Victoria vehicles, and adopted for all new vehicles from April 1962, originated from a Rover 75 motor car seen in the Chatsworth House car park in 1961, and reported as being in 'these very smart colours', which were considered to be equally distinctive, whether the coach was parked at Chatsworth, or in a pub car park. The first vehicle in two-tone grey was the April 1962 arrival, PFA 438, a Plaxton bodied Leyland L2 type, and thereafter all new vehicles were finished in this livery. After several coaches had been repainted, it became apparent that in foggy weather conditions, the rear end of a two-tone grey liveried coach was much less visible than a more distinctly painted rear panel. As a result, and in the interests of road safety, the rear boot doors of all coaches were painted bright yellow with lettering and telephone numbers in black.

Shortly after the rear door panels had been painted yellow, the directors became aware that they were receiving a greater number of private hire enquiries from across a much wider geographic area, than the generally recognised area of Viking's long established hire business. (Plate 247)

The opening of the 73 mile stretch of M1 Motorway between Crick, Northants, and North London in November 1959, was a milestone which brought considerable benefits for all road transport sectors. Much of the time-consuming A5 route between the Midlands and the metropolis was eliminated at a stroke, and shorter journey times allowing longer times in London, provided new opportunities for coach operators. The principal Midlands bus operator, Midland Red, spotted their opportunity and built a fleet of high speed CM5 coaches to inaugurate the first dedicated Motorway Express services between Birmingham-London, and Coventry-London. These services were an instant success.

Other operators including Viking quickly took advantage of the more direct route afforded by the M1.

In 1963, two of the four directors of Viking, Mr. Don Leitch and Mr. Horace Atkins, decided the time had come for them to retire from the business. Whilst Mr. Bill Lloyd and his son, Mr. John Lloyd, who had joined the Company in 1957, indicated their wish to continue running the business, the entire business was made open to offers. Barton Transport of Chilwell, Nottingham, who had operated an hourly bus service between Swadlincote and Nottingham since well before the Second World War, made the only formal offer. The Barton offer effectively established a market price for the business, and in the absence of any further offers, the Lloyds matched what Barton's were offering and took control of the business, with Don Leitch & Horace Atkins retiring on 26th September 1963.

Two new Plaxton bodied AEC Reliance coaches, UFA 593 & AFA 134B, finished in the two tone grey livery, arrived in April/May 1964, whilst the first of three Duple bodied six wheel Bedford VAL14 type's joined the fleet in May 1965.

In 1966, a Mr. John Holmes joined Viking as General Manager, having gained considerable operational experience with Southdown Motors based in Brighton, and whose fleet exceeded 1200 buses and coaches. His experience and enthusiasm was soon directed towards creating new opportunities for both Viking and Victoria, and John has very kindly provided first hand recollections of his time with the Company from 1966 to 1975, and agreed that his notes can be included as the second part of the Viking story.

Viking Motors (Burton) Ltd.

Section 2 - 1966 to 1975

This section has very kindly been contributed by Mr. John Holmes, who joined Viking as General Manager in 1966. His summary of personal recollections during nine years spent with the Company, provides much detailed information on the company's operational activities, and the background to decisions taken, as well providing a very interesting insight into his own thoughts and modus operandi in relation to various situations which arose. Moreover, a so interesting an account as this, could only have been written by someone who was at the heart of the Viking operation, and whose own contribution added so much to the smooth running of the Viking-Victoria operation. The style in which John wrote this account has not been changed.

1. Introduction

Before joining Viking Motors in 1966, I had been working in a large company, running over 1,200 buses and coaches with a complex organisational structure. Viking had less than thirty vehicles and I found myself undertaking all sorts of tasks. Burton-on-Trent and the Swadlincote area was quite industrial. Besides the breweries in the former, there were a number of manufacturers. Swadlincote was a centre both for coal mining and the clay working industry. Bill Lloyd was so concerned that I might not settle in an area so different from his perception of Brighton that after my interview he drove me round Burton, Swadlincote, and some of the colliery villages, like Donisthorpe. He need not have worried, Brighton was not quite as he thought and I never regretted the move to the area.

Viking was able to take advantage of people's desire for recreation at a time when car ownership and use was low. Both east and west coast and their holiday resorts offered a day out or longer holiday breaks. The beautiful Peak District lies nearby to the north with the Cotswolds not much further way to the south. The expansion of the motorway network in the sixties and seventies brought other areas of natural beauty such as the Lake District and the Welsh Mountains within reach.

2. Express Services

In 1966, for those looking for a seaside holiday, Viking operated four express services: Blackpool; Great Yarmouth; the Yorkshire Coast Resorts of Bridlington, Filey, and Scarborough; and Torquay and Paignton. They ran every Saturday, leaving Friday nights for the Devon resorts, for varying periods over the summer.

The most important was that to Blackpool which started on Whit Saturday and ran until the end of the Blackpool Illuminations towards the end of October. During the Illuminations period, services were also run on Monday and Friday, so that people could take short breaks in the resort. The route started picking up in Coalville and then right through the area to Uttoxeter, with up to ten vehicles being operated on some Saturdays. The peak weeks started on the first Saturday in July when Leicestershire schools, factories, and collieries shut down for their holidays. This continued through July with Swadlincote and Burton on Trent main holiday weeks being at the end of July, beginning of August. When the August Bank Holiday was moved to the end of the month, that week began to become another popular holiday week.

Blackpool had been holiday resort for people from the Burton/Swadlincote area for many years. Leicestershire, however, looked more toward the east coast and Skegness, in particular. One regular passenger told me that he and his wife had taken a week's holiday in Blackpool in the same hotel every year since the thirties. One consequence was that the other services ran for shorter periods and were less busy, although the Yarmouth service needed relief coaches in the main holiday weeks.

Two more Summer Saturday services were started before 1975. The first was to Portsmouth and Southsea which ran during July and August. Passengers could book through to the Isle of Wight, using the hovercraft from Southsea. This service started in Burton on Trent and picked up throughout South Derbyshire together with Ashby de la Zouch and Coalville.

The other service, jointly operated with Midland Red, ran between Burton on Trent and Victoria Coach Station, London. Besides giving opportunities for breaks in and around London, it provided connections for a variety of south eastern resorts. Viking had made an attempt to provide a daily express connection with the capital. This had been in the mid sixties, at the time when the M1 was being extended through Leicestershire. The licences to run the service had been refused. I have wondered how successful such a service would have been. There was no direct rail service between Burton on Trent and London and by this time the rail passenger service between the town and Leicester, serving South Derbyshire and North West Leicestershire, had been withdrawn. It is interesting to note that National Express now provide such a daily service, albeit via Leicester.

PLATE 36
The 'revised Panorama' six-wheel Bedford VAL 70, KFA 777F, one of two delivered in May 1968.

Viking had insufficient vehicles to cope with all those who wished to travel on the peak Summer Saturdays, even though other work, such as the advertised excursions and private party was kept to a minimum. A number of vehicles were hired from other local operators, such as Arterial Motors in Derby and Aaron Hart's Cosy Coaches, based in Donisthorpe. In the seventies, Lewis's Coaches of Pailton near Rugby were regularly used for this work. That company had a modern fleet of coaches used on regular contracts in the Coventry, Rugby, Lutterworth area, which were available at weekends.

As a personal aside, after I left Viking to go to University, I drove occasionally for Lauds of Moira. I remember driving on both the Scarborough and London express services.

3. Advertised Excursions

It is difficult to remember that until 1980, any coach operation carrying passengers at separate fares, had to be licensed. The routes of Viking's many tours were faithfully set down. When new ones were wanted, applications had to be made to all the traffic areas through which they travelled. During the late sixties and early seventies, we pursued a policy of expanding the range of day tours with longer distance destinations. Day trips to the Lake District and parts of mid and South Wales became regular events in the summer. Because of the time involved two drivers would have to be used to comply with the driving hours regulations. On busier days, two vehicles would be needed and then three drivers could cover the work. With the expansion of the motorways more places came within our range, resorts such as Bournemouth. We even started running 'No passport' trips to France by connecting with the Hoverlloyd hovercraft near Ramsgate in Kent.

There were a full range of excursions to the more local seaside resorts along with trips into the Peak District and other beautiful country areas, as well as half day shopping excursions to the local cities, such as Birmingham and Leicester. In the winter trips to theatres for pantomimes provided useful work for both drivers and coaches which would not otherwise be used. A niche business that we built up at this time was to pop concerts both in the Midlands and further afield. Each week we bought the New Musical Express and combed through it for upcoming tours. Then it was on the phone to see whether we could get enough tickets to make it worthwhile running. We wore out the dialling mechanism of one of the Union Street phones as we tried time and again to get through when lines were busy. The most memorable event I recall was the "Monkees" concert at Wembley. We had managed to buy 82 tickets. It was two coach loads of screaming teenage girls, the main followers of that particular group. Well actually 80 teenage girls, one boy, and his mother if I remember aright. One of the coaches came home with its external paintwork covered in lipstick as a result of the concert goers attentions.

The most humble of our advertised excursions were the Sunday evening trips that ran through the spring into the summer. A group of faithful regulars would go for a local tour, taking one's mind back to a time when urban dwellers had little opportunity to see the countryside. One evening we included running along the

relatively new section of the M1 with a visit to the Leicester Forest service area. This caused great excitement with some of the regulars who had not travelled on a motorway before and certainly never visited a service area.

This had an odd consequence in that it resulted in Viking's name appearing in the national press. Remembering the excitement the M1 trip caused, I suggested when the M6 was being built through the Midlands and there was much talk of Spaghetti junction, that we should apply for an excursion licence covering this new section of motorway. A licence application was dispatched to the Traffic Commissioners and in due course a notice appeared in Notices and Proceedings. This was a publication by which the Traffic Commissioners informed all who were interested of new applications. It must have been a slow news day because a reporter on the Birmingham Post phoned and asked me about the background to the application. I told him the story, and the next day, his report appeared. It must have been a very slow news day because it appeared on the bottom of the front page. If I remember correctly the headline read something like "Trips to the sea …… of concrete". The article itself was good humoured, somewhat tongue in cheek, and after a few chuckles we thought that would be that but that was not to be. Suddenly the phone went mad, all parts of the media wanted a comment from local radio to the Daily Telegraph. I was even quoted in the 'News of the World', but all in the best possible taste. The day the M6 opened, a Viking coach was one of the first through Spaghetti junction. The Birmingham Post sent along one of their reporters, and so we had another write up in that paper.

4. Traffic Court Hearings

As I mentioned before, every coach or bus operation that involved passengers paying separate fares had to have a Road Service Licence. These had to be applied for and anyone who felt there was a justifiable reason for objecting to the application could do so. On most occasions, applications for excursions went through without challenge but there were several occasions when there were objections to Viking's applications. Express services usually resulted in applications.

PLATE 39. *The chrome 'upperworks' (Plate 35) were discontinued on the 1975 Plaxton Panorama bodied Ford, GUT 795N, seen here turning into Guild Street, Burton on Trent on its way to Viking's Union Street coach station and Nottingham.* Courtesy T.W.W.Knowles

The consequence would be a Traffic Court hearing before the Traffic Commissioner for the area. We took some care over such events, employing experienced lawyers and preparing our case carefully with suitable evidence. This could take the form of details of loadings or other written documentation but most effective were witnesses, members of the public who wished to make use of the service.

Three particular Traffic Court cases, involving Viking, come to mind. The first involved the Southsea express service mentioned above. At the time, if anyone from the area wanted to holiday in Southsea, they either had to travel via London or Cheltenham, involving a change in very busy coach stations. This was unpopular with many prospective passengers who were concerned that they might not catch the right coach. For many who were to make use of the proposed Viking service, using the alternatives would have meant them

PLATE 41. *Two Air Stewardesses were hired from British Midland Airways for a series of promotional photographs, and they are seen here with driver Ron Ratcliffe during the 'photoshoot' c.1970/1. The May 1970 Plaxton bodied Leyland PSU3A seen here, PFA 791H, was the last new Leyland purchased by Viking.*

PLATE 40. *GFA 480L carries the 'Travel Viking' lettering and a full load of passengers during one of Viking's London Tours, following the granting of the London licence.*

travelling to Burton on Trent and London. Viking's application drew an objection from the powerful Associated Motorways consortium which operated Derby – Cheltenham, Cheltenham – Portsmouth services. They promised to run through coaches on Summer Saturdays. We were able to bring evidence to the Traffic Court Hearing of usage of our existing services together with a number of witnesses. They explained how they did not want to have to travel to Burton or Leicester, or change in Cheltenham. We were successful but for at least one summer Associated Motorways ran their through service, but without much success.

Another case heard in the West Midlands Traffic Court related to Viking's application to run a shopping trip to Birmingham. For some years, we had been running such trips to Nottingham and Leicester. Our application drew an objection from Midland Red, which ran a regular service between Burton on Trent and the city. Once again we turned up with written evidence, in the form of the company's advertising of such trips to other Midland cities and our witnesses, who wanted the quick, direct coach trip, as opposed to the slower bus service. Immediately prior to the hearing, we suggested to Midland Red's representative, the company's Traffic Manager, that we would be prepared to accept a limit of running on no more than 12 occasions a year. The offer was refused and so into court. At first, the course of the hearing did not seem to be going our way, particularly when the Traffic Commissioner refused to admit evidence of similar trips operated by Viking. However, The Commissioner was sitting with a Deputy, a Birmingham businessman, who was interested in trade going to other centres. This is where the value of a good lawyer came to the surface. Our man, recognising this interest, returned to this evidence and this time it was admitted. Our application was successful although operation was limited to 24 days a year.

"I suppose you think you've won" was the comment from the Midland Red representative. "Well, we did" was my reply. I should make it clear that he had been a colleague of mine when we had both worked for another company.

One of the most interesting Traffic Court cases was that relating to Viking's application for a London excursion including a tour of the capital. On this occasion, the opposition came from the then operators of London tours, Evan Evans, Frames, and Rickards. Because they opposed the part of the application affecting the London part of the

PLATE 42. *An offside view of NFA 163G, with two small gold edged black 'VIKING' transfers above the grill, with one of the Duple bodied Ford R226's parked behind.*
Courtesy P. Yeomans per J. Bennett

tour, the hearing was heard before the Metropolitan Commissioner in London. We arrived with thirty witnesses, willing to explain why they would not, or could not, make use of the opposition's tours. Clearly, the Metropolitan Traffic Court was not used to such large number of witnesses, more chairs had to be sent for.

The opposition clearly did not think their rural cousins would put up much of a fight because they sent one person from Evan Evans, to represent all three. I remember their representative having one of those beautiful Welsh speaking voices that could only be described as mellifluous. As he flowed on, explaining how much spare capacity the three existing operators had and how damaging tours provided by upstarts like Viking would be, my heart began to sink. Then it was time for cross-examination and once again we seemed like David fighting triple Goliaths until we reached a real turning point, that you think only happens in fictional court room dramas. Our lawyer had been doing a little digging and found that Evan Evans was not a single company but a group of companies, the vehicles were actually owned by Woburn Garages. Suddenly their representative found himself in difficulties when he was asked what company had all these spare seats on London tours.

"This is not germane" claimed their representative, suddenly less sure of himself.

The Traffic Commissioner who had been sitting, eyes closed, apparently asleep, looked at him and said, quietly: "That's for me to decide, you must answer the question".

The latter never seemed to regain his confidence. The message was hammered home by our witnesses. When a young lady told the court that this was her first visit to London, I think the Commissioner was genuinely surprised. He asked for a show of hands among the witnesses, who had not been to London before that day: a number had not been before. The next witness was an older lady. "You have been to London before?" asked the Commissioner. "Oh

PLATE 43
Plaxton bodied Ford R226, BFA 435L, is believed to have been the only coach to have carried the 'European & Executive Travel' transfer seen in this view.
Courtesy T.W.W.Knowles

yes" she replied, "I came through London with my husband, a sailor, on our way to Portsmouth in 1915".

Once again Viking was successful and the London excursion with its tour became a popular addition to our excursion list.

It should not be thought that we had a poor relationship with other operators, even with our bigger neighbours, Midland Red and Trent, both National Bus Company subsidiaries after 1968. The former did offer private hire and excursions with vehicles based in the local garage. The latter were relatively few and I recall the Swadlincote Superintendent telling me that he always knew when our tours were fully booked because then passengers would start coming to them.

5. Private Hire

Private Hire work was undertaken for a wide variety of local clients, both individuals and businesses. Quality, in terms of vehicles, drivers, and other help, such as booking tickets, hotels etc., was the key word. Viking was by no means the cheapest local coach firm, others were willing to undercut our prices but, with few exceptions, we provided reliable service. Sometimes, clients were tempted away by the costs but often returned to us after poor experiences. I remember one occasion when a Burton school approached us about a two vehicle day's hire. It was a busy time of year and our price reflected that but another operator was cheaper. However, two days before the trip, the other operator told the school that they could not provide the vehicles after all. The teacher in charge came to me - "Could Viking help and would we match the other's price?" By this time, our vehicles were fully booked on that day and the answer was "No" to both questions. He was upset but I had to point out that the cheapest price is not always the best.

We took considerable care in costing our private hire work. We recognised that there were certain days of the year when resources were at premium and others when vehicles and drivers might be idle. Our prices were calculated to take these factors into account. We were also honest with our enquirers. For example we could not afford to tie up a coach and driver on a Summer Saturday when our express services kept us fully occupied by taking on a local trip to Twycross Zoo or Drayton Manor. We would explain this to the client and sometimes were able to work out a satisfactory solution for both by changing to another day.

Many smaller independent operators rely heavily on regular contract hire for home to school or home to factory

PLATE 44
Mr. W.J.Lloyd, founder of Viking, is seen with four of the Plaxton Panorama bodied Ford R226 coaches. There are subtle differences between the two 1969 'G' registered vehicles on the right, and the later 1972 pair on the left.

services. Viking was unusual in having only one such contract, between Linton and the William Allitt School, involving two vehicles. Fitting this work could be difficult on busy school days. The morning run usually was not a problem with coaches going out later in the day. The return run in the afternoon could be more difficult, although one journey could be provided by a Victoria bus before taking up its evening peak service working.

Among the more interesting private hire working undertaken by the company were those involving aircraft diversions into East Midlands Airport. The late sixties saw the phenomenal growth of the package tour business to the Mediterranean, and during the winter, for skiing. One firm in particular, Clarkson's, was heavily involved, owning its own airline, Court Line, and hotels in popular resorts both on the Spanish mainland and the Balearic Islands. In order to utilise these resources during the quieter periods, winter breaks were offered. This was all well and good, providing there were satisfactory weather conditions at the company's Luton base. However, that airport could be affected by fog and then planes were diverted to East Midlands and other airports away from the South-east. Coaches were hired to take incoming passengers back to their scheduled airport and outgoing passengers to wherever their plane might be.

The airport authorities had used Barton Coaches, then one of the country's largest independent operators. Unfortunately they were not impressed with the service, particularly when one coach became bogged down when fully loaded with passengers on the grass verge opposite the airport entrance. They turned to Viking and for about eighteen months, we catered for this traffic.

We had some exciting times when Luton Airport closed, on one occasion for more than forty-eight hours. Our coaches spent much time pounding up and down the M1 but Viking could still not meet the demand. Coaches were hired in from many other operators across the Midlands, including, ironically, Barton. We all got involved and worked long hours. I can particularly recall one New Years Eve being rung at about 10.30 pm. All available drivers were out - could I help and so I, along with one of our part-time drivers saw the New Year in drinking coffee out of plastic cups in the airport terminal. Shortly after midnight,

PLATE 45
KNR 442P, the first of four Ford R1014 Plaxton Panorama vehicles, seen near Stoneleigh in Warwickshire in July 1977, the second of two Viking coaches en-route to the Royal Show.
C. T.W.W. Moore

one of the officials came to us. He wanted a party of about forty taken to a hotel in Nottingham and that, he thought, would be all that would be needed that night.

"You go home to bed" I said, "I'll take them. You've got to be up in the morning for the day job".

New Year's Day was not a public holiday in those days. So I loaded up for Nottingham and just before I set off, the official asked if I would be coming back via the airport. That was no problem for me as it was on the way back to Woodville. When I returned, the terminal was in semi-darkness and all seemed very quiet. As the coach stopped, people poured out of every door and surrounded the coach.

"Are you going to Luton?" went up the shout when I managed to open the door.

"I don't know yet, just wait please," was my reply and I went in search of someone in charge.

It appeared that after I had left for Nottingham, another plane with about 100 passengers had turned up. Our other coach was well on the way down the motorway. So after loading all the bags, I set off with a full load of 52 passengers. For most of the way it was slow going, thick fog meant I had to keep down to about thirty miles an hour. It was so cold that the engine never really warmed up and despite the full load, the coach never really warmed through. Everybody was pretty tired by the time we reached Luton, especially the family of mother, father and two boys, one of whom had broken his leg skiing. The father had put his back out carrying him about. The parents went off to find a trolley whilst the children waited on the coach, the younger one quietly crying with tiredness. The fog had lifted when I set off for Woodville and the return journey was uneventful. I was just coming through the door at 7.30 am as my wife came down stairs to get ready to go to work.

The other memory of that work was more pleasant, certainly as far as the weather was concerned. One Friday we received a call from the airport asking if we could provide eight coaches on the Sunday for London. As it happened all our coaches were booked but our friends Lewis's had coaches available, so I replied in the affirmative, but why seven. A plane was coming from Canada with up to 250 passengers. Even allowing for luggage, I could not see why more than five 50 seaters would be needed but eventually we agreed on six. The owner of the firm, Norman Lewis, was one of the drivers and I joined him in going up to Castle Donington. The plane landed and passengers started to stream through. Soon we had dispatched three well loaded coaches for London. Then the stream turned to a trickle and we sent off a fourth coach little more than half full. A search of the terminal suggested that all the passengers were through and so the fifth coach went off with a handful of passengers. No sooner had it left the airport grounds but two more passengers suddenly materialised. Norman Lewis, who had been helping his drivers load their coaches, was not particularly concerned that he would not be needed. However, he was less than amused when the airport official suggested that he take the couple on their own to London in his coach.

After a brief exchange of words, the official was persuaded that a taxi was more appropriate. We pointed out to its driver that the last coach was actually

VIKING

Wed. May 1
SPALDING TULIP FIELDS TOUR
Dep. Union St. 1.00 p.m.—Fare 13/9
" Woodville 1.15 p.m.—Fare 14/6

Compton Superama, Derby, for
" SOUTH PACIFIC "
Dep. Woodville 6.15 p.m.
" Union St. 6.45 p.m.
Fare 16/6 inc.

Fri. May 3
Coventry Theatre for
" 1968 SPRING SHOW "
starring The Bachelors,
The Kaye Sisters,
Mike Yarwood, etc.
Dep. Woodville 5.30 p.m.
" Union St. 6.00 p.m.
Fare 25/- inc.

Sat. May 4
BLACKPOOL
Dep. Woodville 7.30 a.m.—Fare 21/-
" Union St. 8.0 a.m.—Fare 19/6

SPALDING FLOWER PARADE
Dep. Union St. 9.0 a.m.—Fare 14/9
" Woodville 9.20 a.m.—Fare 15/3

MANCHESTER UNITED v. NEWCASTLE UNITED
Dep. Woodville 9.30 a.m.—Fare 14/6
" Union St. 10.0 a.m.—Fare 13/3

LEICESTER
Dep. Union St. 12 noon—Fare 7/6
" Woodville 12.20 p.m.—Fare 7/9

Sun. May 5
BOURNEMOUTH
Dep. Union St. 7.0 a.m.—Fare 34/3
" Woodville 7.20 a.m.—Fare 32/6

TWYCROSS ZOO
Dep. Woodville 2.0 p.m.
Fare 7/6 inclusive of admission
" Union St. 2.30 p.m.
Fare 7/9 inclusive of admission

Evening Tour calling at
CASTLE DONINGTON AIRPORT
Dep. Union St. 5.30 p.m.—Fare 5/3
" Woodville 5.50 p.m.—Fare 5/3

Wed. May 8
BLACKPOOL
Dep. Woodville 7.30 a.m.—Fare 20/3
" Union St. 8.0 a.m.—Fare 19/-

BIRMINGHAM CANNON HILL PARK TULIP FESTIVAL
Dep. Woodville 1.0 p.m.
" Union St. 1.30 p.m.
Fare 8/-

PLATE 46
Viking regularly advertised coach trips in local newspapers, and this is but a part of an advertisement in the Burton Daily Mail on 29 April 1968, announcing the programme of trips later that week.
Courtesy Burton Daily Mail

PLATE 47
If the close proximity of the three Midland Red double deckers is anything to go by, then EFA 496D, a Plaxton bodied Bedford VAM5 is at the wrong stop, and appears to be loading at one of the dedicated Midland Red stops in Burton Wetmore bus park.

Courtesy R.Marshall

setting down two passengers at the Northampton junction and he could transfer the couple there if he did not want to go to London.

The male passenger was watching this pantomime with some bewilderment and asked: "Who picks up the tab for this?" as Norman loaded his cases in the taxi's boot. "Oh!" said Norman, "you're in England now, everything's free".

The taxi pulled away with two very bemused Canadians. I hope they enjoyed their stay in England. I know a lot of people who we carried when undertaking this work were anything but pleased because of their treatment by the airlines and tour companies. On that particular occasion, one of the passengers came to me very concerned because, as with all them, he had expected to land at one of the London airports, and he was flying onto Germany, a connection he would never make. I explained that we had known nothing of this transfer until 48 hours earlier. "We didn't know until we were on the plane!" was his reply.

There were other occasions when passengers were delayed for no real purpose. Sometimes it was because no one would take responsibility for taking action. I remember an occasion when a tour representative could not make his mind up whether two coaches, loaded with passengers and their luggage, should leave or not. I am afraid I told him quite forcibly that his customers had had enough and we were taking them home. As Norman Lewis said that Sunday afternoon: "If I treated the people who travel on my works services like this, I would lose every contract within days."

A final memory concerns a 'might have been'. Viking were approached by Rolls Royce, the aeroplane engine manufacturers about a five day a week operation between the

PLATE 48. *CFA 645C was the first Bedford VAL14 six-wheel Duple coach purchased by Viking in May 1965. It is parked alongside an Eastern Counties service bus, suggesting the location could be Great Yarmouth, one of Viking's popular summer express services.*

company's headquarters in Derby and another site the company had at Barnoldswick in Lancashire. There was considerable travel between the sites. Although the company sought to institute car sharing arrangements, some days the cost of twenty such journeys was being reimbursed to employees. Discussions were progressing, involving the use of what later became known as an executive type coach, when Rolls Royce went into liquidation.

6. Football Excursions

I have separated the carrying of football supporters because at different times it was run as advertised excursions and others as private hire. The regular half-day excursion to Leicester was, officially, a football excursion. The licence only allowed it to run when Leicester City was playing at home. There were, in fact, two regular supporters who travelled, but the rest of the passengers, usually 40 or 50 were going for an afternoon shopping in the city.

One of the first excursions run specifically for football supporters

PLATE 49
This type of line-up was a regular feature alongside the Viking Motors' Woodville Travel Office, itself at the entrance to the Company's main base.

Courtesy Burton Daily Mail Ltd, per 'The Magic Attic'

after I joined was to the Molineux Ground, home of Wolverhampton Wanderers. Wanderers were playing Manchester United and we were successful in filling two coaches, useful revenue in winter. It was very noticeable that the majority of passengers were United supporters. So we started to run on a regular basis to Old Trafford and some other grounds, such as Everton's, when the Old Trafford team was playing there. Usually there was a full coach, sometime two, but I can recall one occasion when United were playing a continental team, four coaches ran.

However, Manchester United found themselves in danger of relegation to the second division. Three of our regulars, a young couple and a young man came to me. They realised that supporters might not be so keen and we be unwilling to run excursions in such circumstances. They asked if we would hire a coach to a group of supporters. It was useful revenue, without risk at a quiet time so I encouraged them. They placed an advert in the Burton Mail for a meeting and were surprised when more fifty people turned up. Agreement was reached and that season we ran to every home and away match. We had few hooligan problems, our group were very careful not to flaunt their colours near away grounds but there was one unfortunate incident when a local youth threw a brick through a window in Sunderland.

Manchester United was not the only team we followed. Occasionally Burton Albion would play a 'big' match, usually in one of the cup competitions and that would bring us in some valuable work. Strangely enough it was when carrying Albion supporters that we suffered two other examples of vandalism. Fortunately, both had a lighter side. The first involved an evening match at Stourbridge whose ground was, apparently, down a side street. Not surprisingly for a cup match, there was a big crowd and Viking's three coaches were trapped in the traffic coming away after the match. Burton had been victorious and a home supporter took exception and thrust his umbrella through the window of one of our coaches. It was not his lucky night because sitting near to the broken window was an employee of one of Burton's breweries. He left the stationary coach, caught up with the wielder of the umbrella, took it from and bent it round his neck like a collar. The local resident was not as strong as the Burton man and was last seen wending his way home, still wearing his new collar.

The other incident occurred at Cheltenham of all places. The driver was not a football fan and had stayed with the coach whilst the match was in progress. However, he had to answer a call of nature. On his return he found a youth adding to the Viking livery with a spray can. He was soon chased away but the coach returned with some graffiti. Fortunately, it had not long been polished, as Viking's coaches were when staff could be spared over the winter. The coating of polish came off along with the spray paint.

7. Victoria Buses
During the period I was with Viking, there were few changes to the Victoria bus service between Burton on Trent, Donisthorpe, and Measham. Although Midland Red covered some of the route, Victoria provided the most direct, in some cases the only link between a number of villages and the town.

There was one particular incident that I remember involving the bus service and that was a near miss, and that could have been a tragedy. One morning, an early bus to Burton was standing at the Castle Gresley bus stop, loading workers, when the driver, to his horror saw an eight wheel tipper truck heading towards him. It had clearly lost its brakes coming down Castle Gresley hill, and he had no chance to get out of its way. There was no room for the lorry to overtake. The lorry driver, with some skill, took to the footpath and avoided the stationery bus on the nearside. Fortunately, the last passenger had boarded otherwise they would have been swept away by the runaway.

8. Tudor Transport
In addition to the buses and coaches, a small lorry fleet was operated under the name 'Tudor Transport'. These were operated under a restricted "B" licence that enabled them to be used for carrying the products of the Woodville Pipe Works. There were two or three regular lorry drivers, but during the winter period, coach drivers, both full and part-time would sometimes fill in on the haulage side.

9. The Vehicles
When I joined Viking Motors, the company had just overcome a difficult time with regard to vehicle reliability. In the late fifties, the mainstay of the coach fleet had been the A.E.C. Reliance but these had experienced engine problems, leading to a number of breakdowns. This had not enhanced Viking's reputation but help was on the way.

In the mid sixties, Bedford had introduced the VAL type. This had three axles and could provide up to 52 seats in its 36 foot length. The Viking examples had 49 seats, the reduced number giving more leg room and making them more comfortable. Despite the reduction, the new coaches offered 8 more seats than the rest of the fleet, increasing revenue without increasing costs. Bedford also offered a shorter version, the VAM, on two axles and seating up to 45. The two Viking examples had 41 seats, giving greater comfort. Although the VAMs had Bedford engines the first VALs were fitted with Leyland engines.

Two further VALs were bought in 1968, fitted with the new Bedford 70 engine. Although this new engine was more powerful than the Leyland, it was also considerably noisier, a fact noted by some of the private hire customers. We only kept them for a year, although some of the earlier versions were kept for up to six years. From 1969 on, Fords were purchased. There was one exception was in 1970 when a single Leyland Leopard coach was bought. My one memory of this vehicle was that, without power assisted steering, it was extremely heavy to manoeuvre round the yard.

This was to continue until 1974 when due to a strike, production of Fords was stopped. That year a single Bedford YRT was purchased. At the time, government was supporting bus routes through grant aid to new buses. The YRT was such a vehicle and as such licensed to Victoria Motorways. Although it had to undertake a certain proportion of mileage on the bus service, it was available for coach work as well. One summer it spent most Saturdays on the Yarmouth express service.

Victoria had already taken advantage of the bus grant through the purchase of Bedford and Ford service buses. Four Bedfords were purchased in 1966. These were replaced by four similar vehicles in 1967. Three years later these were replaced by three Fords, which in turn were replaced in 1973.

This concludes John Holmes' invaluable personal account of the nine years he spent with Viking.

Viking Motors (Burton) Ltd.

Section 3 – 1975 to 1987

The third stage in the history of Viking Motors commences in 1975 and covers the period to November 1987, when Viking Motors (Burton) Ltd., and Victoria Motorways services, but not the Company, were sold. Many new customer initiatives were introduced during this period, all aimed at maintaining the company's activities as the principal coach provider in the South Derbyshire and East Staffordshire areas.

The 50th Anniversary of the launch of Viking Motors in 1926-7, was celebrated in 1977 in fine style. The Company hosted employees and their families for a day out in London, including sightseeing tour and time for their own interests, as a prelude to an enjoyable 50th Anniversary dinner at a Lutterworth hostelry on the homeward journey. The two coaches used were driven by Mr. John Lloyd, Director, and Mr. Ernie Elliott. Sadly, the founder of the Company, Mr. W. J. Lloyd, passed away on 24th March 1977, during the 50th Anniversary year.

Viking achieved a great deal in the thirty year period between 1946 and 1975, successfully positioning the company as the area's principal coach operator for the day tour, private hire and seasonal holiday services market. The emphasis and focus had always been on improving the standards of customer service and reliability and building the public's confidence in travelling by Viking, as a result of which the company could rightly claim to have created an enviable reputation across the wider Burton and Southern Derbyshire area.

A large part of Viking's customer base had always been generated through private hire and corporate hire sectors, and as part of the company's strategy for enhancing their presence within both of these sectors, it was decided to host a 'thank you' outing each year for 'private party organisers' who had previously used Viking, with booking staff providing ideas and information with the aim of securing further hire bookings. The Company's booking agents were also invited each year to a 'thank you' outing, in recognition of the support they gave in publicising the tours and holiday express services. Another key service aspect was the fact that every passenger was greeted and welcomed aboard the coach by the driver, with booking office staff also welcoming passengers joining at the Derby, Burton Union Street and Woodville garage pick-up points. Feeder services for passengers from the out-lying areas, and returning them near their own homes, was also a key element in the customer care package which helped the company increase passenger numbers, and set the company apart from most, if not all, of their competitors in the area.

Training in public speaking was provided for all drivers and booking office staff, by the Head of the 'Little Theatre' in Guild Street, to ensure they could make announcements by microphone when required, and also to ensure they were able to make announcements on arrival at a destination. Trips for route training to different parts of the country were

also used.

At the beginning of 1975 the Viking fleet was ten strong, six of which were Ford type R226, three Ford type R1114, and a solitary Leyland type PSU3A/4RT, No. PFA 791H new in May 1970. Nine carried Plaxton C53F bodies, whilst Ford R226 TFA 225J, new in February 1971, was the sole Duple C53F bodied example. PFA 791H was sold in March 1975, and two further new Plaxton bodied Ford R1114's, GUT 795N/796N, arrived in the same month.

In August 1975, two further Plaxton bodied Ford type R1014's, KNR 442P/443P brought the fleet number up to eleven vehicles, all with Plaxton bodies.

The successful acquisition of the London Tour licence in 1975 gave the company a major boost, inasmuch as passengers would now be able to enjoy seeing around London in the 'homely' surroundings of the Viking coach on which they had commenced their journey, in marked contrast to the hustle and bustle of having to find a London Tour bus, and moving between attractions less speedily than Viking's own tour. The London Tour licence necessitated Viking drivers and couriers undergoing familiarisation training of the Capital city's attractions, to at least meet the standards required, and identify where the Viking 'touch' could be applied to ensure the 'London' standards were exceeded.

A training trip to London, took place on Sunday 9th November 1975, and in true Viking 'family tradition', the following 'notice' was circulated to all employees:

"On Sunday 9th November we are joining Bryant Peers and some of his guides in London for a session in sightseeing tour training. If any members of the firm would to like to accompany us they are invited to do so and at the same time wives and families are invited to come along.

Depart Woodville	*7.30am*
Meet B.Peers	*10.30am*
Tour of London & Training	*4.00pm*

Wives and children will be welcome on the first tour and then have free time to do things while we continue training, and a picnic lunch will be provided and dinner on the homeward journey arriving back 8.30pm (no later). Come along and make a day out."

Mr. John Lloyd, Managing Director, was joined by 27 employees, with family members and 18 children totalling 82, and he recalls the day was a huge success for

PLATE 50
GFA 588L was new in 1973, a July delivery. The body style was unchanged, except for the 'destination blind' window now beneath the windscreen, moved from the lower grill panel.

Courtesy T.W.W. Knowles

were already established as Funeral Directors, and their name would doubtless have been a well-known one around the Burton area before the coach business was started. By the time Mr. W. J. Lloyd started Viking operations in late 1926, Wellings were operating three charabancs, and it is believed a summer season express service from Burton to Skegness, in addition to private hire and day trips. Viking acquired the business on 1st January 1977, taking over the two remaining coaches. Duple bodied Bedford No.MRR 473K, was used by Viking before being sold in September 1977. It was numbered 7 in the Viking fleet, which suggests it received Viking's two-tone grey livery. The second Welling's vehicle acquired, No.DOK 514C, was not operated by Viking, and it was sold in January 1978.

After the arrival of four new vehicles in 1975, two further Plaxton bodied Ford type R1014's OUT 352R/353R were purchased in 1976, whilst three coaches, XFA 788K, YFA 157K & BFA 435L were disposed of in August that year. The only vehicles added in 1977 were the two from Wellings referred to earlier. A return to the Ford type R1114 came with the arrival of XJF 156S & 157S in May 1978, both fitted with Plaxton C53F bodies, with the 'five horizontal chrome bar' front grill. Four identical coaches were purchased in 1979, two arriving in June, EBC 280T & 672T, and two in October, ERY 790T & GJF 400V, but only two vehicles were disposed of, GJU 686N & GUT 796N. Whilst the fleet strength had been kept at eleven vehicles between 1974-8, the 1979 changes resulted in an increase to 13 coaches.

Two new coaches were added in 1980. Both were the reliable Ford type R1114 with Plaxton C53F body, registered LJF 735V & 742V, both of which were included in the sale of Viking Motors to Stevensons on 31st October 1987. In 1985, LJF 735V was re-registered with the personal number plate from the late Mr. W. J. Lloyd's car, OFA 10.

The last new Plaxton C51F bodied Ford type R1114

the Company in all ways.

Viking's own in-company 'London Guide' expertise was a key factor in ensuring the Company's London Tours were heavily booked throughout each successive season, right through in fact to the time when the Lloyd family ownership ceased in November 1987. The 'families trip' had the added bonus of being able to give something back to the employees' families who were well looked after throughout the day.

Another innovative, if somewhat unusual addition to the Viking programme, were day trips by air to the Bunratty Folk Park in Ireland. Passengers were taken to London Heathrow where they boarded a Jumbo jet chartered by Ian Allan Travel for the trip to Ireland's Shannon Airport, and onto the Bunratty Folk Park by coach. The Jumbo trips were part of a programme of short haul training flights for aircrew, on which passengers could also be carried.

A new 'Viking Travel Club' was launched in 1976 with a reception at the Friary Hotel, Derby, and invited guests were taken to and from the event by coach. Fare reduction incentives and a range of new destinations designed to attract members, were the key elements in the 'club' package. The real benefit for the Company in offering a members' reduced fare, was to get more passengers using the midweek tour programme, when passenger loadings outside the peak summer season were often lower than during the peak holiday periods. The club was a popular innovation, with added incentives such as morning coffee and afternoon tea included in a reduced ticket price, with the cost more than recovered from the increased number of passenger fares taken.

Towards the end of 1976 discussions took place with Viking's long standing local competitor, Wellings (Burton upon Trent) Ltd. The Welling's coach business started when Mr. G. W. Wellings purchased a Ford T 14 seater charabanc in March 1921. However, Welling's

PLATE 52
KNR 443P, one of two August 1975 deliveries, outwardly identical to GUT 796N in the previous illustration. The 'Viking' name and warrior head are seen more clearly in this illustration.

Courtesy K.West

coach was delivered with registration NAY 791W in late 1980, and whilst one photograph of it in this form is included (Plate 257), it was re-registered RJU 383W and taxed from 1st April 1981.

Viking's first purchase of a D.A.F. vehicle was in June 1983, by which time the Plaxton C53F body styling had taken on a more dynamic appearance. The vehicle was registered JGL 53, a personal number plate purchased by Mr. J. L. Lloyd, Managing Director. A second 'nearly new' acquisition in July 1983, was LFO 800Y, a Duple C53F bodied Leyland, which had been delivered new in May 1983 to C.G.& D.R.Morris of Bromyard.

A number of corporate incentive trips were undertaken for overseas visitors to the Uttoxeter headquarters of JCB, with the package including collection from and return to either Heathrow or Gatwick airports, and outings for spouses to the Cotswolds area.

All-in holidays to Scarborough, ski parties to the Cairngorms, and a Christmas tour to Scotland, were other popular destinations, whilst a six day holiday package to the Scilly Isles included a first night in Penzance, with the last leg of the journey to the Isles was by SS Silonian steamer after breakfast on the second day. The return from the Scillys to Penzance was by helicopter. A one-day excursion to the Scillys had required an overnight coach journey to Penzance with breakfast on arrival, before catching the ferry to the Isles. The return journey to Penzance was late afternoon, before boarding the coach for the return journey, with arrival in Burton around mid-night.

Another popular if somewhat unusual 'Coast to Coast' tour, included visits to both the East and West coasts of England. Arrival in Scarborough in time for lunch was followed by a journey through some of the most beautiful parts of the Yorkshire Dales and Pennines, before an arrival in Morecambe for afternoon tea and a leisurely stroll. The third leg of the tour was usually completed around 11pm.

What must have been the longest 'one-day' Viking excursions ever undertaken, were those to Guernsey in the Channel Islands. Departure from Woodville garage was late afternoon on Day 1, arriving in Poole, Dorset to catch the midnight ferry. Lounge chairs or beds were available, and breakfast was taken on arrival in St.Peter Port, Guernsey. The teatime ferry from St. Peter Port to Poole was used, with the Viking coach returning the weary souls to Burton around midnight on Day 2. Another of the popular one-day excursions, with a near midnight return to Burton , was to the Isle of Wight, with ferries between Portsmouth and Fishbourne, and a visit to Blackgang Chine.

Excursions to the Ascot Race meetings for the Royal Hunt Cup and Ladies Days were other popular attractions, with a need for an early departure. Lunch packs were collected by Viking prior to leaving Woodville. The outward journey was timed to allow for a stop at the George Hotel, Kilsby, Northants, for breakfast, whilst the return journey included dinner at the Bridge Hotel, Shillingford.

Meanwhile, the seasonal holiday services and daily tour programme continued almost as if by clockwork, and such was the demand for seats, additional coaches were often required, including some hired in from other operators.

Private hire bookings were a large part of the Viking business, particularly as the costs of running private hire bookings were up to 30% less than those for advertised day excursions.

In 1984, Viking won a number of School Contracts from both the Derbyshire and Staffordshire County Councils for Monday to Friday school term services. This was a new area of activity under the 'Viking Motors' name, and because of the potentially large numbers for some schools, two second-hand Daimler double-deck buses were purchased in August 1984, for the purpose. They were Daimler chassis with Northern Counties H43/33F bodies, BHL 621K & BHL 625K, both new in March 1972, to West

PLATE 53
One of only two double deckers ever owned by the Viking and Victoria companies. BHL 625K is seen leaving Swadlincote bus station bound for Newhall & Burton on the Victoria X22 service, in September 1987. Courtesy D.J.Stanier

Riding Automobile Co. Ltd., Wakefield. They were delivered in the National bus red livery, but were soon repainted at the Woodville garage workshops into a striking new Viking two-tone blue and white livery, with large Viking head on the front, and bold advertisement panels for the 'Viking Travel Agency British & Continental Holidays on each side. In the early days of these contracts arrangements were made for the two double deckers to be parked in a farmyard each day, near to the first and last pick-up/drop off points so that the costly and repetitive dead mileage between Woodville and the school catchment area could be kept to a minimum. However, the two vehicles returned to Woodville garage after the afternoon run, allowing time for any necessary repairs and servicing.

Three of the coaches used on morning school services were parked in New Street Bus Station, Burton until required for the afternoon services. Victoria buses and Viking coaches were also used on some of the school contracts.

When not required for school contracts, the two double deckers were used on Victoria services into and out of Burton. In addition to the formal School Contract work, Viking had been regular suppliers of coaches to schools in the East Staffordshire and South Derbyshire areas since the

1950's, for journeys which were part of an individual school's own extra-curricular programme of outside visits and sports related visits.

Viking were members of the nationally recognised 'Bus & Coach Council – Independent Sector', with Viking's Managing Director, Mr. John Lloyd, serving on the East Midlands Regional Committee.

In early 1984, Mr. Lloyd was one of a group of Rotarians from the Swadlincote, Ashby and Coalville Rotary Clubs, who visited Russia in the days of very strict communism, and recalls all luggage was searched on arrival, and they were conducted and directed everywhere they went.

Whilst on this trip he met a Coalville Rotarian, who had recently returned from America and who, over a number of visits, had made friends with a Rotarian who was also a travel agent in Connecticut. The travel agent was wanting to arrange a trip for American Rotarians to attend the Rotary International Convention which was to be held at the National Exhibition Centre, Birmingham, in June 1984, but he had been unable to sort out hotel accommodation and transportation in the London area for a proposed group of up to 350 Rotarians/their wives/partners. On hearing that Mr. Lloyd was in the travel business, the Coalville Rotarian introduced him to the Connecticut travel agent.

John Lloyd offered to provide an 8 day package consisting of hotel accommodation in Derby area hotels rather than in London, travel to and from the NEC each day, a daily programme of sightseeing tours to popular venues for wives/partners, with transportation from Heathrow or Gatwick airports to Derby on arrival, and return as required at the end of their stay, and this proved to be a more competitively priced package than one based on using London hotels. The arrangements were made through the Viking Travel Agency, and included an undertaking by Mr. Lloyd that only Viking coaches and the company's own staff would be used, and this proved acceptable to the Connecticut organiser.

A good variety of optional sightseeing tours were part of the package, including a specially constructed sightseeing tour of Birmingham. Prior to the visit, three Viking employees, Eric Nicholls, Arthur Prince, and Sue Gardner, accompanied Mr. Lloyd on a fact finding and route planning trip to Birmingham. The specially compiled itinerary included the City's Victorian Town Hall and Law Courts, the Jewellery quarter of the city, art galleries, John Peel's statue, Edgbaston Cricket Ground, the parks, University, and Birmingham's never-to-be-forgotten Spaghetti Motorway Junction. There was the obvious name connection between Birmingham England and the several Birmingham's in the United States, and many of the visitors were impressed and moved by the sight of the bombed church and graveyard near the Jewellery quarter.

A number of the visitors expressed a desire to experience the delights of having dinner in an English country house, and Callow Hall, near Ashbourne, was the chosen venue, with Viking providing transportation.

An apparent tendency for American visitors to travel with more than the average number of items of luggage per person was anticipated by Mr. Lloyd, and vans were hired to transport the visitors' luggage between airports and the Derby hotels.

The final three days of the package were based on using

several London hotels, with Viking coaches used for London sightseeing, trips to Windsor, Hampton Court and other locations, all of which helped to complete a very successful package for the company. Viking staff co-ordinated movements between hotels and the NEC, and they also acted as courier and tour guides on the coaches. The arrangements were a great success, and at the end of the London stay, Viking coaches returned the visitors to either Heathrow or Gatwick.

Viking's seasonal express services had been well patronised over many years, resulting in high loadings for most of the available weeks each year. Some weeks, however, a small number of seats were not taken, and in an effort to increase passenger loadings, it was decided to try to fill the empty seats by offering 'Away-Day Saver' tickets to Weston-super-Mare and Minehead (Ilfracombe service), Banbury & Oxford (Bournemouth service), and to Nottingham, Newark and Lincoln (Skegness service). The

PLATE 54
A marked change in the 1976 front grill design, if anything a more simple style. A paper sticker for 'Red Funnel Services Southampton-Isle of Wight', is behind the windscreen, and the photograph was taken at a Sandown IOW hotel.
Courtesy T.W.W. Knowles

PLATE 55.
The only D.A.F. powered vehicle purchased by Viking, fitted with Plaxton's new 1982 'Paramount' body design in replacement for the long running Panorama styling. The JGL 53 plate reflected Mr.J.G.Lloyd's initials, re-registered to 82 HBC when sold to Stevensons in 1987. It is seen on Pastures Hill, Littleover, Derby in June 1983.
Courtesy D.J.Stanier

Saver tickets could only be booked in the seven days before date of travel.

The last vehicle to be purchased by Viking Motors (Burton) Ltd., before the 1987 sale to Stevensons, was a March 1984 registered Leyland with Plaxton C55F body A834 PPP, which joined the Viking fleet in March 1986.

In April 1986 the *'The Viking Norseman Club'*, was launched, offering a range of unusual destinations and special 'member' fares, as a way of securing customer loyalty for Viking following de-regulation of the bus and coach industry, and the probability of new operators becoming competitors of Viking.The first welcoming note sent to members stated that over 2,000 people had joined, and that such overwhelming demand would mean the Company having to allocate Burton area members a time for the coach from the Viking coach station in Union Street, Burton, which would take them to the first Social Event to be held on 9th April. A monthly Newsletter detailing the 'club events' was sent to all members, and such was the popularity of the club, that in some months as many as six trips were set aside for members.The February 1987 Newletter records that the 1986 Christmas Party event held at the Gresley Old Hall, was attended by 250 members and partners, with a number of lucky prize draw winners receiving prizes from free Viking coach holidays to Christmas puddings.

In 1986 a number of additional drop off/pick-up points were added to the Holiday express services which offered passengers a greater choice of destinations as follows:
TORQUAY Express
- Weston super Mare (this had been the overnight Torquay service convenience stop since the early 1960's)
- EXETER - with connections by Devon General services to Dawlish, Teignmouth, Exmouth, Sidmouth, Budleigh Salterton, and Plymouth
- TORQUAY & PAIGNTON
BOURNEMOUTH & ISLE OF WIGHT Express
- via Southampton, and Red Funnel ferry to and from East Cowes, Isle of Wight. Arrangements were made with Moss Paul coaches to transfer passengers between ferry and the major holiday towns on the island. Red Funnel ferry and

PLATE 56.
EBC 280T, delivered in June 1979, was the first of Viking's seven Ford R1114 Plaxton 'Supreme' style bodied coaches.

Moss Paul tickets were issued by Viking.

The Bournemouth & Isle of Wight (via Portsmouth) service was acquired from Hanfords of Barton.
ILFRACOMBE - MINEHEAD for Butlins Holiday Camp, and Somerwest World

The company's first foray into Europe came in 1987, when a number of spare seats on a privately organised twelve day tour of France, Switzerland, Italy and the Black Forest, were advertised by Viking.   In October 1986, Mr. Alan Paling, a coach driver with considerable driving experience in Europe, had joined Viking and was the ideal choice as driver for the 1987 tour.   The price including all meals was £380, and the company's last new coach, the 1983 DAF with Plaxton 53 seat body, carrying the Managing director's personalised number plate, JGL 53, was used for the tour. Seating was reduced from 53 to 49, with the re-arrangement

PLATE 57. *Four of the seven Plaxton 'Supreme's are seen in this line-up in the Woodville garage yard circa 1981. GJF 400V arrived Oct 1979; LJF 742V & 735V were July 1980 arrivals, whilst RJU 383W did not enter service until 1981.*

allowing more leg room for each passenger.

The following summer season Express Services were operated in the final year of 1987:

-WESTON-SUPER-MARE-EXETER-TORQUAY-PAIGNTON
Saturdays from 23 May to 12 September, and Tuesdays 4, 11, 18 & 25 August

-KINGS LYNN-NORWICH-CAISTER-GREAT YARMOUTH, also picked up and set down at WEST BRIDGFORD-GRANTHAM   Saturdays 23 May to 12 September

- BRIDLINGTON-FILEY-CAYTON BAY-SCARBOROUGH
Saturdays 18 July to 29 August

- BANBURY-OXFORD-SOUTHAMPTON Royal Pier, Dock Gate 7 (for Isle of Wight passengers)-BOSCOMBE-BOURNEMOUTH   Saturdays 23 May to 12 September

- NOTTINGHAM-NEWARK-LINCOLN-SKEGNESS
Saturdays 23 May to 12 September

- BLACKPOOL
Saturdays 23 May to 31 October (Saturdays October 3,10,17,24 depart Blackpool 11pm, and on 31 October, depart 5pm) Mondays 13 July to 26 October
Fridays 27 July to 30 October Sundays 4,11,18,25 October
Extra journeys were run over Bank Holidays

Sadly, the Lloyd family's ownership of Viking, stretching over sixty-one years, came to an end on the 31st October 1987.   Throughout this long period, the name 'Viking' had been synonymous with first class quality coach travel and service, and whilst other smaller operators in the area, including Lauds Coaches of Moira and Cosy coaches of Donisthorpe, had also provided private hire and a limited range of day trips, none had – *in the opinion of the author* - quite commanded the coach market in the same way as Viking had achieved down the years.

As outlined in the section on 'Regent', Midland Red had secured the local bus services in the South Derbyshire area, apart from those operated by Viking's associate company, Victoria Motorways, but despite Midland Red also offering a limited programme of day and half day trips from Swadlincote each Spring and Summer, Viking were by far the most dominant coach operator in the area over a very long period.

LFO 800Y was new in May 1983 to Morris of Bromyard, and it was purchased by Viking in July 1983. It was photographed at Weston super Mare in 1984, most probably during the afternoon return journey from Torquay.
Courtesy T.W.W.Knowles

School Contract S10

	7.45	Dep. Woodville, proceed to Edingale (arr.8.15) via Overseal and Lullington
	8.15	Edingale School, via Croxall & Alrewas
	To	JOHN TAYLOR HIGH SCHOOL, Barton under Needwood
THEN:	8.40	Dep. Tatenhill Cross Roads, Acorn Inn, Aviation Lane, Needwood New Inn,
	To	RANGEMORE ALL SAINTS SCHOOL

School Contract S20

	7.45	Dep Woodville garage to Burton and Barton
	8.35	Oakfield Rd, Fox Lane & Co-op store, Alrewas
	To	JOHN TAYLOR HIGH SCHOOL, Barton under Needwood

School Contract S30

	7.45	Dep Woodville garage to Burton and Barton
	8.40	Alrewas Village Hall, Wychnor Lane lay-bye
	To	JOHN TAYLOR HIGH SCHOOL, B-u-N

School Contract S40

	7.45	Dep. Woodville garage to Beam Hill, Burton
	8.10	Beamhill Road corner, Anslow School, Burnt Gate, Tatenhill Post Office, Tatenhill Crossroads, Tatenhill School, Rangemore School
	To	JOHN TAYLOR HIGH SCHOOL, B-u-N

School Contract S50

	7.45	Dep. Woodville garage, to Burton
	8.15	Wellington St. Post Office. Forest Road, Aviation Lane End, Henhurst Hill PO, Acorn Inn, Burnt Gate, Anslow School, Brickmakers Arms,
	To	WULFRIC SCHOOL (Harehedge Lane & Rolleston Rd. Junc) then to
	To	DE FERRUS HIGH SCHOOL, Rolleston on Dove

School Contract S60

	8.00	Dep. Woodville garage to Linton
	8.25	Linton Post Office
	To	PINGLE SCHOOL, Swadlincote
THEN:	8.45	Black Horse Hotel, Stanton, Short St. Stapenhill, Bretby Lane, Hawfield Lane, Dalebrook, Hawkins Lane, Wetmore Road, Stretton Church,
	To	BITHAM SCHOOL, Stretton

School Contract S65 – Mon, Tues, Wed only

	8.00	Dep. Woodville garage to Linton
	8.30	Red Lion Inn, Linton
	To	PINGLE SCHOOL, Swadlincote
THEN:	8.43	Elmsleigh Drive, Poplar Avenue, Lime Tree Avenue, Midway
	To	GRANVILLE SCHOOL, Midway

School Contract S70

	4.10	PINGLE SCHOOL
	To	Red Lion Inn, Linton, via Rickmans Corner & Heath House

School Contract S80

	3.25	BITHAM SCHOOL
	To	Black Horse Hotel, Stanton
THEN:	4.10	PINGLE SCHOOL, Swadlincote
	To	Linton

School Contract S90

	3.15	RANGEMORE ALL SAINTS SCHOOL
	To	Tatenhill Cross Roads
THEN:	3.50	JOHN TAYLOR HIGH SCHOOL, Barton under Needwood
	To	Alrewas, Croxall, Edingale School

School Contract S100

	4.00	DE FERRUS HIGH SCHOOL, Rolleston Road, Burton upon Trent
	4.05	WULFRIC SCHOOL (Harehedge Lane & Rolleston Rd Junc)
THEN:		ANSLOW SCHOOL
	To	Burnt Lane, Acorn Inn, Henhurst Post Office, Aviation Lane, Henhurst Hill

School Contract S110

	3.50	JOHN TAYLOR HIGH SCHOOL, Barton under Needwood
	To	Alrewas Village Hall, Wychnor Lane End

School Contract S120

	3.50	JOHN TAYLOR HIGH SCHOOL, Barton under Needwood
	To	Oakfield Road, Fox Lane & Co-op store, Alrewas

School Contract S125 – Mon, Tues only

	4.00	PINGLE SCHOOL
	To	Red Lion Inn, Linton

SBA Baths Contract – Wednesday only

S10 Schools Contract vehicle

THEN TO:		ALL SAINTS SCHOOL, NEWBOROUGH pick-up
	9.15	To Abbots Bromley Baths
THEN TO:		RANGEMORE ALL SAINTS SCHOOL pick-up
	9.40	To Abbots Bromley Baths
WAIT	10.10	From Baths to ALL SAINTS SCHOOL, NEWBOROUGH
THEN TO:		ST. PETERS SCHOOL, YOXALL pick-up
	10.30	To Abbots Bromley Baths
	10.40	From Baths to RANGEMORE ALL SAINTS SCHOOL
	11.40	From Baths to ST. PETERS SCHOOL, YOXALL

SBB Baths Contract – Tuesday & Fridays only

DE FERRERS SCHOOL Swimming Contract

	1.05	WULFRIC SCHOOL, St. Mary's Drive, Rolleston-on-Dove
	To	DE FERRERS SCHOOL
	2.40	Return WULFRIC SCHOOL

VIKING MOTORS – List of vehicles

Mr. Lloyd's departure from Regent Motor Services in 1926 was so that he could start his own company. He ordered his first coach, an Albion *'Viking'* chassis with W.D.Smith bodywork, and the *'Viking Coaches'* name was adopted from the chassis type name.

However, Albion records state the chassis was ordered in 1926 in the names of Messrs. Lloyd, Power & Dennis, (partners in Regent Motor Services), but as Mr. Lloyd had left Regent in the latter half of 1926, he took delivery of this vehicle in May 1927. With the help of The PSV Circle and the Albion Motors archive at the Biggar Museum Trust, the registration of this first vehicle, although unconfirmed, is now believed to have been RA 2838. The Albion chassis No. 5037F for this vehicle, is recorded in the end pages of Mr. Lloyd's 1927 diary.

Regn Number	Type	Body by:	Seating	New in:	To Viking:	Date w/drawn	Pre-Viking ownership & disposal
Vehicles listed in year of acquisition							
1927							
RA 2838	Albion *'Viking'* chassis	W.D.Smith West Bromwich	C26	5/27	5/27	7/30	Alton, Nottingham 7/30 Last licensed 3/36
The following is the first Viking vehicle recorded in the PSV Circle Fleet List PD18:							
1928							
FA 3271	Albion PK26	Rushton & Wilson	C26	5/28	5/28	2/29	To unknown owner Argyll 6/32 Last reg'd owner J.Reekie, Dunoon Last Licensed 3/49
	(a bus chassis with straight frame at the rear and no space for a boot, originally intended for the Sandwell Motor Co., Birmingham. Vehicle had limited luggage space without a boot, and this may have been the reason for disposal by Viking after ten months).						
1929							
FA 3518	Albion PNC26	W.J.Smith	C26R	2/29	2/29	3/36	Churchbridge Motor Garage, Cannock 4/36 To unknown owner Middx as showmans goods 9/45 Last Licensed 12/47 LRO P.M.Davis, Hayes, Middx
	(re-bodied to FC32 by 1932 – builder unknown)						
FA 3760	Albion PNC26	Dixon	C26	5/29	5/29	10/34	not known
1933							
FA 4960 Fleet No. 1	Leyland TS4	Burlingham	C30F	1/33	1/33	9/53	To Ada Coaches, Leicester Unknown owner, Surrey (no date) To Reading owner 8/55 as S'mans Spec. LRO J.Matthews,Caversham,Reading Last licensed 9/55
	(received new Burlingham C32F body and re-seated to 33, in post-war years)						
1935							
FA 5740	Albion PV70	"	C31C	4/35	4/35	7/51	V&M Coaches, Grendon 7/51 Evans, Bedworth -/55, LL 9/55
	(re-seated to 32 after 1945)						
1936							
FA 6199	AEC Regal	"	C32F	3/36	3/36	2/52	V&M Coaches, Coventry 2/52 Last licensed 9/55 as goods LRO G.L.Ogle, Coundon, Coventry
	(re-seated to 33 postwar)						
1938							
FA 7205	Albion CX13	"	C32F	6/38	6/38	11/53	Ada Coaches, Leicester 1.54 Last licensed 12/54 LRO L.C.Pratt,Leicester (Ada)
1940							
VT 2901	AEC Reliance	Dixon	B32F	5/29	c/40	12/42	New to Buckley, Basford, Stoke-on-T 5/29 Caswell, Tunstall 3/30 Victoria Motorways 4/31 No further operator after Viking, Believed destroyed by war action 12/42
FA 3999	Daimler CF6	Charlesworth	C28	3/30	1/41	12/45	New to Wellings, B-o-T 3/30 Machins, Ashby-de-la-Zouch 3/40 To Viking Motors 1/41, No further optr.
1944							
FV 1689	Leyland TS2	Burlingham Harrington	C25DT C32F(1938)	3/31	?/44	4/48	New to Wood Bros, Blackpool 3/31 Standerwick, Blackpool 9/36 Broadhead (dealer) Bollington 3/38 J.C.Broadhead, Bollington 7/38 Victoria Motorways c/40 Gee's Motors, Swinford 4/48, w/d 12/52
GG 4946	Albion PMB28	Cowieson	C31	11/31	?/44	4/49	New – Baillie Bros.Dumbarton 11/31 Central SMT, Motherwell 6/36 W/D 39 Victoria Motorways c/43 No further operator after Viking

VO 4066 B.A.T.Cruiser	?		C20F	6/30	by 1945	10/50	New to H.Wilson, East Retford To Viking Motors during 1939-45 war period No further operator after Viking
BR 8228 B.A.T. Cruiser	?		C20D	7/30	c/45	10/50	New to G.E.Dunay, Pity Me 7/30 H.Wilson, East Retford ?/?? To Viking Motors c/45 No further operator after Viking

Note: *Until about 1947 the rear seat was only allowed to seat 4, then 5 were allowed, but no physical change in the seats was made.*

1948

FA 8882 AEC Regal III No.22 named 'Valorous'	Burlingham	C33F	1/48	1/48	5/58	Whitley Motors, Coventry 6/58 Marchant, Cheltenham 8/60 w/d12/62 Not licensed after Marchant Last known owner Stevens (scrap Dealers) Gloucester
FA 8883 AEC Regal III No.23	"	C33F	2/48	2/48	2/54	Harper, Stockport 2/54 Abbott Motor Tours, Timperley 5/57 Contract Bus, London 7/60, LL 4/63 LNO F.Furman, Pengam, Pontypool
FA 8961 AEC Regal III No.21	"	C33F	3/48	3/48	8/54	Harper, Stockport 2/55 Unidentified owner London 7/60
FA 9073 Daimler CVD6 No. 2 named 'Viceroy'	"	C33F	6/48	6/48	3/58	Say's Luxury Coaches, Gloucester 3/58 LL UK 1/61 Autobuses, Las Palmas, Gr.Can. 9/61 Scrapped Arucas Depot

1949

FA 9325 Daimler CVD6 No.25 named 'Vamoose'	Burlingham	C33F	3/49	3/49	2/58	Say's Luxury Coaches, Glou. 2/58 Last licensed (Say's) 1/61 Autobuses, Las Palmas, Gr.Can. 7/61 Withdrawn by 1973
FA 9326 Daimler CVD6 No.26 named 'Vampire'	"	C33F	2/49	2/49	-/55	Ogle, Coventry -/55 Vanguard, Bulkington 5/57 W/drawn 3/63, Scrapped 5/63
FA 9354 AEC Regal III No.24 named 'Valiant'	"	C35F	3/49	3/49	10/54	Cottons Coaches, Bilton 11/54 Court, Chapel End Coaches 7/59 Edwards & Son Ltd., Joys Green 11/60 Last licensed 10/64

1951

AFA 499 AEC Regal IV No. 9 named 'Vigilant'	Burlingham	C39C	6/51	6/51	5/62	Hart, Donisthorpe 5/62 Last known owner – J.R.Buxton, Broughton Astley, Leics. LL 11/66

1952

AFA 953 AEC Regal IV No. 3 named 'Valkyrie'	"	C39C	6/52	6/52	12/61	Whitley Motors, Coventry 2/62 Vanguard, Bulkington 2/65 w/d 6/69 Exported to Australia, re-registered with Hunter Valley Coaches, NSW 1/71

1953

BFA 565 AEC Regal IV No. 5 named 'Vanguard'	Plaxton	C41C	4/53	4/53	4/65	Wilson, Contractor, Northampton 5/65
BFA 566 AEC Regal IV No. 6 named 'Venturer'	"	C41C	5/53	5/53	4/65	Wilson, Contractor, Northampton 5/65

1954

RMB 159 AEC Regal IV No. 3 named 'Viscount'	"	C41C	7/53	3/54	10/65	New to Altrincham Coachways Ltd. Reliant Coaches, Ibstock 4/66 Hylton & Dawson, Glenfield 11/66 Leversley, Fulbeck 2/70 Yeates, Loughborough (dealer) scrap
RMB 240 AEC Regal IV No.8 named 'Voyager'	"	C41C	7/53	3/54	10/65	Leese, Barlaston 11/65 Bassetts Coachways, Tittensor 4/67 (Vehicle in preservation 2003)

1955

DFA 548 AEC Reliance No. 8	Willowbrook	DP41F	5/55	5/55	?/61	To Victoria Motorways ?/61

Reg	Chassis	Body	Seating	New	In	Out	Notes
DFA 550 No.10	AEC Reliance	"	DP41F	5/55	5/55	?/61	To Victoria Motorways ?/61

1957

Reg	Chassis	Body	Seating	New	In	Out	Notes
FFA 811 No.11	AEC Reliance	"	DP41F	6/57	6/57	3/66	Lilac Coaches, Barlestone 4/66 Kenneally, Dungarvan 7/68 Re-registered BWI 717 Used as workshop 9/68, scrapped by 4/85
BJP 271 No. 15	Leyland PSUC1/2	Alexander C41F		4/55	9/57	c/60	New to Smith & Co. Wigan To Victoria Motorways ?/60
BJP 387 No. 14	Leyland PSUC1/2 named 'Valorous II'	"	C41F	5/55	9/57	c/60	New to Webster, Wigan Silver Grey, Morecambe 4/56 To Victoria Motorways ?/60

1958

Reg	Chassis	Body	Seating	New	In	Out	Notes
HFA 3 No.13	Leyland PSUC1/2 named 'Viceroy II'	Willowbrook	C41F	5/58	5/58	5/62	To Victoria Motorways 5/62

1959

Reg	Chassis	Body	Seating	New	In	Out	Notes
203 ARB No. 21	Bedford SBG	Duple	C41F	1/56	1/59	3/67	New to Brooks Bros. Castle Gresley Cream & Blue Coaches, Guildford 7/67 Alpha Coaches, Brighton 5/70
JFA 519 No.12	AEC Reliance named 'Vamoose'	Willowbrook	C41F	3/59	3/59	?/63	To Victoria Motorways ?/63
JFA 798 No. 2	Bedford SB3 named 'Vampire'	Duple	C41F	6/59	6/59	9/67	Unidentified Operator, Gwynedd 9/67

1960

Reg	Chassis	Body	Seating	New	In	Out	Notes
LFA 153 No.23	Bedford SB3 named 'Valiant'	"	C41F	5/60	5/60	7/69	Ashcroft, Leicester 9/69

1961

Reg	Chassis	Body	Seating	New	In	Out	Notes
833 ERR	Bedford SB3	"	C41F	3/60	3/61	5/71	New to Netherfield Coaches, Netherfield Unid. Contractor, Kingswinford 11/74 In use as site hut at Swindon by 5/76
NFA 316 No.16	AEC Reliance	Plaxton	C41F	4/61	4/61	4/66	Reliant Coaches, Ibstock 4/66 Hylton & Dawson, Glenfield 11/66 28th Leicester Scout Grp 1/77 Broadbent Motors (dealer) 2/82
NFA 317 No.17	AEC Reliance	"	C41F	4/61	4/61	3/66	Pugh & Sons, Towyn 3/66 Regina Coaches, Blaenau Ffestiniog 6/76, W/d 7/78

1962

Reg	Chassis	Body	Seating	New	In	Out	Notes
PFA 438 No. 3	Leyland L2	"	C41F	4/62	4/62	3/72	Rosemary Coaches, Terrington St.Clement 5/72
PFA 439 No. 9	AEC Reliance		C41F	5/62	5/62	3/66	Reliant Coaches, Ibstock 4/66 Ward, Middlesbrough 7/74

1964

Reg	Chassis	Body	Seating	New	In	Out	Notes
UFA 593 No.15	AEC Reliance	"	C41F	4/64	4/64	4/72	Pugh, Towyn 5/72 w/d 6/73
AFA 134B No.14	AEC Reliance	"	C41F	5/64	5/64	4/72	Brownrigg, Egremont 6/72 Unidentified owner, Newtownards, N.I. By 9/78

1965

Reg	Chassis	Body	Seating	New	In	Out	Notes
CFA 645C No. 5	Bedford VAL14	Duple	C49F	5/65	5/65	3/71	Castle Coaches, Kirby Muxloe 4/71
CFA 646C No. 6	Bedford VAL14	"	C49F	5/65	5/65	1/72	Hopkins, Ogmore Vale 1/72 Nth Somerset Coaches, Nailsea 1/78 Swanbrook Tr'pt, Staverton 7/78 w/d 6/80 Breakdown tender 8/80 sold for scrap 12/80

1966

Reg	Chassis	Body	Seating	New	In	Out	Notes
EFA 494D No. 4	Bedford VAL14	"	C49F	4/66	4/66	12/72	To Victoria Motorways 12/72
EFA 495D No.16	Bedford VAM5	Plaxton	C41F	3/66	3/66	5/68	Tagg, Sutton-in-Ashfield 6/68 Trow, Bolton-on-Dearne 7/72

Reg / No.	Model	Body	Seating				History
EFA 496D No.17	Bedford VAM5	"	C41F	3/66	3/66	3/71	Broomhill Motors, Hucknall 3/71 Penrhyn Service Station Ltd., Rhos-on-Sea 11/71 Gold Star C/ways, St. Asaph 9/74 W/d post 1975

1967

Reg / No.	Model	Body	Seating				History
GFA 601E No. 1	Bedford VAL14	"	C49F	3/67	3/67	5/70	Pugh, Towyn 5/70 to 6/73 Pied Bull Coaches, Mold 8/73 W/d by 4/82

1968

Reg / No.	Model	Body	Seating				History
KFA 776F No.12	Bedford VAL70	"	C49F	5/68	5/68	7/69	Longdale Coaches, Ravenshead 9/69 Burnt out 8/70
KFA 777F No.11	Bedford VAL70	"	C49F	5/68	5/68	7/69	Arnold, Redcar 8/69 Begg, Thornaby-on-Tees 12/71 w/d 6/72 Yeates (dealer) Loughborough to Longdale Coaches, Ravenshead 7/72

1969

Reg / No.	Model	Body	Seating				History
NFA 163G No.16	Ford R226	Plaxton	C52F	5/69	5/69	2/74	Frost & Heath, Leigh 3/74
NFA 164G No.18	Ford R226	"	C52F	5/69	5/69	7/75	Beeline, Coventry 7/75 Enterprise Coaches, Coventry 5/80, W/d 8/83 Gerry Cottle Circus (showman) by 3/88
NFA 547G No.12	Ford R226	Duple Northern	C53F	7/69	7/69	11/74	Copeland & Bowers, Hanley 5/75 Hirst Tours, Longton 5/76 Return to Copeland & Bowers 2/79 H.T.Copeland, Hanley 5/79 Copeland Tours, Hanley 3/80 w/d 7/82 Goodwin (dealer) Carlton 6/86 for scrap
NFA 548G No.11	Ford R226	"	C53F	7/69	7/69	7/73	Johnson Coaches, Hanslope 10/73

1970

Reg / No.	Model	Body	Seating				History
PFA 791H No.1	Leyland PSU3A/4R	Plaxton	C53F	5/70	5/70	3/75	Tay Valley Coaches, Invergowrie 3/75 D.C.Gorman, Cambusland 4/79

1971

Reg / No.	Model	Body	Seating				History
TFA 225J No.5	Ford R226	Duple	C53F	2/71	2/71	7/75	Adkins, Upper Boddington 11/75 W/d 9/87, dismantled for spares 3/89
TFA 226J No.6	Ford R226	"	C53F	4/71	4/71	11/74	Glantawe Motors, Pontardawe 11.74 T.Roberts & Son, Meinciau 7/87 Jenkins Tours, Llanelli 11/87 for spares
UFA 517J No.17	Ford R226	"	C53F	6/71	6/71	12/73	To Victoria Motorways 12/73

1972

Reg / No.	Model	Body	Seating				History
XFA 788K No.14	Ford R226	Plaxton	C53F	3/72	3/72	8/76	Westward Travel, Kingswood 10/76 Buglers, Bristol 9/81 Re-registered 280 GHT by 1985 Re-registered XEU 63K by 3/88 Hayne's Tours, Davidstowe 4/88
YFA 157K No.15	Ford R226	"	C53F	3/72	3/72	8/76	Horton's Coaches, Ripley 8/76 Express Coaches & Minicoaches, Rugby 6/78
YFA627K No.3	Ford R226	"	C53F	4/72	4/72	5/77	Overlander Coaches, Chessington 11/77
BFA 435L No.2	Ford R226	"	C53F	8/72	8/72	8/76	Overlander Coaches, Chessington 8/77

1973

Reg / No.	Model	Body	Seating				History
GFA 480L No.4	Ford R1114	Plaxton	C53F	7/73	7/73	1/77	Jones, Eccles, Lancs. 1/77
GFA 588L No.11	Ford R1114	"	C53F	7/73	7/73	8/77	Sapwell, Emberton 10/77

1974

Reg / Notes	Chassis	Body	Seating				Disposal
GJU 685N No.6 re-numbered 23 by 6/80	"	"	C53F	11/74	11/74	3/81	Westward Travel, Kingswood (Brown & Simmons) 3/81 (Simmons & Sim.) 9/81
GJU 686N No.12	"	"	C53F	11/74	11/74	6/79	Wrights of Wrexham, Penycae 7/80 Kavanagh, Urlingford by 3/82 Re-registered 994 MIP

1975

Reg / Notes	Chassis	Body	Seating				Disposal
GUT 795N No.1	"	"	C53F	3/75	3/75	3/81	Hunter, Hucknall 4/81
GUT 796N No.17	"	"	C53F	3/75	3/75	10/79	Westward Travel, Kingswood (Brown & Simmons) 7/80 Westward Travel, Kingswood (Simmons & Simmons) 8/81 – received Plaxton Supreme IV front end in 1984, scrapped 3/88
KNR 442P Ford R1014 No.5		"	C45F	8/75	8/75	3/80	E.Williams & Son, Bala 3/80 w/d by 6/88 Huxley, Threapwood ?/89
KNR 443P No.18	"	"	C45F	8/75	8/75	7/80	Westward Travel, Kingswood (Brown & Simmons) 8/80 Westward Travel, Kingswood (Simmons & Simmons) 8/81 Received Plaxton Supreme V front panel in 1985

1976

Reg / Notes	Chassis	Body	Seating				Disposal
OUT 352R No.14	"	"	C45F	8/76	8/76	10/81	Darragh, Kilrea 10/81 Re-registered EW 523, and to Buick, Cullybackey (NI) by 12/88
OUT 353R No.15	"	"	C45F	8/76	8/76	3/82	Bestwick, Tibshelf 3/82

1977

Reg / Notes	Chassis	Body	Seating				Disposal
DOK 514C Bedford SB5 *Not numbered in Viking fleet*		Duple	C41F	6/65	1/77	1/78	New to Ashted Coaches, B'ham, w/d 3/67 To Wellings, Burton on Trent 6/67 To Viking 1/77,(when Viking bought Comp) Elizabethan Travel, Walsall 1/78, w/d 1/79
MRR 473K Bedford YRQ *Not numbered in Viking fleet*		"	C45F	?/72	1/77	9/77	New to Makemson Bros, Hucknall Wellings, Burton-on-Trent 8/75 To Viking 1/77, (when Viking bought the Wellings coach business) Aberfeldy Motor Coaches Ltd., 9/77 Andrews (dealer) Stair 8/86

1978

Reg / Notes	Chassis	Body	Seating				Disposal
XJF 156S Ford R1114 No. 11		Plaxton	C53F	5/78	5/78	8/83	Island Coaches, Sittingbourne 10/83
XJF 157S Ford R1114 No.4		"	C53F	5/78	5/78	5/83	E.Williams & Son, Bala 5/83 Tanat Valley Coaches, Pentrefelin 5/88

1979

Reg / Notes	Chassis	Body	Seating				Disposal
EBC 280T Ford R1114 No. 6		"	C53F	6/79	6/79	10/87	Stevensons, Uttoxeter 11/87 E.W.Kisbee, Sutton on Hull 4/88
EBC 672T Ford R1114 No.12		"	C53F	6/79	6/79	10/87	Stevensons, Uttoxeter 11/87 E.W.Kisbee, Sutton on Hull 4/88
ERY 790T Ford R1114 No.17		"	C53F	10/79	10/79	9/85	Westward Travel, Kingswood 9/85
GJF 400V Ford R1114 No.1 Re-registered 834 GYD by 8/88		"	C53F	10/79	10/79	10/87	Stevensons, Uttoxeter 11/87 R.A.Bugler, Bristol 12/87

1980

Reg / Notes	Chassis	Body	Seating				Disposal
LJF 735V Ford R1114 No.5 Re-registered OFA 10 by 10/85 Re-registered LJU 965V by 3/89		"	C53F Re-seated to 49 in 1983 Seating re-instated to 53 by 1987	7/80	7/80	10/87	Stevensons, Uttoxeter 11/87 L.C.Munden & Sons Ltd., Bristol 2/88
LJF 742V Ford R1114 No.7		"	C53F	7/80	7/80	10/87	Stevensons, Uttoxeter 11/87 L.C.Munden & Sons Ltd., Bristol 2/88

1981

RJU 383W Ford R1114	"	C51F	?/81	?/81	10/87	Stevensons, Uttoxeter 11/87
No.8	(delivered with registration NAY 791W in 1980, but did not enter service until 1981 as shown)						

1983

JGL 53 DAF MB200DKFL600	Plaxton	C53F	6/83	6/83	10/87	Stevensons, Uttoxeter 11/87
No.14						

* JGL 53 cherished registration from new – J.G.Lloyd, Managing Director, Viking
  (Cherished registration retained by Mr. Lloyd when vehicle sold to Stevensons)

(temporarily re-seated to 49 for a European tour in 1987)

LFO 800Y Leyland TRCTL11/2R	Duple	C53F	5/83	7/83	10/87	New to Morris, Bromyard 5/83
No.15							Stevensons, Uttoxeter 11/87

1984

BHL 621K Daimler CRG6LX	N.C.M.E.	H43/33F	3/72	8/84	10/87	New to West Riding Automobile Co.Ltd.
No.21							Wakefield, Fleet No.721
							Stevensons, Uttoxeter 11/87

BHL 625K Daimler CRG6LX	N.C.M.E.	H43/33F	3/72	8/84	10/87	New to West Riding Automobile Co.Ltd.
Not numbered in Viking fleet							Wakefield, Fleet No.725
							Stevensons, Uttoxeter 11/87

1986

A834 PPP Leyland TRCTL11/3R	Plaxton	C55F	3/84	3/86	10/87	New to Armchair Passenger Transport
No.4	(re-seated to 44 in ?/86)						Co.Ltd., Brentford 3/84
							Stevensons, Uttoxeter 11/87

Eleven vehicles, including the two double-deckers, passed to Stevensons of Uttoxeter when they purchased Viking Motors (Burton upon Trent) Ltd., which also included the Victoria bus operations, on 31 October, 1977. The details of the immediate ownership after Viking and any known subsequent overseas ownership details are shown.

```
              VIKING MOTORS (BURTON) LTD.

  Directors' Valuation of Assets        at        5th. April 1944.

  Goodwill.                                        500. 0. 0

  Freehold Premises, High Street, Woodville.      1500. 0. 0

  Freehold Garage, Burton Road, Woodville.         500. 0. 0

  Leasehold Garage Premises, Central Garage, Union
     Street, Burton-on-Trent.                      500. 0. 0

  Motor Vehicles:-

     Coaches.
       Leyland      FA.4960.                       1000. 0. 0
       Albion       FA.5740                         800. 0. 0
       A.E.C.       FA.6199                         1000. 0. 0
       Albion.      FA.7205                         1500. 0. 0
       Daimler.     FA.3990                         100. 0. 0
       B.A.T.       VO.4066                         100. 0. 0
       B.A.T        BR.8228                         100. 0. 0
       Albion.      GG.4946                         150. 0. 0

     Cars:-
       Vauxhall.    FA.5646   (Van)                  30. 0. 0
       Austin.      RC.3545                           50. 0. 0
       Austin.      ARY.485                           40. 0. 0
       Riley.       BKY.307                          100. 0. 0
       Vauxhall.    FA.5655                           30. 0. 0
       M.G.         ?                                100. 0. 0

  Petrol Pumps & Oil Cabinets.                     229. 0. 0

  Plant & Machinery.                               510. 0. 0

  Office Furniture & Fittings.                      56. 0. 0

  Loose Plant & Tools.                              95. 0. 0

  Sundry Debtors, less Specific Reserves for Bad Debts 5935. 0. 0

  Stock in Trade.                                  558. 0. 0

  Directors' Loan Accounts:-

     W. J. Lloyd Esq.                             8389. 0. 0
     D. S. J. Leitch Esq.                         7804. 0. 0
     H. Atkins Esq.                               2855. 0. 0

  Cash in Hand.                                    102. 0. 0

  Unexpired Charges.                               683. 0. 0

                                               £35316. 0. 0
```

PLATE 58

Whilst not a photograph, it is nevertheless a more interesting item. This 1944 Director's Valuation of Assets provides a unique insight into what Viking Motors (Burton) Ltd., actually owned on the list dated for the last day of the Tax year. There was probably a similar asset list prepared for Victoria Motorways Ltd., the company which the directors of Viking, Messrs. Lloyd, Leitch & Atkins, acquired on 26th July 1943. Daimler FA 3990 may well be the Daimler listed as No. FA 3999 in the PSV Circle PD18 fleet list. The Vauxhall Van on the 1944 list of assets is seen in Plate 72. It is interesting to note that Albion FA 7205 (Plate 22), purchased in June 1938, is considered to be Viking's most valuable physical asset, equal in value to the Brewery Yard premises on High Street, Woodville.

PLATE 59 (above) *This Scammell 8-wheel lorry was the last to be purchased before the Viking Motors lorry business was sold in 1943. It was No.14 in the Viking fleet, and was used for long distance heavy haulage. It appears to be in very clean condition, possibly when new, or perhaps after overhaul and repainting.*

PLATE 60 (left) *This advert was one of several 'Viking service' advert included in the 1939 Viking 'Happy Days' booklet featured in Plates 80-84. The nightly trunk service to London returned with deliveries of fresh vegetables and fruit, to be delivered to Derby market before 6am each day.*

PLATE 61 *A Fordson lorry in the 1930's, with 'VIKING' in large lettering just visible to the left of the rear wheel. The print is marked 'No.1' on the reverse side.*

Repairs and Garage facilities....

Viking garage staff were trained by chassis and body manufacturers, and their collective contribution towards ensuring every vehicle was available when required, and performing to the optimum levels, was the key element in Viking's strong reputation for safety and reliability...

PLATE 63.
George Poultney edges GFA 601E, a 1967 Bedford VAL 14, through the coach wash installation.

PLATE 62 (top left)
Whilst this is splendid picture of George Paling, it is against the background of the well equipped garage facilities installed at Viking's High Street, Woodville depot.

PLATE 64 (left)
George Poultney in the picture again, this time replacing the cap on the air pipe after checking the tyre pressures.

PLATE 65 (below)
Jimmy Hassall, who joined Viking in 1933, is seen making adjustments in the confined underside.

PLATE 66
Another advertisement from the 'Happy Days' brochure of tour destinations shown in Plates 80-84. Car servicing and washing, as well as 'in-and-out-all-day' car parking behind Viking's Union Street garage, is being offered.

Booking Offices & Publicity matters....

The company's three booking office locations were instrumental in generating a great deal of revenue for the many sides of the Viking and Victoria businesses, and this selection of illustrations acknowledges the friendly and untiring contributions made by the booking office staff towards their customers and to the success of the two companies.

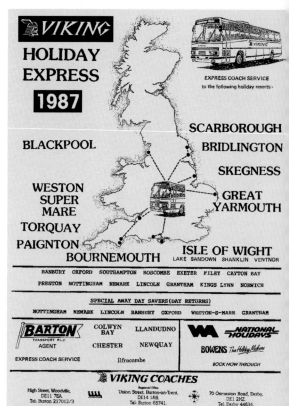

PLATE 67
An early 1930's advert, with a reminder of the 'Regular Service to Blackpool'. The '7 Church Street' address was one of Mr. Lloyd's early addresses, with parking space for one vehicle accessible through a gate onto Church Street, Church Gresley.

PLATE 69. *The 1987 season turned out to be the last for the privately owned Viking & Victoria businesses. This brochure encapsulates not only the extent of Viking's own Holiday Express Services, but also several of the agencies held for well known operators including Bartons, Wallace Arnold and Bowens.*

PLATE 68
The Union Street, Burton upon Trent, booking office, which was alongside the garage facilities. Viking first occupied the rented premises in 1926, before Mr. Lloyd purchased them in 1955. As well as taking bookings for Viking's own tours, they were appointed agents for a range of other travel providers and holiday resort facilities, including Butlins Holiday Camps as evidenced by the Butlins advert on the entrance door.

PLATE 70
Details of two of Viking's own holiday express services, which show fares, pick-up feeder services, pick-up points and timings to ensure passengers were not left behind.

PLATE 71 (right)

This advertisement was placed in the 1937 Coronation brochure. Viking sold Burton Road Garage, Woodville, after the war and moved the maintenance and repair workshops to the former Brunt & Bucknall's brewery site on High Street, and this remained the centre for both the Viking & Victoria vehicles until 1987.

PLATE 72 (below)

This was formerly Don Leitch's (Viking director) Vauxhall car, No. FA 5646, valued at a mere £30 in the 1944 Director's Valuation of Assets, (Plate 58). The section behind the front doors was removed, and local carpenter, George Shuttleworth, built the van body section and roof headboard, and it became a useful publicity vehicle for Viking as seen here. Legend has it that its longest journey was to collect a Viking passenger who had unfortunately died whilst in Blackpool. The photograph is believed taken at one of the Woodville Carnival days.

It costs no more
to travel by
VIKING
than it does by an ordinary Coach.

Enquiries :—

BURTON ROAD GARAGE.
'Phone : 7212 — 7196.

PLATE 73 (right)

The Woodville Booking Office & Travel Agency, High Street, Woodville – Head Office ! - formerly the brewery offices.

PLATE 74 (below)

Inside the Woodville booking office, normally a hive of activity most days.

PLATE 75 (top left) *Viking's Derby Office, at 70 Osmaston Road. The bottom left poster advertises a coach to Wembley Stadium on 27th June 1971, for the fight between South Derbyshire Boxing hero, Jack Bodell and Joe Bugner, a contest which saw Jack win and become the European and British Heavyweight Champion.*

PLATE 76 (top right) *The 1987 poster Viking used to advertise spare seats on a privately organised 12 day tour into Europe.*

PLATE 77 (left) *The wide area covered by Viking appointed Agents is evident from this 1964 advertisement.*

PLATE 78 (bottom left) *Interior of the Derby office.*

PLATE 79 (bottom right) *A sample price guide directed at North American tour operators bringing parties to Britain.*

Party travel….

Route 16.

Worcester & Holt Fl

Choice of routes to Worcester e
Malvern Hills, Lunch at Worcester, by
Holt Fleet for Tea and rejoining coach.
enjoyable trip.

River Trips can be arranged. It is bett
your party beforehand and so avoid any disapp
The river trips are always enjoyed, there a
regular service boats about 2-0 p.m.

Route 17.

Malvern Hills.

Burton, Lichfield, Birmingham, B
Droitwich, Worcester, Malvern Hills.

Approx. Miles 6

Note routes to Worcester alternative

After leaving Worcester by the river bridg
through numerous hop fields you approac
like a big black shadow in the sky, gettir
realize it is the Malvern Hills and you
houses. etc., you are soon gradually rising
back it is a surprise to see how high
Malvern is a very interesting and healthy
who is energetic can climb to the top, tho
ride can have a most enjoyable run round
at the British Camp. This solitary clum
be seen to be appreciated.

14

Route 51. **Manchester**.

Burton, Uttoxeter, Tean, Cheadle, Leek, M
field, Stockport, Manchester, Approx. 6
Burton, Derby, Ashbourne, Buxton,
Bridge, Stockport, Manchester. Approx. 6
Choice of either routes outwards.

One of the leading catering places in the v
every kind of Sport and Amusement, wonderful
and Zoo. Everywhere has been recently broug
date, anyone not having been for several year
greatly surprised at the wonderful impro
Belle View Fireworks are well known, and
need no comment.

Route 52.

Cheddar Gorge.

Burton, Tamworth, Coleshill, W
Stratford-on-Avon, Cheltenham, Bath, (
Gorge. Bristol, Gloucester, Tewkesbury, We
Droitwich, Birmingham, Lichfield, Burton
Approx. 274-

The journey to Cheddar is exceptionally pretty.
Stratford the route is fairly well known to local peo
through Cheltenham, the beautiful Spa with its
and Fountains, onwards to Bath, the old Roma
noted for its Baths and Abbey. Passing throug
noted for its Cathedral, we come to Cheddar. H
famous Gorge which cuts through the Mendip Hi
wonderful sight. The caves are well worth a vi
some of the most wonderful in the world. Our ne
Bristol, another very old town, here you will see th
Clifton Suspension Bridge. The return journey
through Gloucester, noted for its Englands Glory
and Tewkesbury, where the Abbey can be seen,
Old Mill, scenes of "John Halifax Gentleman."
Worcester the road is described in other route
enjoyable trip.

38

Route 53.

LONDON.

Let us take you on a conducted tour
of London, and show you the places of
interest; Ride, Meals and Theatre, all
inclusive.

Trips to look forward to

Route 54.
Aldershot Tattoo and Ascot Races.

Route 55.
Tour of the Tulip Fields (Spalding).

Route 56.
Navy Week, Portsmouth.

Route 57.
Tissington Well Dressing.

Route 58.
Eyan Plague Service.

Route 59.
Twenty-four hour trip to Blackpool
Illuminations.

39

PLATES 80-84 *In 1939 Viking published a 40 page 'Happy Days' brochure for tour organisers, with over fifty suggested routes for day outings, and a selection of the pages is shown.*

Party travel was a large part of the agenda for Viking, who sought to secure repeat bookings year on year. Each year the company organised events for the previous year's clients and the appointed agents, to brief them on new destinations and added value attractions.

PLATE 85. *Two Viking coaches, 1938 Albion FA 7205, and (far left) 1935 Albion FA 5740, with a party outside what is believed to be the new Coventry Hippodrome theatre to see one of the singing legends, Deanna Durbin. The two white-coated drivers are Don Newbold and Stan Parkes.*

PLATE 86 (below)
Another 1930's group of happy travellers in front of FA 5740, with driver Don Newbold kneeling (5th from R). Note the rather elaborate chrome edging separating the antique red and tan panelling.

PLATE 87
This appears to be a family group assembled behind FA 5740, again with Don Newbold holding the little girl (bottom left).

Party Groups....

This selection of photographs shows party groups enjoying the use of Viking coaches for various types of annual outing. Viking's use of Enquiry cards was the catalyst which brought many first time enquirers, and the sense of occasion for many was supplemented by the white-clad driver arriving to start the day.

PLATE 88
Customers of the Forest Gate public house in Burton, seen before setting off for a day out on FA 6199, the 1936 AEC Burlingham coach.
Courtesy G.Wheildon

PLATE 89 (above) *Photographs of the coach rear end are, understandably so, few and far between, and whilst the group are enjoying their outing, this picture is important in that it is the only rear end view of one of the stylish 1948 Burlingham coaches the author has found. A similar Viking is alongside.* Courtesy E.Goodwin

PLATE 90 (above right) *Burlingham Seagull coach AFA 953, with group on one of the high roads.*

PLATE 91 (right) *One of the Enquiry Cards distributed widely to generate interest in Viking private coach hire.*

PLATE 92 (below) *Ernest Newbold in drivers white, with a men's group alongside one the 1948 Burlingham coaches.*

PLATE 93 (below right) *Three Viking coaches with picnic group – BJP 271 – BJP 387 (centre) – HFA 3.*

56

Mr. E. M. Sales (trading as 'Victoria')   1919-1930
&
Victoria Motorways Ltd.   1930-1987

A taxi business, started in the village of Netherseal, South Derbyshire, by a Mr. E. M. Sales in 1919, was expanded into a bus service between Netherseal and Burton upon Trent, and led to the formation of Victoria Motorways Ltd., in 1930.   In 1943, the Company was acquired by the three directors of Viking Motors (Burton) Ltd.,but retained its separate Victoria identity as a bus company until 31st October 1987. The services and four buses were sold, and from that date the Company name was retained by Mr. J. G. Lloyd and his family.

The organisation which is remembered as 'Victoria Motorways' or perhaps better known as 'Victoria buses', has its' origins in a taxi business in the small South Derbyshire village of Netherseal, in the heart of what was essentially open farming countryside for miles around, except for Netherseal Colliery and other small colleries within a few miles.   The area was otherwise unspoilt, with a spread of small villages and hamlets across the undulating terrain, and for those who were not employed in farming or mining, who sought to ply other trades, travel to places such as Measham (3miles), Tamworth (7m), Church Gresley (4^1/$_2$ m), or Burton upon Trent (8m) before the first bus service commenced, was either on foot, by taxi, horseback, bicycle, or pony and trap. The nearest railway station was a 1^1/$_2$m trek to Donisthorpe station on the Ashby to Nuneaton line, and in 1920 there were eight trains in each direction each day, which at least gave the area the opportunity to visit the larger towns of Ashby-de-la-Zouch 7 miles distant, or Nuneaton, approximately 15 miles or so away.

A Netherseal resident, Mr. Ernest Marcus Sales, started a taxi service from a garage in the village and began trading as 'Sales Brothers'. It is believed the first vehicle was a six seat Renault vehicle, R3205, which is listed in a 'PSV Circle' fleet listing (PD18) as acquired by Sales Brothers in April 1921 (see plate 94). The service was successful and it was soon decided to expand the business and provide a bus service operating as 'Victoria', using a second-hand 14 seat Ford T, Registration No. FA 727, and whilst this was new in February 1921, the date when it was acquired by Sales Brothers is not known. The 'Victoria' name was Mr. Sales wife's second name – *Mrs. Minnie Victoria Sales.*

Early fleet history is unfortunately sparce and therefore incomplete, because the Ford T is recorded as being scrapped in June 1925, and there appears to have been no further vehicle acquisitions recorded until the arrival of two new vehicles in June 1927, one an Overland bus No. RA 3155, and a RIO bus, No. UT 1173. Seating capacities are not known.

The arrival of the first motor bus allowed passengers to be carried between Netherseal and other villages in the area, notably Measham, Overseal and Donisthorpe.   By December 1927, a service from Measham to Burton upon Trent, via Netherseal, Overseal, Linton and Castle Gresley, was in operation, this being licensed by Burton upon Trent County Borough Council in February 1928.

In June 1928, it is believed Mr. Sales was experiencing financial difficulties, and some limited financial support may have been given by Mr. W. J. Lloyd, who had formed a partnership with a Mr. D. J. S. Leitch, as 'Lloyd & Leitch' and were trading as 'Viking Motors' of Burton.

However, some interesting information has been found in the official vehicle registration records, namely, two vehicles - UT 1173, new in June 1927, and UE 5951, new in March 1928 - which had first been registered in the name of

E. M. Sales, were re-registered in the joint names of 'Sales and Lloyd' in June 1928.   Such re-registration could have provided Mr. Lloyd with some security for any monies which may have been loaned to Mr. Sales, and would have given Mr. Lloyd control over the two vehicles.   It is interesting to note that No. UE 5951, a Reo Pullman coach new in March 1928, was sold in August 1928, only two months after the re-registration, and this raises the question as to whether the sale may have been necessary to generate sufficient funds to allow Mr. Lloyd to recover his loan.

Whilst the PSV Circle Fleet List (PD18) states that Mr. E. M. Sales formed 'a short-lived partnership' with Mr. W. J. Lloyd (of Viking Motors) in 1928, Mr. Lloyd's son, Mr. J. G. Lloyd, states this is not correct, as his father had never referred to forming any sort of business partnership with E. M. Sales, but limiting his support to providing a short term financial loan.

Licensing of the Measham to Burton service by Victoria in February 1928 was unlikely to have gone un-noticed by other operators in the South Derbyshire area.

One such operator was, The Birmingham & Midland Motor Omnibus Co. Ltd. (widely known as 'Midland Red') which had taken over some of the bus services of the North Warwickshire Motor Omnibus and Traction Co. Ltd., in the Tamworth area on 1 February 1918, and in the early 1920's began sending buses from their Tamworth garage, to start a service from Ashby-de-la-Zouch to Burton upon Trent via Woodville & Swadlincote, in direct competition with the Burton & Ashby Light Railway tramcars, and the part of the Regent Motor Services Gresley and Burton between Swadlincote and Burton. When Midland Red's Coalville garage opened on 6 December 1925, it took over operation of the Ashby-Burton service, and Midland Red became a more formidable competitor in the South Derbyshire area.

The financial difficulties of the E. M. Sales bus service operation, may have led Mr. Sales in June/July 1929, to offer to sell the E. M. Sales bus business and the Netherseal to Burton service. It is probable however, that the predominantly country route was not sufficiently lucrative nor had the potential for expansion, to interest 'Midland Red' in purchasing the business. Instead, 'Midland Red' came to an agreement with E. M. Sales, under which they purchased the 'goodwill' of the Sales business, but 'authorised' him to continue running the Netherseal – Burton service only.

As a result, under the Assignment dated 29th July, 1929, Mr. Sales agreed *"....to sell the Purchasers (BMMO) the goodwill of the said business (E.M.Sales) and the full benefit thereof except as hereinafter provided at the price of £285, ...the Vendor shall not at any time during the term of Five years from the First day of July 1929, either alone or jointly with any other person or persons directly or indirectly either on his own account or as Manager, Agent,*

Driver, Conductor or otherwise howsoever be concerned engaged or interested in the operation of Motor Omnibus services or Workmen's services within an eighty miles radius from the Town Hall, Swadlincote,.....or allow his name to be used for the purpose of any such business provided always that nothing in these presents shall prevent the Vendor from continuing to operate a through service only of Motor Omnibuses (the times and fare for such service having been previously approved by the Purchasers (BMMO)) between Netherseal and Burton on Trent by way of Overseal, Mount Pleasant Main Road, Castle Gresley, Cauldwell Cross Roads, Stanton and Stapenhill only and terminating at Wetmore Road Park, Burton on Trent."

The agreement to acquire the goodwill and rights of Sale's business for £285. yet allow Sales to continue operating a *".....through service only, between Netherseal and Burton upon Trent"*, gave 'Midland Red' total control over service timings and fares for the five years from 1st July 1929, and effectively prohibited E. M. Sales from starting new bus services, or being involved directly or indirectly in any other bus operation, within an 80 miles radius of Swadlincote Town Hall, during the five year period expiring on 30th June, 1934.

The name of E. M. Sales as vendor in the agreement with BMMO, suggests the 'Victoria' name was only applied to vehicles, as Plate 94 shows.

The relatively modest £285. received from Midland Red in July 1929, may have been insufficient to satisfy Sales' creditors, and records indicate that 'Messrs. Eadie & Co'., reportedly of Netherseal, had helped with finance and acquired an interest in the E. M. Sales 'Victoria' business.

Registration of the business as a Limited Company, may well have been demanded by Eadie & Co., so that ownership of all assets would be vested in the Company's name, rather than in the name of a partner or partnership, and shares could be issued in proportion to the value of each party's investment.

As a result, the proposed new company was registered as 'Victoria Motorways Ltd.', of Victoria Garage, Netherseal, on 12th March, 1930, the previously used name of 'The Garage' in Netherseal, being re-styled 'Victoria Garage'.

However, in the same month, a further party gained an interest in ownership of Victoria Motorways Ltd. The Arlington Motor Company, vehicle dealers and also providers of commercial vehicle finance, are believed to have provided finance for the purchase of two new buses in July/August 1928. Arlington required security for the monies loaned, and they were given a Debenture which gave them a legal charge over all Victoria Motorways Ltd.'s assets. Under the Debenture, if Victoria failed to meet the scheduled repayment dates of loans, under the terms of the Debenture, Arlington would have had the authority to appoint a Receiver to take charge of the Company's assets and liabilities, thereby giving them ownership of the Company. However, such situation did not arise.

The presence of 'Midland Red' in South Derbyshire was strengthened considerably when they opened a Swadlincote garage in September 1931. New routes were started, but under the July 1929 agreement between E. M. Sales and 'Midland Red', there could be no encroachment of Victoria's Netherseal – Burton route by 'Midland Red'. However, the agreement also prevented Victoria from being involved in opening or operating any further services in the

PLATE 94. *This splendid picture was taken in Horninglow Street, Burton, in 1927. The Burton & Ashby trams stopped running on 19th February that year, and as the three buses are parked on the B&ALR tracks, it appears permission was given for 'out-of-town' bus services to stand on the disused tram tracks in Horninglow Street. The centre vehicle is the one of most interest, in that it is believed to be Victoria's first bus – a six seat Renault No. R 3205, purchased by E.M.Sales in April 1921. The front vehicle is Blue Bus Services No. NU 6959, a Halley chassis with 28 seat bodywork by Smith of Castle Bromwich, purchased in July 1925. The side panels are lettered: DERBY REPTON BURTON. The Trent bus is a 1926 Midland Red 'Standard SOS' chassis, with Ransomes body, one of 32 purchased in 1925/6.*
Courtesy Derby Evening Telegraph

PLATE 95
Reo Pullman with 26 seat Bracebridge body, No. UE 5643. The relatively pristine condition suggests it may have been photographed when new in February 1928. The addition of 'Safety Coach' on the sides may have been adopted from the Regent vehicles of Church Gresley. This Reo was sold in March 1929 to Ace Coaches of Twogates. Courtesy R.Marshall

area, or from allowing any other body to use their name, until after expiry of the five year period on 29th July 1934.

It is, therefore, interesting to note that by March 1933, Victoria Motorways Ltd were operating two separate daily services - the original route between Netherseal and Burton, and another between Netherseal and Measham, which one presumes was approved by Midland Red. The two services connected in each direction at Acresford, a hamlet astride the main A444 trunk road between Burton and Nuneaton, so that inter-change of passengers between the two services could take place.

A further interesting feature of the Victoria timetable commencing on 18 March 1933 (Plate 98), is the reference in the heading to the service being '*Joint* Daily Omnibus Services', suggesting that another operator – presumably 'Midland Red' - was involved with this service.

The following explanation is offered:-

E. M. Sales (and any successors in title) was prohibited from being associated with, or starting any new bus services within an 80 mile radius of Swadlincote Town Hall, before 29 July, 1934, when the 5 year agreement between 'Midland Red' and E. M. Sales would expire.

It is probable, therefore, that Victoria Motorways Ltd., (as 'E. M. Sales' successors), having identified demand for a new service which would allow interchange of passengers with their Netherseal-Burton service, approached 'Midland Red' for their permission to apply for a licence for a new Netherseal-Measham service. 'Midland Red' may well have agreed to allow Victoria to make application for a 'joint licence', subject to it being designated a 'Joint Service', and by so-doing retaining for themselves the right to be party to all discussions relating to the route, and possibly to benefit from the route should it become a lucrative one in the future. An interesting point is that whilst the Netherseal-Burton and Measham-Netherseal timetables coincided at Acresford Mills, allowing passengers to switch between services at this point, there is no evidence of through ticketing or pricing arrangements, which would have required approval of the Licensing Authority.

In December 1933, Victoria Motorways Ltd., obtained Licensing Authority approval to take over the licences for excursions and tours, and a seasonal service to Blackpool, which had been operated by Messrs. Clamp & Bailey, garage proprietors of Market Street, Church Gresley – see advertisement Plate 96. The licence references were:

ECC52/1 Excursions & Tours ex Church Gresley
ECS52/2 Church Gresley - Blackpool service

PLATE 96. *A Clamp & Bailey's tours advert c.1930.Their garage was opposite the Boot Inn, Church Gresley, which was the start point for Regent Motor Services Burton service route. Clamp & Bailey's licences for excursions and tours, and their seasonal Blackpool excursion licence, were acquired by Victoria in February 1934.*

PLATE 97. *The Burlingham bodied Leyland LT5A, registered BEH 401 in the Potteries, brought to Victoria by a Mr.J.Hawthorn in December 1934. It was originally ordered for his own Potteries based Company, which he sold prior to delivery of this vehicle.* Courtesy R.Marshall

VICTORIA MOTORWAYS, LTD.

BURTON—NETHERSEAL—MEASHAM. Joint Daily Omnibus Services.

VIA STANTON, CASTLE GRESLEY, OVERSEAL AND ACRESFORD.

Commencing on Saturday, March 18th, 1933, the following revised Services will come into operation.

MONDAY, TUESDAY, WEDNESDAY AND FRIDAY.
To and from Wetmore Bus Park only.

Depart—	a.m.	a.m.		p.m.	p.m.	p.m.	p.m.	p.m.	p.m.
Netherseal	8 0	9 10	1040	1 10	2-55	5 30	6 35	9 0
Acresford	8 5	9 12	1042	1 12	2 57	5 35	6 40	9 5
Overseal	8 15	9 18	1051	1 18	3 3	5 40	6 45	9 10
Castle Gresley	8 20	9 30	11 0	1 30	3 12	5 45	6 50	9 20
Stanton	8 25	9 40	1110	1 40	3 20	5 52	6 57	9 25
Burton Arrive	8 30	9 50	1120	1 50	3 30	6 0	7 3	9 35
Depart— Burton	8 35	10 0	1145	2 0	4 10	6 10	7 15	1010
Stanton	8 40	10 5	1150	2 5	4 15	6 15	7 20	1020
Castle Gresley	8 45	1015	12 0	2 15	4 25	6 22	7 30	1025
Overseal	8 50	1020	12 5	2 20	4 30	6 27	7 35	1030
Acresford	8 55	1025	1210	2 23	4 32	6 32	7 40	1033
Netherseal Arr.	9 0	1027	1212	2 26	4 35	6 35	7 45	1035

THURSDAYS.

	a.m.	a.m.	a.m.	p.m.	p.m.	p.m.	p.m.	p.m.	p.m.	p.m.
	8 0	9 10	1130	1 10	2 30	3 45	5 0	7 10	9 0
	8 5	9 12	1132	1 12	2 32	3 47	5 2	7 12	9 5
	8 15	9 18	1140	1 18	2 40	3 53	5 8	7 18	9 10
	8 20	9 30	1150	1 30	2 50	4 0	5 15	7 30	9 20
	8 25	9 40	1155	1 45	3 0	4 15	5 35	7 40	9 30
	8 30	9 45	12 8	1 50	3 8	4 20	5 40	7 45	9 35
	8 35	10 0	1215	1 55	3 8	4 20	5 45	8 0	1010
	8 40	10 5	1220	2 0	3 15	4 30	5 55	8 5	1020
	8 45	1015	1230	2 10	3 25	4 35	6 5	8 15	1025
	8 50	1020	1235	2 15	3 30	4 40	6 10	8 20	1030
	8 55	1025	1237	2 20	3 35	4 45	6 12	8 27	1033
	9 0	1027	1240	2 22	3 37	4 49	6 15	8 35	1035

SATURDAYS.

Depart—	a.m.	a.m.	a.m.	a.m.	p.m.	p.m.	p.m.	p.m.	p.m.	p.m.	p.m.	p.m.	p.m.	p.m.	p.m.	p.m.	p.m.	p.m.
Netherseal	8 0	9 10	9 45	1055	12 0	1 10	2 10	2 40	3 40	4 38	5 30	6 0	6 45	8 0	8 30	9 22	9 50
Acresford	8 5	9 12	9 47	1057	12 2	1 12	2 12	2 42	3 42	4 40	5 32	6 3	6 56	8 2	8 32	9 25	9 52
Overseal	8 15	9 18	9 55	11 3	1210	1 18	2 15	2 50	4 0	4 45	5 38	6 10	6 58	8 10	8 40	9 30	9 58
Castle Gresley	8 20	9 30	10 0	1110	1215	1 30	2 20	3 0	4 5	4 55	5 45	6 18	7 5	8 20	8 50	9 40	1010
Stanton	8 25	9 40	1010	1115	1230	1 35	2 30	3 10	4 20	5 10	6 0	6 28	7 20	8 30	9 0	9 45	1015
Burton Arrive	8 30	9 45	1025	1130	1235	1 47	2 40	3 20	4 25	5 15	6 5	6 38	7 28	8 35	9 5	9 50	1020
(Bus Pk) Dep.	8 35	10 0	1055	1145	1 25	1 55	3 0	3 55	4 30	5 20	6 10	6 35	7 45	8 45	9 20	10 0	1025
Stanton	8 40	10 5	1150	1 35	2 0	3 5	4 0	4 35	5 30	6 20	6 40	7 55	8 55	9 25	10 5	1030
Castle Gresley	8 45	1015	1115	12 0	1 45	2 10	3 15	4 10	4 45	5 35	6 30	6 48	8 0	9 0	9 35	1010	1040
Overseal	8 50	1020	1125	12 5	1 55	2 15	3 20	4 20	4 50	5 45	6 35	6 55	8 5	9 5	9 40	1015	1045
Acresford	8 55	1025	1130	1210	2 0	2 20	3 25	4 25	4 55	5 50	6 38	6 58	8 10	9 10	9 42	1020	1047
Netherseal Arr.	9 0	1027	1135	1212	2 5	2 22	3 30	4 27	5 0	5 55	6 40	7 0	8 12	9 15	9 47	1025	1050

SUNDAYS.

	B	B						
	p.m.	p.m.	p.m.	p.m.	p.m.	p.m.	p.m.
	1 10	3 20	6 20	7 30	8 45	10 0
	1 15	3 22	6 25	7 33	8 47	10 3
	1 25	3 25	6 30	7 35	8 53	10 8
	1 30	3 35	6 40	7 40	9 10	1012
	1 40	3 45	6 45	7 45	9 15	1022
	1 50	3 50	6 55	7 53	9 20	1030
	B					
	2 50	4 0	6 58	7 55	9 25	1035
	3 0	4 10	7 15	8 10	9 30	1040
	3 15	4 15	7 15	8 10	9 40	1050
	3 15	4 20	7 20	8 15	9 45	1055
	3 20	4 27	7 25	8 25	9 55	11 0

B This Bus arrives and departs Infirmary.

MONDAYS, TUESDAYS, WEDNESDAYS AND FRIDAYS.

	a.m.	a.m.	a.m.	noon	p.m.	p.m.	F	T.W.	p.m.	p.m.
Netherseal dep	7 30	8 50	1020	12 0	2 18	4 25	5 45	6 40	7 35	..
Acresford "	7 35	8 55	1025	1210	2 23	4 32	5 50	6 45	7 40	9 5
Measham arr	7 45	9 5	1035	1220	2 33	4 42	6 0	6 55	7 50	9 15

	a.m.	a.m.	a.m.	p.m.	p.m.	p.m.	F	T.W.	p.m.	F
Measham dep	7 55	9 5	1035	1 0	2 48	5 25	6 0	7 0	8 55	9 30	1045
Acresford "	8 5	9 15	1042	1 12	2 57	5 35	6 10	7 10	9 5	9 40	1055
Netherseal arr.	8 10	9 20	1045	1 15	3 0	5 40	6 15	7 15	..	9 45	11 0

* Fridays excepted. F Fridays only. T.W. Tues. & Weds. only.

SATURDAYS.

	a.m.	a.m.	a.m.	noon	p.m.	p.m.			p.m.	.p.m.
Netherseal dep	7 30	8 50	1120	12 7	2 15	..	..	7 30	9 38	1015
Acresford "	7 35	8 55	1125	1210	2 20	4 15	5 45	6 56	7 35	9 10	9 42	1020
Measham arr.	7 45	9 5	1135	1220	2 30	4 25	5 52	7 10	7 45	9 20	9 52	1030

	a.m.	a.m.	a.m.	noon	p.m.	p.m.	p.m.	p.m.	p.m.	p.m.
Measham dep.	7 55	1030	1152	1 0	2 32	4 30	5 54	7 15	7 50	9 25	10 0	1045
Acresford "	8 5	1042	12 2	1 12	2 42	4 40	6 3	7 25	8 0	9 35	1010	1055
Netherseal arr.	8 10	1045	12 5	..	..	..	..	7 28	8 5	9 38	1015	11 0

THURSDAYS.

	a.m.	a.m.	p.m.	p.m.	p.m.	p.m.
	7 30	8 50	1232	3 30	6 8	8 22
	7 35	8 55	1237	3 35	6 12	8 27
	7 45	9 5	1247	3 45	6 22	8 37

	a.m.	a.m.	p.m.	p.m.	p.m.	p.m.
	7 55	1125	1 0	4 50	7 0	8 55
	8 5	1135	1 12	5 2	7 12	9 5
	8 10	1140	1 15	5 5	7 15	9 10

SUNDAYS.

	p.m.	p.m.	p.m.	p.m.	p.m.
	1245	3 14	4 22	8 15	..
	1248	3 17	4 25	8 20	9 40
	1258	3 27	4 35	8 30	9 50

	p.m.	p.m.	p.m.	p.m.	p.m.
	1 0	3 30	6 15	8 35	9 52
	1 10	3 40	6 25	8 47	10 0
	1 13	3 45	6 30	..	10 5

The Company cannot be held responsible for any loss or delay, although every effort will be made to maintain these services.

Phone (Office and Garage): Overseal **34**.

E. M. SALES, Managing Director, Victoria Garage, Netherseal.

H. J. TILL, Printer, Swadlincote 20170

Return Fares.

Burton (Wetmore Park) to Castle Gresley 9d.
Burton (Wetmore Park) to Overseal 1/1
Burton (Wetmore Park) to Netherseal 1/4

Fares.
Netherseal to Measham— Single, 4d. Return, 7d.
Netherseal to Acresford — Single, 1d.
Acresford to Measham— Single, 3d. Return, 5d.

	Netherseal	Acresford	Overseal	Mount Pleasant Inn or Rickman's Corner	Castle Gresley or Cadley Hill	Stanton Chapel or Council Farm	Piddocks Road	Black Horse Inn	Stapenhill	Burton (Wetmore Park)
Netherseal	1d.	3d.	4d.	5d.	6d.	7d.	8d.	9d.	1/1
Acresford	3d.	—	2d.	4d.	5d.	6d.	7d.	8d.	9d.	1/-
				1½d.	3d.	4½d.	5½d.	6½d.	7½d.	
			2d.	2d.	3½d.	4½d.	5½d.	6½d.	

PLATE 98 *March 1933 Victoria timetable and fare table.* Courtesy The Omnibus Society

---

Clamp & Bailey had started a garage business in 1919, and by coincidence, the garage was directly opposite the Boot Inn, which was the original start point for the Regent bus service from Church Gresley to Burton upon Trent.

It is also interesting to note that the Regent company appears to have concentrated solely on the bus service and did not appear, even before operator licensing became mandatory, to have attempted to run excursions and tours. However, the presence of Clamp & Bailey as excursion and private hire operators on Regent's doorstep in Church Gresley, may have been one of the factors which led Mr. W.J.Lloyd to base his new business in Burton upon Trent rather than South Derbyshire, after he left Regent in 1926. Mr. Lloyd may well have noted the demand for such excursions and the Blackpool service, and led him to leave Regent to form Viking Motors in Burton.

One Clamp & Bailey vehicle – Reg'n No. RB 3764, an Albion PKA26 with Rushton & Wilson 26 seat front entrance coach body, new to Clamp & Bailey in March 1931, joined the Victoria fleet.

In May 1934, a Mr. Manners of Netherseal Hall, a director of Bass, Ratcliffe & Gretton Ltd., purchased an interest in the Company and became a director, with Mr. E. M. Sales continuing to operate the business.

In June 1934, close to the expiry of the 1929 agreement with 'Midland Red', the Company acquired garage premises in Russell Street, Burton upon Trent, providing an overnight base for vehicles, a step which no doubt had benefits for the operation of early morning and late evening services .

A Mr. J. Hawthorne, who had sold his Potteries based bus and coach business in July 1934 to the Potteries Motor Traction Co. Ltd., in Stoke-on-Trent, became a director of Victoria Motorways Ltd. in December 1934. Prior to selling his Company, they had ordered a Leyland LT5A type chassis with a Burlingham 34 seat coach body, which, prior to delivery, had been registered in Stoke as BEH 401. This vehicle was delivered new in December 1934, after the sale of the Hawthorne business, and was therefore lettered in 'Victoria Motorways' livery.

The financial structure of Victoria Motorways Ltd., must have improved by 1935, sufficiently so, to allow the Company to order a new Leyland TS6 chassis with Burlingham flat front 31 seat coach body, Reg'n No. FA 5840, and this arrived in June that year. The livery was

60

PLATE 99
Whilst this photograph is slightly out of focus, the rarity of 1930's illustrations of Victoria buses on service routes, over-rides, in the opinion of the author, the quality of such pictures when no others are available for consideration. The bus is a Gilford with an unknown body type, No. UE 7866, seen passing the Robin Hood crossroads in Overseal in the direction of Acresford and Netherseal.

Courtesy The Magic Attic

PLATE 100
This Leyland TS6 type, with Burlingham full-fronted coach body, was, according to comments by one or two people who can remember travelling on it, or seeing it, 'Mark Sales pride and joy'.   FA 5840 was affectionately known as 'The Black Hawk', a name which no doubt came from the 'diving hawk' bird image on each side. The destination panel above the front windows shows – Victoria Motorways, and ownership is marked on the lower side panel.
Courtesy R.Marshall Collection,
per Keith West

PLATE 101
FA 5840, new to Victoria in June 1935, was used extensively on the seasonal Blackpool service acquired from Clamp & Bailey in 1934, and on other tours and private hire assignments.   It was sold by Victoria in December 1940 to Mann's Superlux Coaches of Smethwick.

Courtesy A.Wood Collection,
per D.Wilkinson

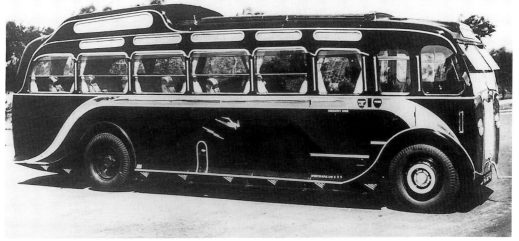

VICTORIA MOTORWAYS.
TIME TABLE

Between MEASHAM, NETHERSEAL, OVERSEAL, CASTLE GRESLEY and BURTON.

MONDAYS, TUESDAYS, WEDNESDAYS and FRIDAYS.

		a.m.	a.m.	a.m.	a.m.	p.m.	p.m.	p.m.	p.m.	p.m.	p.m.
Netherseal	dep.	6 55	8 0	9 10	10 40	1 10	2 55	5 30	6 35	9 0	
Acresford	,,	7 0	8 5	9 12	10 42	1 12	2 57	5 35	6 40	9 5	
Overseal	,,	7 10	8 15	9 18	10 51	1 18	3 3	5 40	6 45	9 10	
Castle Gresley	,,	—	8 20	9 30	11 0	1 30	3 12	5 45	6 50	9 20	
Stanton	,,	—	8 25	9 40	11 10	1 40	3 20	5 52	6 57	9 25	
Burton (Wetmore Pk.)	arr.	7 25	8 30	9 50	11 20	1 50	3 30	6 0	7 3	9 35	

			C	C		C		C		
		a.m.	a.m.	a.m.	a.m.	p.m.	p.m.	p.m.	p.m.	p.m.
Burton (Wetmore Pk.)	dep.	..	8 35	10 0	11 45	2 0	4 10	6 10	7 15	10 10
Stanton	,,	..	8 40	10 5	11 50	2 5	4 15	6 15	7 20	10 20
Castle Gresley	,,	..	8 45	10 15	12 0	2 15	4 25	6 22	7 30	10 25
Overseal	,,	..	8 50	10 20	12 5	2 20	4 30	6 27	7 35	10 30
Acresford	,,	..	8 55	10 25	12 10	2 23	4 32	6 32	7 40	10 33
Netherseal	arr.	..	9 0	10 27	12 12	2 26	4 35	6 35	7 45	10 35

C Connection for Measham.

THURSDAYS.

		a.m.	a.m.	a.m.	a.m.	CB p.m.	p.m.	p.m.	p.m.	p.m.	p.m.
Netherseal	dep.	6 55	8 0	9 10	11 30	1 10	2 30	3 45	5 0	7 10	9 0
Acresford	,,	7 0	8 5	9 12	11 32	1 12	2 32	3 47	5 2	7 12	9 5
Overseal	,,	7 10	8 15	9 18	11 40	1 18	2 40	3 53	5 10	7 18	9 10
Castle Gresley	,,	—	8 20	9 30	11 50	1 30	2 50	4 0	5 15	7 30	9 20
Stanton	,,	—	8 25	9 40	11 45	1 40	3 0	4 15	5 20	7 40	9 30
Burton (Wetmore Pk.)	arr.	7 25	8 30	9 45	12 8	1 50	3 8	4 20	5 30	7 45	9 35

			C		C		C		C		
		a.m.	a.m.	a.m.	p.m.	p.m.	p.m.	p.m.	p.m.	p.m.	p.m.
Burton (Wetmore Pk.)	dep.	—	8 35	10 0	12 15	1 55	3 8	4 20	5 45	8 0	10 10
Stanton	,,	—	8 40	10 5	12 20	2 0	3 15	4 30	5 55	8 5	10 20
Castle Gresley	,,	—	8 45	10 15	12 30	2 10	3 25	4 35	6 3	8 15	10 25
Overseal	,,	—	8 50	10 20	12 35	2 15	3 30	4 40	6 8	8 20	10 30
Acresford	,,	—	8 55	10 25	12 37	2 20	3 35	4 45	6 12	8 27	10 33
Netherseal	arr.	—	9 0	10 27	12 40	2 22	3 37	4 49	6 15	8 30	10 35

C B—Burton Infirmary.

SATURDAYS.

		a.m.	a.m.	a.m.	a.m.	a.m.	noon	p.m.	p.m.	p.m.	p.m.	p.m.	p.m.	p.m.	p.m.	p.m.	p.m.	p.m.	p.m.	p.m.
Netherseal	dep.	6 55	8 0	9 10	9 45	10 55	12 0	1 10	2 10	2 40	3 40	4 38	5 30	6 0	6 45	8 0	8 30	9 22	9 50	
Acresford	,,	7 0	8 5	9 12	9 47	10 57	12 2	1 12	2 12	2 42	3 42	4 40	5 32	6 3	6 56	8 2	8 32	9 25	9 55	
Overseal	,,	7 10	8 15	9 18	9 55	11 3	12 10	1 18	2 15	2 50	4 0	4 45	5 38	6 10	6 58	8 10	8 40	9 30	9 58	
Castle Gresley	,,	—	8 20	9 30	10 0	11 10	12 15	1 30	2 20	3 0	4 5	4 55	5 45	6 18	7 5	8 20	8 50	9 40	10 10	
Stanton	,,	—	8 25	9 40	10 10	11 15	12 30	1 40	2 30	3 10	4 20	5 10	6 0	6 23	7 20	8 30	9 0	9 45	10 15	
Burton W.P.	arr.	7 25	8 30	9 45	10 25	11 30	12 35	1 47	2 40	3 20	4 25	5 15	6 5	6 28	7 25	8 35	9 5	9 50	10 20	

		C		C		C		C			C		C		C		C		C	C
		a.m.	a.m.	a.m.	a.m.	a.m.	p.m.	p.m.	p.m.	p.m.	p.m.	p.m.	p.m.	p.m.	p.m.	p.m.	p.m.	p.m.	p.m.	p.m.
Burton (W.P.)	dep.	..	8 35	10 0	10 55	11 45	1 15	1 55	3 0	3 55	4 30	5 20	6 10	6 35	7 45	8 45	9 20	10 0	10 30
Stanton	,,	..	8 40	10 5	11 0	11 50	1 20	2 0	3 5	4 0	4 35	5 30	6 15	6 40	7 55	8 55	9 25	10 5	10 35
Castle Gresley	,,	..	8 45	10 15	11 10	12 0	1 30	2 10	3 15	4 10	4 45	5 35	6 20	6 48	8 0	9 0	9 35	10 10	10 45
Overseal	,,	..	8 50	10 20	11 20	12 5	1 35	2 15	3 20	4 20	4 50	5 45	6 30	6 55	8 5	9 5	9 40	10 15	10 50
Acresford	,,	..	8 55	10 25	11 25	12 10	1 40	2 20	3 25	4 25	4 55	5 48	6 38	6 58	8 10	9 10	9 42	10 20	10 55
Netherseal	arr.	..	9 0	10 27	11 30	12 12	1 45	2 22	3 30	4 27	5 0	5 55	6 40	7 0	8 12	9 15	9 47	10 25	11 0

C—Connection for Measham.

SUNDAYS.

		p.m.	p.m.	p.m.	p.m.	CB p.m.	p.m.
Netherseal	dep.	1 10	3 20	6 20	7 30	8 45	10
Acresford	,,	1 15	3 22	6 25	7 33	8 47	10
Overseal	,,	1 20	3 25	6 30	7 35	8 53	10
Castle Gresley	,,	1 30	3 35	6 40	7 40	9 10	10
Stanton	,,	1 40	3 45	6 45	7 45	9 15	10
Burton W.P.	arr.	1 50	3 50	6 55	7 53	9 20	10

		p.m.	CB p.m.	p.m.	p.m.	C p.m.	p.m.
Burton (W.P.)	dep.	2 50	4 0	6 58	7 55	9 25	10
Stanton	,,	3 0	4 10	7 5	8 0	9 30	10
Castle Gresley	,,	3 10	4 15	7 15	8 10	9 40	10
Overseal	,,	3 15	4 20	7 20	8 15	9 45	10
Acresford	,,	3 17	4 25	7 23	8 20	9 50	10
Netherseal	arr.	3 20	4 27	7 25	8 25	9 55	11

C B—Arrives and Departs Infirmary.

NETHERSEAL and MEASHAM.

MONDAYS, TUESDAYS, WEDNESDAYS and FRIDAYS.

		C a.m.	C noon	C p.m.	C p.m.	C p.m.
Netherseal	dep.	8 50	12 0	2 18	4 25	7 35
Acresford	,,	8 55	12 10	2 23	4 32	7 40
Measham	arr.	9 5	12 20	2 33	4 42	7 50

		C a.m.	C p.m.	C p.m.	C p.m.	C p.m.
Measham	dep.	9 5	1 0	2 48	5 25	8 55
Acresford	,,	9 15	1 12	2 57	5 35	9 5
Netherseal	arr.	9 20	1 15	3 0	5 40	9 8

THURSDAYS.

		C a.m.	C p.m.	C p.m.	C p.m.	C p.m.
Netherseal	dep.	8 50	12 32	3 30	6 8	8 22
Acresford	,,	8 55	12 37	3 35	6 12	8 27
Measham	arr.	9 5	12 47	3 45	6 22	8 37

		C a.m.	CB p.m.	C p.m.	C p.m.	C p.m.
Measham	dep.	11 25	1 0	4 50	7 0	8 55
Acresford	,,	11 35	1 12	5 2	7 12	9 5
Netherseal	arr.	11 40	1 15	5 5	7 15	9 10

SATURDAYS.

		C a.m.	C a.m.	C a.m.	C p.m.	C p.m.	C p.m.	C p.m.	C p.m.	C p.m.	C p.m.
Netherseal	dep.	8 50	11 20	12 7	2 15			7 30		9 38	10 15
Acresford	,,	8 55	11 25	12 10	2 20	4 15	5 45	6 56	7 35	9 10	9 42	10 20
Measham	arr.	9 5	11 35	12 20	2 30	4 25	5 52	7 10	7 45	9 20	9 52	10 30

		C a.m.	C a.m.	C p.m.	C p.m.	C p.m.	C p.m.	C p.m.	C p.m.	C p.m.	C p.m.
Measham	dep.	9 5	11 52	1 0	2 32	4 30	5 54	7 15	7 50	9 25	10 0	10 45
Acresford	,,	9 15	12 2	1 12	2 42	4 40	6 3	7 25	8 0	9 35	10 10	10 55
Netherseal	arr.	9 20	12 5				7 28	8 5	9 38	10 15	11 0

C—Connection for Measham and Burton.

SUNDAYS.

		C p.m.	C p.m.	C p.m.	C p.m.	C p.m.
Netherseal	dep.	12 45	3 14	4 22	8 15	—
Acresford	,,	12 48	3 17	4 25	8 20	9 40
Measham	arr.	12 58	3 27	4 35	8 30	9 50

		CB p.m.	C p.m.	C p.m.	C p.m.	C p.m.
Measham	dep.	1 0	3 30	6 15	8 35	9 52
Acresford	,,	1 10	3 40	6 25	8 47	10 0
Netherseal	arr.	1 13	3 45	6 30	—	10 5

C B—Through Bus to Burton Infirmary.

Registered Office and Garage—Overseal 34.
Phone { Russell Street, Burton-on-Trent, Burton Garages
CHURCH GRESLEY, Phone 7572 (C & B Tours)
Booking Offices
Netherseal ...... 3657 Burton Office

NETHERSEAL AND BURTON.

	Netherseal								
1. Netherseal									
2. Acresford (Cricketts Inn)	1d.	Acresford (Cricketts Inn)							
3. Overseal	3d.	2d.	Overseal						
4. Mt. Pleasant Inn or Rickman's Corner	4d.	3d.	2d.	Mt. Pleasant Inn or Rickman's Corner					
5. Castle Gresley (Railway Inn)	5d.	4d.	3d.	1½d.	Castle Gresley (Rly. Inn)				
6. Cadley Hill or Rock House	6d.	5d.	4d.	3d.	1½d.	Cadley Hill or Rock House			
7. Stanton Chapel or Council Farm	7d.	6d.	5d.	3½d.	2d.	—	Stanton Chapel or Council Farm		
8. Black Horse Inn	8d.	7d.	6d.	4½d.	3d.	2d.	—	Black Horse Inn	
9. Stapenhill (Green)	9d.	8d.	7d.	5½d.	4d.	3d.	2d.	2d.	Stapenhill (Green)
10. Burton (Wetmore Park)	10d.	9d.	8d.	6½d.	5d.	4d.	3d.	3d.	—	Burton (Wetmore Park)

MEASHAM FARES.

Netherseal to Measham—
Single, 4d. Return, 7d.
Netherseal to Acresford—
Single, 1d.
Acresford to Measham—
Single, 3d. Return, 5d.

RETURN FARES.

Burton (Wetmore Park) and Castle Gresley	..	9d.
do.	and Overseal	..	1/1
do.	and Netherseal	..	1/4

CHILDREN between 3 and 14 years of age, if not occupying a seat, can travel at HALF FARE as per Schedule in Monthly Time Table. CHILDREN under THREE years of age, if not occupying a seat, can travel FREE, provided not more than one such Child accompanies any passenger. Any additional Children, irrespective of age, MUST BE PAID FOR.

REGULAR WEEKLY SERVICES TO BLACKPOOL THROUGHOUT THE SEASON.
PRIVATE HIRE, ANY DESCRIPTION AND ANY NUMBER CATERED FOR.

20.3.39

PLATE 102
This Victoria timetable does not show a commencement date, but a date of 20.3.39 has been marked in ink at the bottom. The two services licensed are shown with fare details.
Courtesy The Omnibus Society

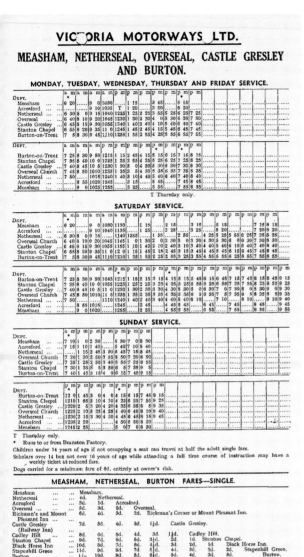

VICTORIA MOTORWAYS LTD.

MEASHAM, NETHERSEAL, OVERSEAL, CASTLE GRESLEY AND BURTON.

MONDAY, TUESDAY, WEDNESDAY, THURSDAY AND FRIDAY SERVICE.

SATURDAY SERVICE.

SUNDAY SERVICE.

T Thursday only.

* Runs to or from Branston Factory.

Children under 14 years of age if not occupying a seat can travel at half the adult single fare.

Scholars over 14 but not over 16 years of age while attending a full time course of instruction may have a weekly ticket at reduced fare.

Dogs carried for a minimum fare of 6d. entirely at owner's risk.

MEASHAM, NETHERSEAL, BURTON FARES—SINGLE.

VICTORIA MOTORWAYS LTD.

TIME TABLE.

MEASHAM, ACRESFORD, NETHERSEAL, OVERSEAL, CASTLE GRESLEY, STANTON, BURTON-ON-TRENT.

Commencing
MONDAY, FEBRUARY 7th, 1944
and until further notice.

The Company will make every effort to maintain these services and will accept no liability for loss, damage, injury or delay sustained by any passenger by reason of unpunctuality or failure to maintain the service.

Head Office :
UNION STREET,
BURTON-ON-TRENT.

Phone : Burton 3625.
Phone : Swadlincote 7212.

FARE SCHEDULE.

	Weekly Ticket to Branston Ord. Depot.	Weekly Fares to Burton Wetmore Park—Shop Asst. Workpeople.	Weekly Fares to Burton Wetmore Park—School Children.
Measham	7/– 6 days In—Out	7/– 6 days In—Out	
Netherseal	7/– ,, ,,	6/6 ,, ,,	4/– 5 days only
Moira	7/– ,, ,,		
Acresford	6/– ,, ,,	6/– ,, ,,	4/– ,, ,,
Overseal	5/6 ,, ,,	5/– ,, ,,	3/3 ,, ,,
Mount Pleasant Inn Rickman's Corner	4/6 ,, ,,	4/6 ,, ,,	2/3 ,, ,,
Linton	4/6 ,, ,,	4/6 ,, ,,	
Castle Gresley	4/– ,, ,,	3/6 ,, ,,	1/9 ,, ,,
Cadley Hill	3/6 ,, ,,		
Stanton	3/– ,, ,,	2/6 ,, ,,	

PLATES 103-5. *A timetable from the war years, commencing 7th February 1944. Note the asterisks * signifying journeys running to and from the Government's Branston Ordnance Factory, which was a base for sending supplies to the British army. The Crosse & Blackwell's 'Branston Pickle' brand name came from the Branston location of the factory producing it.*
Courtesy The Omnibus Society

predominantly black with a diving hawk image on each side, which quickly led to it being known as *'The Black Hawk'*. (Plate 100/1) One young lady, with whom the author worked more than 40 years ago, has lived all her life in Netherseal, can just remember the *'Black Hawk'* coach and the super ride it gave.

Nothing further of note appears to have occurred during the late 1930's, and the Company continued to operate its services through to the commencement of the Second World War in September 1939.

By 1941, control of Victoria Motorways services and vehicles was obtained by Viking Motors (Burton) Ltd., possibly as a result of the war. Continuation of Victoria bus services was a vital necessity throughout the war years, but with cessation of virtually all coach operations, the Victoria and Viking fleets were utilised for transporting people to Ordnance Factories and other installations across the Midlands, which had been turned over to production of items for the war effort.

Mr. W. J. Lloyd of Viking took on a role as co-ordinator of bus transport requirements in the Burton and South Derbyshire area, and such was the wide-ranging brief, vehicles from other operators could be requisitioned for the

war effort. In a presentation some years later, Mr. Lloyd told his audience that by 1941 Viking had responsibility for between 40 and 50 vehicles on a day to day basis, with many drafted in from other operators. It is probable therefore, that under the war arrangements, control of Victoria's fleet came within Mr. Lloyd's responsibilities as wartime co-ordinator. Vehicle records suggest that between Sept 1939 when war started, and 1943, 14 second-hand vehicles came into the Victoria fleet, whilst 1 bus and 3 coaches, all second-hand, were registered for the Viking fleet.

Throughout the war period, and through until the early 1960's, Victoria's 7.05am and 6.55pm arrivals in Burton, continued through to the Branston Ordnance Factory. They were not allowed to pick-up on the morning return into Burton, but two afternoon services from Branston at 5.15pm and 7.15pm, were allowed to pick up passengers on the journey to Burton Wetmore Park providing those passengers had tickets for destinations beyond the Burton Corporation boundary, which was the Black Horse hostelry.

Four vehicles (TF 3172, ATE 77,78,79) were hired from Darwen Corporation in September 1941, followed by five Guy 26 seater buses from Burton Corporation in 1941/2. Blue Bus Services sold Leyland Lion LT5A, No.ARA 172, (new to BBS in June 1934) with Burlingham 26 seat bus body, to Victoria in 1943, and this vehicle remained in service until withdrawn in December 1954. One other vehicle, GG 4946, an Albion PMB28 with 29 seat Cowieson coach body, was added to the Victoria fleet in 1943, and this is the last recorded wartime acquisition by Victoria.

The four ex-Darwen buses hired by Victoria retained their Darwen fleet numbers, (No's 9, 11-13). After the Victoria Motorways business, including the four ex-Darwen vehicles, had been purchased by the three directors of Viking in 1943, fleet numbering appears to have been extended across the Victoria fleet circa. 1946.

The Share Register for Victoria Motorways Ltd., shows the following holdings on 25th July 1943,

Ernest Marcus Sales	*2037 shares of £1. each*
Minnie Victoria Sales	*462 -do-*
Total	*2499 issued*

The 13th Annual General Meeting of Victoria Motorways Ltd., was held at 10am on 26th July 1943 at Russell Street Garage, Burton upon Trent, and Mr. E. M. Sales and Mrs. M. V. Sales had been directors from the March 1930 Date of Incorporation. Minutes of the meeting show that after the Accounts for the financial year ended 28th February 1943 had been approved, and Mr. Ernest Marcus Sales re-elected a director for a further two year period, three further directors were appointed to the Board - Mr. W. J. Lloyd, Mr. D. J. S. Leitch and Mr. H. Atkins, all directors of Viking Motors (Burton) Ltd.

Immediately following the election of the three new directors, the annual meeting closed and the directors then left Victoria's Russell Street Garage and moved to Viking Motors (Burton) Ltd., Central Garage in Union Street, Burton, for an 11am meeting. Mrs. M. V. Sales, who had been the other serving director of the Company, having been re-appointed in 1942, tendered her resignation as Company Secretary, to which position Mr. H. Atkins was then appointed. The meeting also approved a change of Registered Office from Russell Street Garage to Central Garage, Union Street, Burton upon Trent. Mr. Sales resigned as Managing Director, but remained a director.

The appointment of the three new directors followed the purchase by them individually of all but ten of the Victoria shares then issued, as follows:

William John Lloyd	*996 shares*
Donald James Smith Leitch	*996 "*
Horace Atkins	*498 "*
	2490
Ernest Marcus Sales	*10 "*
	2500 shares issued

VICTORIA MOTORWAYS LTD.

Amount payable on completion of the purchase of the Share Capital of the Company by Messrs. Lloyd, Leitch and Atkins from Mr.E.M.Sales and Mrs.Sales.

Purchase price	£10,000	
less deposit already paid	1,000	9,000

Road fund licences on the vehicles taken over from 26th July to 30th September, 1943. (say 2 months) -

	3 months	
FV 1689 Tiger	£15.16.10	
VT 7065 T.S.6	15.16.10	
JD 4828 Bedford	9.18. 0	
FA 3889 Guy	15.16.10	
VT 8132 T.S.4	-	NOT LICENCED
FS 1762 Albion	-	do
	57. 8. 6	

⅔ x £57.8.6 = 38. 5. 8

Insurance of vehicles from 26th July,1943, to 7th September, 1943 - no payment as agreed   NIL

Income Tax to be deducted from Poultney's wages for the week ending 31st July, 1943   4. 2

Mr.Sales undertakes to pay to the Collector all tax deductible from employees wages up to 31st July, 1943.

Total payable   £9,038. 9. 10

PLATE 106
This original 1943 statement sets out the purchase price and adjustments to it, for the acquisition of Victoria Motorways Ltd., personally by the three directors of Viking Motors (Burton) Ltd., W.J.Lloyd, D.J.S.Leitch and H.Atkins, rather than purchased in the name Viking Motors (Burton) Ltd. The effective date of the change of ownership was 26th July 1943.

PLATE 107
Two of the three ex-Darwen Corporation Leyland LT7 buses acquired by Victoria in September 1941. New to Darwen in February 1936, ATE 79 and its unidentified sister vehicle are parked at the Victoria stand in Burton's Wetmore bus park in the Red and Cream livery c.1946.

Courtesy R.Marshall

ATE 79, now repainted
in the antique red (waste
band) and tan livery, is
seen parked in resi-
dential surroundings,
most probably awaiting
the return of football
fans. The type of front
entrance Plaxton
Venturer coach with
entrance door ahead of
the front axle, parked
behind ATE 79, was not
introduced by Plaxton
until 1955, and this
photograph was
therefore not taken until
at least Autumn 1955.
ATE 79 was numbered
13 in the Victoria fleet.
Courtesy P. Yeomans
per. J. Bennett

PLATE 109/110 (above)
*Interior views of Victoria
No.11, ATE 77.*
Courtesy A. Wood Collection,
per D. Wilkinson

PLATE 111
*ATE 78 is in the Red & Cream
livery, suggesting a c.1945/6
date. The background
buildings suggest the
photograph may have been
taken whilst the vehicle was
parked in close proximity to
the Branston Ordnance
factory, on the outskirts of
Burton upon Trent. Certain
weekday morning Victoria
services were licensed to run
beyond Victoria's Wetmore
Park terminal in Burton, to
the factory, with return
workings after 5pm each
weekday.*
Copyright P. Thomas

PLATE 112
Victoria No.10, ARA 172, seen unloading passengers on Trent Bridge, Burton, was new to Repton, Derbyshire operator, 'Blue Bus Services', in June 1934, and it remained in their service until it was bought by Victoria in 1943. It was not included in the July 1943 statement (Plate 106) for the purchase of Victoria by Lloyd Leitch & Atkins, and therefore purchase by Victoria may have been after July 1943. Courtesy R.Marshall

The purchase of Victoria Motorways Ltd. business by Messrs. Lloyd, Leitch & Atkins as individuals, rather than as a takeover by Viking Motors, ensured continuation of Victoria's individual identity, even though the two companies shared premises and existed side-by-side until sold in October 1987. The statement setting out the details of the purchase, is shown in Plate 106.

A Directors Meeting held on 29 October 1943, heard that *"….a satisfactory increase in the service takings since the new directors were appointed"* had been achieved, *.."although this had necessarily been accompanied by an increase in the wages paid.* At the same meeting, Mr. Lloyd stated that: *"…the buses and coaches which were the property of the Company had been hired to Viking Motors (Burton) Ltd., and that the buses used on the service had been hired from Viking Motors. It was decided that the charge as between the two Companies should be finally agreed after 28 February 1944. It was reported that two employees of the Viking motor company were working for Victoria Motorways Ltd., and that the wages paid to such employees were being refunded by the Company."*

At a meeting of Directors held on 10 November 1943, the Secretary advised he had received Mr. E. M. Sales' notice of resignation as a Director, and this was accepted.

However, Mr. Sales retained his 10 shares in the Company until 27 November 1946, when he sold them back to the Company for £1.each.

The Victoria timetable commencing 7 February 1944, shows no reference to the 'Joint Service' arrangement printed on the 1933 timetable, but the Measham-Netherseal and Netherseal-Burton services had been combined into one. The eight Netherseal-Burton services a day frequency in 1933, had increased to eleven each way by 1944.

A meeting of Directors on 20 April 1945, was advised that the Company's Accounts for the year ended 28 February 1945, showed a net profit for the year of £876.9s.2d., the Accounts being approved at the AGM held on 29th April 1945. Whilst in 2005 terms this figure will seem a minute profit return for one year's business activity, by 1945 post-war expectations, this would have been considered as being a fair return.

Another South Derbyshire bus and coach proprietor, based in Castle Gresley, operated as Brooks Brothers, and the Victoria directors held an evening meeting on 28 May 1945, at which Mr. Lloyd reported that he *"... and Mr. Atkins had been in negotiation with Messrs. Brooks Bros. (Castle Gresley) and on behalf of the Company (Victoria), had entered into an agreement to purchase the Goodwill of*

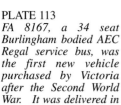

PLATE 113
FA 8167, a 34 seat Burlingham bodied AEC Regal service bus, was the first new vehicle purchased by Victoria after the Second World War. It was delivered in April 1946, and is seen at Victoria's stand in Burton Wetmore Bus Park, in red and cream livery. It was sold by Victoria in June 1959.

Courtesy R.Marshall

the Brooks' business for the sum of £11,000., together with a Maudslay bus No. OV 9147 for £1,000."

The directors approved the purchase. Mr. Lloyd also reported that he: *"and Mr. Atkins had completed long and difficult negotiations with the B&MMO Co. Ltd. (Midland Red), as a result of which Victoria had sold the business purchased from Brooks Bros to the B&MMO Co.Ltd., for £10,000, and in addition, had obtained the agreement of that company (B&MMO) to the following:-*

"1. The B&MMO Co. Ltd., to withdraw the Service at present operated by them between Donisthorpe (Bulls Head) and Burton-on-Trent via Short Heath, Overseal

PLATE 114
New in June 1946, Burlingham/AEC Regal FA 8224, is seen alongside FA 8791, a Daimler CVD6 type with a Burlingham 35 seat body, delivered new in September 1947, both awaiting their next turn of duty in Wetmore Park, Burton.
Courtesy R.Marshall

& Cadley Hill, and also to withdraw all services between Overseal and Burton-on-Trent via Castle Gresley and Cadley Hill, and not to apply for the re-instatement of the journeys operated by them in 1939 and since discontinued."

"2. The B&MMO Co.Ltd., to raise no objection to any application by Victoria Motorways Ltd., for journeys between Donisthorpe (Bulls Head) and Burton, via Short Heath, Overseal & Cadley Hill, and to any service between Measham or Netherseal and Burton, via Overseal, Castle Gresley and Cadley Hill."

"3. The B&MMO Co. Ltd., to operate no services between Castle Gresley & Stanton, via Cadley Hill."

The Company on their part had undertaken to raise no objection to any application by the B&MMO Co. Ltd., for journeys between Measham & Burton-on-Trent via Donisthorpe (Masons Arms) & Moira (Toll Gate)." It was further recorded that: *"The Directors were satisfied that substantial benefits would accrue to the Company as a result of the agreement which had been reached, and it was resolved that the sale to the B&MMO Co. Ltd., and the Agreements be approved by the Board."*

Brooks sold the service buses but retained their coaches and concentrated on private hire coach provision, including hiring coaches to Viking Motors and other operators at peak times, until the Brooks' business finally closed at the end of the 1961 summer season, and the vehicles sold.

Brooks' main service was between Swadlincote and Linton, via Church Gresley and Castle Gresley, with an extension to Newhall on Thursdays only. This service operated in a clockwise direction from the cross roads in Castle Gresley, via Mount Pleasant, Rickman's Corner,

Linton Heath, and Linton before returning to the road junction in Castle Gresley, on what was then effectively the return journey to Swadlincote. The Midland Red Swadlincote to Linton service No.706 served exactly the same route via Castle Gresley and Linton, but in the anti-clockwise direction. Brooks also ran a Swadlincote to Overseal service via Castle Gresley and Rickman's Corner into Overseal, taking the same route between Castle Gresley and Overseal as Victoria's Burton to Measham service. Service frequency on both Brook's services was hourly.

'Midland Red's' acquisition of the former Brooks' services enabled them to extend their original 705 service from Swadlincote to Castle Gresley, by taking the Brooks 'clockwise' route through Linton and back to Castle Gresley, whilst continuing the original anti-clockwise Swadlincote-Linton No.706 service.

During the war period, 'Midland Red' had started a new service between Swadlincote-Castle Gresley-Overseal (Service No. 720). However, this service was severely restricted to afternoons only, so as not to conflict directly with Brook's long established Swadlincote-Overseal service. The 'Midland Red' service was two return trips every Friday, from Swadlincote at 5.20pm and 6.20pm, four return trips on Saturdays, leaving at 2.20pm, 5.20, 6.20, 7.20pm, and three return services on Sundays, leaving Swadlincote as service No.716 at 2.10pm, 4.10 and 6.10pm. The afternoons only restriction was designed to prevent competition for passengers during the period Monday to Thursday with the Brooks' service, and with Victoria's Measham-Burton services which ran between Overseal and Castle Gresley. However, once the former Brooks' Swadlincote-Overseal service was sold by Victoria, Midland

Red's No.720 service became an hourly one throughout the day in both directions.

After the war had ended, the Victoria bus services did not enjoy the same growth prospects which were gradually evolving for the Viking coach operations. Demand for day, half-day, and evening theatre trips, and the increasing popularity of Viking's Blackpool service, were providing opportunities for more rapid growth than could be achieved by Victoria's routine bus services.

A Directors' meeting held on 14 December 1945, was advised that the Interim Accounts for the half year ended 31 August 1945, showed that a net profit of £378.16s.6d. had been achieved.

PLATE 115
Between May 1950 and May 1966, there were no new vehicles purchased by Victoria for stage carriage work, but four Viking coaches each with a front entrance ahead of the front wheel arch, were transferred to Victoria. Willowbrook bodied AEC Reliance No. DFA 550, was one of the four, and it is seen here repainted with Victoria's Staffordshire Knot badge, before departure on the Donisthorpe service.
Courtesy R.Marshall

In April 1946 two new Burlingham half-cab 35 seat AEC Regal service buses joined the Victoria fleet. Three identical Burlingham bus bodied Daimler CVD6's followed late in 1947, whilst the last half-cab bus to be purchased by Victoria, a Daimler CVD6 with Willowbrook dual purpose 35 seat front entrance body, arrived in May 1950. This vehicle (FA 9847), which had the Viking coach badge rather than the Victoria Staffordshire Knot badge on the sides until at least April 1952, remained with Victoria until December 1964, and whilst preservation was seriously considered, it was eventually decided it should be scrapped.

A meeting of the Board on 27 November 1946, approved transfer deeds covering the purchase of the ten shares which had been retained by Mr. M.V.Sales after he had ceased to be a director. The ten shares were allocated to Mr. W. J. Lloyd (4 shares), Mr. D. J. S. Leitch (4) and Mr. H. Atkins (2), to round-off their respective holdings to 1,000, 1,000 & 500.

Further Director's meetings were advised of the following:
"5 November 1947 - Year ended 28 February 1947 produced trading profit of £1407.16s.10d."
"3 November 1948 - Year ended ....1948, increase in profit to £3,166. noted".
"23 September 1950 – Accounts presented – the fall in takings noted and it was decided to make application for an increase in fares."

Victoria succeeded in developing a new service from Donisthorpe Masons Arms, via Moira Crescent to Overseal Church, and this was operational by December 1948, linking with the Measham to Burton services at Overseal Church crossroads. A second licence was also obtained for a new Saturday's only service between Overseal Spring Cottage and Burton, increasing the service frequency between Overseal Church and Burton, and this was in operation by 1951.

Draft accounts for the year ended 28th February 1951, presented at a Directors' meeting on 24 August 1951, revealed *"...a substantial rise in fuel costs, and the running of buses with oil engines was considered. Mr. Lloyd reported that an increase in fares had been granted from the end of July 1951, but as the maximum increase was 20%, it was clear that this increase alone would not enable the Company to operate at a profit, and further increases would have to be obtained, or economies made in running costs."*

It was also decided *"to depreciate the buses by 20% for the year ended 28 February 1951."*

A Directors' meeting on 4 November 1952 noted the *"improved results"* for the year ended 29 February 1952.

The accounts presented to the Board for year ended 29 February 1953 revealed *"...further increases in the cost of petrol, maintenance and wages....as a result of which a Loss of £365. had been incurred."*

On the 13th August, 1953, Mr. W. G. Lloyd's son, Mr. John G Lloyd, was appointed a Director of Victoria Motorways Ltd.

A part of the garage premises owned by Viking Motors at Burton Road, Woodville, was sold to Victoria Motorways Ltd., for £800. on 26 July 1954, and in May 1955, a Mr. P. H. Smith purchased the Burton Road premises for £3,000. All Viking and Victoria vehicles moved to the more extensive garage and yard premises in High Street, Woodville.

Victoria could only increase the service frequency on the services they already had, always providing that sufficient passenger demand could be created. The presence of 'Midland Red' on Victoria's 'doorstep', and the stranglehold they could exercise over development of any new bus services, left Victoria with few new opportunities.

The following table shows the increase in service frequency between the 1944 and 1951 timetables, whilst the 1958 and 1970 figures show slight reductions. The 1983 figures show all services from Measham going via Donisthorpe, with no Sunday services whatsoever :

PLATE 116

	Feb 1944 Mon-Fri	Feb 1951 Mon-Fri	Jun 1958 Mon-Fri	1970 Mon-Fri	1983 Mon-Fri
Measham- Burton) via	6	11	10	10	-
Burton-Measham) Netherseal	7	12	11	10	-
Netherseal- Burton *Thurs only	4 + 1*	1	1	-	-
Burton-Netherseal	4	2	1	-	-
Donisthorpe-Moira-Burton	-	14	13	12	1
Burton-Moira-Donisthorpe	-	12	12	11	1
Overseal Church-Burton M-F	-	1	-	-	1
-do- -do- Thurs only	-	5	-	-	-
Burton-Overseal Church M-F	-	-	-	-	1
-do- -do- Thurs only	-	5	-	-	-
Measham-Donisthorpe-Netherseal-)					
-Overseal-Linton-Burton)	-	-	-	-	5
-do- -do- Fri only	-	-	-	-	2
Burton-Linton-Overseal-Netherseal-)					
Donisthorpe-Measham)	-	-	-	-	5
-do--do- Fri only	-	-	-	-	2
Measham-Donisthorpe-Moira-Burton	-	-	-	-	4
Burton-Moira-Donisthorpe-Measham	-	-	-	-	4
Castle Gresley-Netherseal-Measham (Mon-Thurs only)					1
Measham-Donisthorpe-Castle Gresley (Mon-Thurs only)		-		-	1
Donisthorpe-Netherseal-Moira- Overseal-Linton-Burton)	-	-	-	-	1
Burton-Overseal-Moira-Donisthorpe	-	-	-	-	1

	Sat	Sat	Sat	Sat	Sat
Measham-Burton) via	6	19	17	13	-
Burton-Measham) Netherseal	5	20	18	14	-
Measham-Burton) not via	4	-	-	-	-
Burton-Measham) Netherseal	5	-	-	-	-
Netherseal-Burton #Acresford-Burton	7	1	-	# 1	-
Burton-Netherseal	8	-	-	-	-
Donisthorpe-Moira-Burton	-	20	20	15	-
Burton-Moira-Donisthorpe	-	21	19	14	-
Overseal Spring Cottage-Burton) Sats	-	5	-	-	-
Burton-Overseal Spring Cottage) only	-	4	-	-	-
Measham-Donisthorpe-Netherseal-Burton	-	-	-	-	9
Burton-Netherseal-Donisthorpe-Measham	-	-	-	-	10
Measham-Donisthorpe-Moira-Burton	-	-	-	-	3
Burton-Moira-Donisthorpe-Measham	-	-	-	-	2

	Sun	Sun	Sun	Sun	No
Measham-Burton) via	5	8	7	6	Sunday
Burton-Measham) Netherseal	5	8	6	5	service
Netherseal-Burton	1	-	-	-	
Burton-Netherseal	3	-	-	-	
Donisthorpe-Moira-Burton	-	10	6	6	
Burton-Moira-Donisthorpe	-	10	6	6	

The 1950's was the period when an increase in private car ownership gradually became evident, and whilst bus passenger numbers remained relatively stable up to the mid-50's, a decline in numbers began to show towards the end of the decade.

Between 1950 and 1966, there were no vehicle acquisitions by Victoria and as stated earlier, several wartime acquisitions and the six half-cab buses acquired new between April 1946 and May 1950, were the mainstay of services until they were sold between 1957 and February 1961, the last remaining until December 1964.

From 1960, a new and potentially very cost-effective policy of transferring redundant Viking coaches to Victoria for use on the stage carriage services, was introduced, with six such vehicles being switched between 1960 and 1973. The six vehicles were DFA 548, DFA 550, HFA 3, JFA 519, EFA 494D and UFA 517J, all designated DP (dual purpose) vehicles with the entrance door at the front nearside corner, which ensured passengers had to pass the driver position on entry, therefore making them suitable for one-man operation. An added advantage was retention of the coach style seating, which allowed them to be used for coaching duties if Viking required additional vehicles. There were no further transfers from Viking, nor any other vehicle acquisitions in years 1964-65.

In May 1966, a new fleet purchasing policy emerged with the arrival of four Strachan bodied Bedford VAM5's, No's EFA 497D-500D, and these were sufficient to maintain services, before being disposed of in June 1967, when a further four buses to the same specification , No's HFA 207E-210E, arrived as replacements. One of these, No.HFA 208E, was sold after one year, reflecting a reduced service requirement, whilst the remaining three were sufficient to maintain the required level of services through to March 1970. No further vehicle acquisitions were made in years 1968-69.

In March 1970, three Ford R192 Willowbrook bodied vehicles were acquired, No's OFA 917H-919H, and these remained with the Company until January, 1973, when they were replaced by three more vehicles to the same specification, No's DFA 125L-127L.

One vehicle, a Bedford three axle VAL14 with Duple front entrance coach body seating 49, No. EFA 494D, was transferred from Viking Motors in December 1972, and sold in July 1973. In December 1973, a Duple 53 seat coach bodied Ford R226, No. UFA 517J, became the sixth vehicle transferred from Viking, remaining on Victoria service work until it was sold in January, 1976.

The growth of car usage continued in the early 1960's and the bus services gradually became less well loaded. When nationalisation of the UK bus industry took place in 1968, Victoria and Viking remained in the private sector, and they were able to continue their well established activities serving a loyal and appreciative customer basis.

By 1970, the timetable shows a slight reduction in frequency on the Measham-Burton Monday-Friday service with ten throughout journeys from Measham and eleven from Burton, with twelve Donisthorpe-Burton and eleven Burton-Donisthorpe services. Saturday frequency was 13 from Measham, 14 from Burton, 15 from Donisthorpe and 14 to Donisthorpe. The 1970 Sunday services were afternoon only, with 6 from Measham and also Donisthorpe, with 5 to Measham and 6 to Donisthorpe. Evening services on both routes up to 10.30pm ran every day, but by the early 1980's evening patronage had declined markedly.

The reality of passenger decline can be gauged by the leaflet issued by Derbyshire County Council in April 1983, seen on Plate 123.

Prior to these additional services, the last service from Measham left at 17.15, arriving Burton at 18.01, and in the return direction the 17.30 from Burton arrived Measham at 18.14. There was a later bus departing Burton at 18.15 arriving Donisthorpe 18.51. The last Saturday services are shown as leaving Measham and Burton simultaneously at 18.30, arriving at 19.11 and 19.10 respectively. A poignant note on the timetable states: NO SUNDAY SERVICE .

It is not known what level of passengers these 'late' Friday services attracted, but the fact that there were no services running after 19.11 on Mondays to Thursdays, and none on Sundays, illustrates the decline of the long established and what some might call, the 'traditional' bus services in the semi-rural South Derbyshire-Northwest-Leicestershire area.

PLATE117

In May 1966 four new Bedford VAM5 with Strachan 45 seat bus bodies, joined the Victoria fleet, and EFA 498D seen here, was the second of the batch. However, the four were sold in June 1967, because they were considered not suitable for Victoria's requirements. Note the simple 'VICTORIA' lettering style. Courtesy K.West

PLATE 118. HFA 207E, one of four replacements for the 1966 'EFA' group with similar Bedford VAM5/Strachan specification as the 1966 batch.

PLATE 119

HFA 3 joined the Viking fleet in May 1958 before being transferred to Victoria in May 1962. The Viking warrior badges were removed when coaches were found to be returning to Woodville garage without the badges, but it retained the Viceroy II name, and when not in use on Victoria services, was available to provide additional seats for Viking tours. It is seen in the standard two-tone grey livery adopted for both fleets.

Courtesy R.Marshall

PLATE 120

One of the June 1967 arrivals, HFA 209E is crossing the town-end of Trent Bridge before entering Wetmore Park for its next journey to Donisthorpe. Normal practice was to discharge passengers at the town-end of the bridge, but on this occasion it appears the four passengers are content to remain on board and alight in Wetmore Park. Courtesy R.Marshall

PLATE 121

The next batch of new buses for Victoria arrived in March 1970, to replace the 1967 HFA series. They were 45 seat Willowbrook bodies on Ford R192 chassis, No's OFA 917H-919H. The company lettering style on the front was in plain block capitals, smaller than earlier styles used.

PMPhotography

PLATE 122

An increase to 47 seats came with the batch of three new arrivals in January 1973. DFA 127L is also seen at the town-end of Trent Bridge heading with passengers for Wetmore Park. The Willowbrook badge on the front grill was later removed from the three vehicles.

From Monday 16 July 1984, with assistance from the Derbyshire County Council, Public Transport Unit, a 'New Improved Timetable' was introduced.The features listed are shown in Plate 123.

However, de-regulation of the bus industry which took effect from 26th October, 1986, blew the old restrictive route licensing regulations out of the window, and created conditions which allowed operators greater flexibility to take on more popular and remunerative services, whilst providing new and smaller concerns with an opportunity to make an entry to the bus service industry. Whilst the Victoria operations continued to be viable, profit margins were under considerable pressure, and there was greater competition for some of the private hire work.

The era of de-regulation heralded the introduction of 'X' designated services by Victoria.

The timetable for the first three 'X' routes (X11, X12, X22) was not dated, but it is believed they were introduced in 1985, one being the long-standing Measham-Burton route (X11), the other two routes (X12 & X22) were new for Victoria, with both Swadlincote and Church Gresley on Victoria timetables for the first time. From 19th April 1986, some changes were made to two of the routes, and all three were re-designated. When the 2nd edition of the X22/X23/X33 timetable was issued, also effective from 19th April 1986, a more detailed diagrammatic route plan was provided. Further changes were also made to the 'X' routes (see Plate 193).

The growth of dedicated school services was encouraged and financially supported by County authorities and Government, and Victoria/Viking successfully tendered for several new school services. Two second-hand double-deck buses were purchased by Viking for this work and reference is made to them in the 'Viking' section of this book. The designation of school services as Viking, was to distance them from the Victoria stage carriage services.

By mid-1987, the potential sale of the Viking & Victoria businesses was being considered. De-regulation had in many ways revived bus service operations and the industry had become ultra-competitive, but amalgamations and formation of new groups began to gather pace, with economies of scale becoming the predominant factor. The rise of Stagecoach was perhaps the most significant new grouping, but other groupings were beginning to build.

By 31st October 1987 the sale of Viking Motors (Burton) Ltd., & the Victoria services, but not the Victoria Motorways Ltd., name nor the company itself, had been agreed, with ownership passing to Stevensons of Uttoxeter. The 'Viking' name was continued by Stevensons and they re-badged their own coaches as 'Viking'. Subsequently, Stevensons were swallowed up by Arriva, whose only interest was stage carriage services, and not coaching, and the 'Viking' name was then sold to another operator.

An interesting sequel from a Mr. C. J. Taylor of Cardiff, to whom thanks are extended: The sale of a Bedford front entrance 25 seat bus, registered FA 6627, (new to Victoria in May 1937), to a Mr. Williams of Treorchy, in 1938, led to him re-naming his own Welsh bus company as 'Victoria Motorways', Treorchy, and he also re-painted his other vehicles in the Victoria livery carried by FA 6627.

VICTORIA MOTORWAYS

Measham to Burton Service

Commencing Friday 8 April 1983

A new Friday evening service is being introduced on an experimental basis following requests from passengers.

The additional Friday journeys are:

```
1815 Measham - Netherseal - Burton 1901
2015 Measham - Netherseal - Burton 2058
1930 Burton - Netherseal - Measham 2010
2100 Burton - Netherseal - Measham 2144
```

See overleaf for full timetable and sample fares.

Publicity prepared by:

DERBYSHIRE County Council

Derbyshire County Council
County Planning Department
Public Transport Unit
County Offices
Matlock
Derbyshire DE4 3AG

PLATE 123
Derbyshire County Council sponsored leaflet promoting new Friday evening 'experimental' services.

PLATE 124
TRY 3S, a Ford R1114 with 53 seat front entrance Plaxton 'Supreme' body, seen here on 27 April 1979, was delivered new to Victoria in August, 1977, but the coach seating made it suitable for use by Viking, should the need arise, and it was certainly a seat upgrade from the standard bus type seat.   Apart from small print legal lettering, no other fleet identification was carried by this coach, and it remained in use with Stevensons after they had purchased the Victoria services in October 1987.
Courtesy R.Marshall

BUSES LEAVE	TO SWADLINCOTE	TO BURTON
LINTON	6.40(n) 9.20 10.20 11.20 12.20 1.20 2.20 3.20 3.50 4.50 5.20 5.50 6.20	6.40(n) 7.55(n) 8.20 9.00(s) 9.20 9.50 10.20 10.50 11.20 11.50 12.20 12.50 1.20 1.50 2.20 2.50 3.20 5.20 7.20(f) 9.06(f)

CODES (n)= NOT ON SATURDAYS (s)= SATURDAYS ONLY (f)= FRIDAYS ONLY (x)=THURSDAY, FRIDAY, SATURDAY ONLY
BUSES UNDERLINED OPERATE DIRECT TO BURTON via A444

TIMETABLE
VICTORIA MOTORWAYS

X22
BURTON – NEWHALL – SWADLINCOTE
LINTON – OVERSEAL – MEASHAM

X23
BURTON – NEWHALL – SWADLINCOTE
CHURCH GRESLEY

X33
BURTON – LINTON (DIRECT)

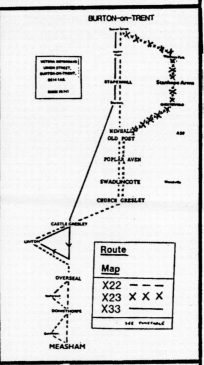

Route Map	
X22	– – –
X23	X X X
X33	——

UNION STREET, BURTON-ON-TRENT, DE14 1AB. (0283) 65741
HIGH STREET, WOODVILLE, BURTON-ON-TRENT, DE11 7EA. (0283) 217012

BURTON – NEWHALL – SWADLINCOTE – CH. GRESLEY – LINTON – OVERSEAL – MEASHAM Service X22
BURTON – LINTON (DIRECT) Service X33

BURTON – NEWHALL – SWADLINCOTE – CH.GRESLEY – LINTON – OVERSEAL – MEASHAM   SERVICE X22 X33

Not Sat X22	Not Sat X33	Sat Only X33	X22	X33	X22	X33	X22	X33	X22	X33		X22	X33	X22	X33	X22	X33	X22	X33	X22	X33	Fri Only X22	Fri Only
											BURTON (STATION STREET)	1.05	1.35	2.05	2.35	3.05	3.35	4.05	4.35	5.05	5.35	5.55	8.05 10.05
7.25	—	—	—	9.05	9.35	10.05	10.35	11.05	11.35	12.05 12.35	STAPENHILL (Post Office)	1.09	1.39	2.09	2.39	3.09	3.39	4.09	4.39	5.09	5.39	5.59	8.09 10.09
7.29	—	—	—	9.09	9.39	10.09	10.39	11.09	11.39	12.09 12.39	STANTON (Black Horse)	1.12	1.42	2.12	2.42	3.12	3.42	4.12	4.42	5.12	5.42	6.02	8.12 10.12
7.32	—	—	—	9.12	9.42	10.12	10.42	11.12	11.42	12.12 12.42	NEWHALL (Old Post)	1.20	—	2.20	—	3.20	—	4.20	—	5.20	—	6.10	—
—	—	—	9.20	—	10.20	—	11.20	—	12.20	—	NEWHALL (Poplar Aven)	1.23	—	2.23	—	3.23	—	4.23	—	5.23	—	6.13	—
—	—	—	9.23	—	10.23	—	11.23	—	12.23	—	SWADLINCOTE (Bus Park)	1.30	—	2.30	—	3.30	—	4.30	—	5.30	—	6.20	—
—	—	8.48	9.30	—	10.30	—	11.30	—	12.30	—	CH.GRESLEY (Miners Arms)	1.35	—	2.35	—	3.35	—	4.35	—	5.35	—	6.25	—
7.38	—	8.53	9.38	9.46	10.38	10.46	11.38	11.46	12.38	12.46	CASTLE GRES (Burton Rd)	1.38	1.46	2.38	2.46	3.38	3.46	4.38	4.46	5.38	5.46	6.28	8.16 10.16
7.40	—	8.56	9.40	9.50	10.40	10.50	11.40	11.50	12.40 12.50	LINTON (Red Lion)	1.40	1.50	2.40	2.50	3.40	3.50	4.40	4.50	5.40	5.50	6.30	8.20 10.20
7.46	—	9.00	9.46	—	10.46	—	11.46	—	12.46	—	OVERSEAL (Church)	1.46	—	2.46	—	3.46	cont	4.46	cont	5.46	cont	6.36	8.26 10.26
7.49	cont	—	9.49	—	10.49	—	—	—	12.49	—	MOIRA (Short Heath)	—	—	2.49	—	—	on	4.49	on	—	on	6.39	8.29 —
—	on	—	9.50	—	—	—	11.50	—	—	—	NETHERSEAL	1.50	—	—	—	3.50	to	5.50	to	—	—	—	— 10.30
7.52	7.25 B.OT	8.54	9.55	—	10.52	—	11.55	—	12.52	—	DONISTH. (Masons Arms)	1.55	—	2.52	—	3.55	Ch.G	4.52	Ch.G	5.55	Ch.G	6.42	8.32 10.35
7.55	—	8.57	—	—	10.55	—	—	—	12.55	—	OAKTHORPE (Square)	—	—	2.55	—	—	&	4.55	&	—	Swad	6.45	8.35 —
7.59	7.29	—	8.59	9.59	—	10.59	—	11.59	—	12.59	MEASHAM (High Street)	1.59	—	2.59	—	3.59	Swad	4.59	Swad	5.59	W/Vi	6.49	8.39 10.39

MEASHAM – OVERSEAL – LINTON – CH.GRESLEY – SWADLINCOTE – NEWHALL – BURTON   SERVICE X22 X33

Not Sat X22	Not Sat X33	Sat Only X33	X33	X22	X33	X22	X33	X22	X33		X22	X33	X22	X23	X22	Sat Only X33	X22	X22	Fri Only	Fri Only	Fri Only
—	—	8.00	—	9.00	—	—	—	11.00	—	MEASHAM (Jerrams D.I.Y.)	1.00	—	—	—	3.00	—	5.00	—	7.00	8.45	—
—	7.35	—	—	—	10.00	—	—	—	12.00	MEASHAM (Bradfords Shop)	—	2.00	—	4.00	—	6.00	—	7.04	—	10.39
—	7.39	—	—	—	10.04	—	—	—	12.04	OAKTHORPE (Square)	—	2.04	—	4.04	—	6.04	—	10.43
—	7.43	8.05	—	9.05	—	10.08	—	11.05	—	12.08	DONISTH. (Masons Arms)	1.05	2.08	—	3.05	—	4.05	—	5.05	6.08	7.45	8.50 10.47
—	—	8.10	—	9.10	—	—	—	11.10	—	NETHERSEAL	1.10	—	3.10	—	5.10	—	6.12	7.10	8.55
6.32	7.46	—	—	—	10.11	—	11.11	—	12.11	MOIRA (Short Heath)	1.14	—	2.14	—	4.11	—	5.14	—	6.15	7.14	9.00
6.35	7.49	8.14	—	9.14	—	10.14	—	11.14	—	12.14	OVERSEAL (Church)	1.20	1.50	2.20	2.50	3.14	1.50	4.50	5.20	5.50	6.20	7.20 9.06
6.40	7.55	8.20	9.00	9.20	11.50	10.20	11.50	12.20 12.50	LINTON (Red Lion)	1.25	1.53	2.25	2.53	3.25	3.53	4.18	4.53	5.25	5.53	7.24 9.11
6.45	8.00	8.25	9.05	9.25	9.53	10.25	10.53	11.25	11.53	12.25 12.53	CASTLE GRES (Burton Rd)	1.28	—	2.28	—	3.28	3.55	4.55	5.28	5.55	6.28	—
6.48	—	9.28	10.28	—	11.28	—	12.28	CH.GRESLEY (Miners Arms)	1.33	—	2.33	—	3.33	4.00	5.00	5.33	6.00	6.33	—
6.53	—	9.33	10.33	—	11.33	—	12.33	SWADLINCOTE (Bus Park)	1.37	—	2.37	—	3.37	—	5.37	cont cont	—
6.57	—	9.37	10.37	—	11.37	—	12.37	NEWHALL (Poplar Aven)	1.40	—	2.40	—	3.40	—	5.40	on on	—
7.00	—	9.40	10.40	—	11.40	—	12.40	NEWHALL (Old Post)	—	2.11	—	4.11	—	5.48	to to	—
7.05	8.05	8.30	9.10	9.48	9.58	10.48	10.58	11.48	11.58	12.48 12.58	STANTON (Black Horse)	1.48	1.58	2.48	2.58	3.48	—	4.23	5.51	W/Vi W/Vi	7.29 9.16
7.09	8.09	8.33	9.13	9.51	1001	10.51	11.01	11.51	12.01	12.51 1.01	STAPENHILL (Post Office)	1.51	2.01	2.51	3.01	3.51	—	4.26	5.55		7.32 9.19
7.13	8.13	8.37	9.17	9.55	10.05	10.55	11.05	11.55	12.05	12.55 1.05	BURTON (STATION STREET)	1.55	2.05	2.55	3.05	3.55	—	4.30	—		7.35 9.23

PLATE 125. *Victoria 1980's timetable*

73

VICTORIA BUS SERVICES
DRIVER SHIFT PATTERNS – Mid-1980'S

SHIFT A

REPORT GARAGE 6.00am   FIT DESTINATION BOARDS TO COACH
Proceed direct to ASHBY ROYAL HOTEL, then do the following service as per Company Timetable
(ALL TIMES TO BE OBSERVED)

DEP. TIME	ROUTE No.	ROUTE
6.18am	X22	ASHBY-MEASHAM-DONISTHORPE-LINTON-SWADLINCOTE-BARGATES-BURTON-PIRELLI FACTORY
		PRIVATE TO WETMORE PARK
7.24am	X22	WETMORE PARK-SWADLINCOTE-LINTON-C.BRIDGE- DONISTHORPE-(THEN VIA B5861-MOIRA TOLLGATE- NORRIS HILL-ASHBY
		PRIVATE TO LINTON
8.30am	—	LINTON RED LION-PINGLE SCHOOLS
	(Contract No.1)	
8.43am	(10p fare)	EMSLEIGH DRIVE-POPLAR AVENUE-LIME TREE AVENUE-GRANVILLE SCHOOL
		PRIVATE TO DONISTHORPE MASONS ARMS
9.09am	X22	DONISTHORPE-ACRESFORD-NETHERSEAL-OVERSEAL-LINTON-SWADLINCOTE-BURTON
9.45am	X33	BURTON-LINTON-OVERSEAL
10.45am	X33	OVERSEAL-LINTON-BURTON
11.05am	X22	BURTON-SWADLINCOTE-LINTON-SLACKY LANE-MOIRA-ASHBY-MEASHAM
12.02pm	X22	MEASHAM-DONISTHORPE-LINTON-SWADLINCOTE
		(Monday – Thursday relief Driver 'D' Shift)
		(Fridays only) Continue into Burton
(Fridays only)		
12.45pm	X33	BURTON-LINTON-OVERSEAL-ACRESFORD-NETHERSEAL
(Fridays only)		
1.40pm	X33	NETHERSEAL-OVERSEAL-LINTON-BURTON
(Fridays only)		
2.05pm	X23	BURTON-MEASHAM-ASHBY SERVICE (As far as Swadlincote) RELIEF DRIVER 'E' SHIFT
	FINISH	MON-Thursday 1.00PM 7 HOURS
		FRIDAYS ONLY 2.45PM 8³/₄ HOURS

SHIFT B

REPORT GARAGE 7.00am   FIT DESTINATION BOARDS TO COACH
Proceed direct to SWADLINCOTE ALEXANDRA ROAD then do the following service as per Company Timetable (ALL TIMES TO BE OBSERVED).

DEP.TIME	ROUTE No.	ROUTE
7.24am	X22	SWADLINCOTE-LINTON-SLACKY LANE-MOIRA-ASHBY-MEASHAM
8.02am	X22	MEASHAM-ACRESFORD-NETHERSEAL-OVERSEAL-LINTON-SWADLINCOTE-BARGATE- BURTON HIGH STREET
9.05am	X22	BURTON-SWADLINCOTE-LINTON-SLACKY LANE-MOIRA-ASHBY-MEASHAM
10.02am	X22	MEASHAM-DONISTHORPE-LINTON-SWADLINCOTE-BURTON
10.45am	X33	BURTON-LINTON-OVERSEAL-ACRESFORD-NETHERSEAL
11.40am	X33	NETHERSEAL-OVERSEAL-LINTON-BURTON
12.05pm	X23	BURTON-SWADLINCOTE-LINTON-DONISTHORPE-MEASHAM-ASHBY
1.00pm	X23	ASHBY-MOIRA-SLACKY LANE-LINTON-SWADLINCOTE-BURTON
1.45pm	X33	BURTON-LINTON-OVERSEAL
2.45pm	X33	OVERSEAL-LINTON-BURTON (Pick up Mrs. Sandal & Mrs. Thornhill at Copper Hearth)
		(DURING SCHOOL HOLIDAYS CHECK WORK SHEETS)

Then private to BITHAM LANE SCHOOL picking up Mrs. Robinson at Dallow Street Lights en route (3.10pm) transfer Mrs. Sandal & Mrs. Thornhill on to S80 bus at Bitham School.

| 3.35pm | - | Depart BITHAM SCHOOL setting down passengers at Rolleston Rd/St. Andrews Drive-Rolleston Road-Harper Av/Horninglow Rd-Farringtons-Derby St.-Waterloo St.- Queens St./Uxbridge St.- Branston Rd/Queen St-Branston Rd-Anglesey Rd-Mellor Rd. |

After last passenger set down proceed direct to FOREST OF NEEDWOOD HIGH SCHOOL via A38 and Clay Mills

| 4.00pm | | Depart FOREST OF NEEDWOOD HIGH |

SCHOOL

4.05pm		Depart WULFRIC SCHOOL (Junction of Harehedge Lane & Rolleston Road) then via ANSLOW SCHOOL (Also pick up if required)-BURNT GATE-ACORN INN-HENHURST POST OFFICE-AVIATION LANE-THE ALBION (Dropping passengers as required)
		After last passenger set down take break then proceed to do
5.05pm	X22	BURTON-SWADLINCOTE-LINTON-SLACKY LANE-ASHBY-MEASHAM
6.02pm	X22	MEASHAM-DONISTHORPE-ACRESFORD-NETHERSEAL-LINTON-SWADLINCOTE.
		Then return PRIVATE to depot

SHIFT C

REPORT GARAGE 8.15am   FIT DESTINATION BOARDS TO COACH
PROCEED DIRECT TO RICKMANS CORNER

DEP. TIME	ROUTE No.	ROUTE
8.23am	——	RICKMANS CORNER then all stops to RED LION
		Then to PINGLE SCHOOL (Contract No.3)
		THEN PROCEED DIRECT TO SWADLINCOTE ALEXANDRA ROAD THEN DO THE FOLLOWING SERVICE AS PER COMPANY TIMETABLE (ALL TIMES TO BE OBSERVED)
8.54am	X23	SWADLINCOTE-LINTON-DONISTHORPE-MEASHAM-ASHBY
9.31am	X23	ASHBY-MOIRA-SLACKY LANE-LINTON-CASTLE GRESLEY (THEN A444)-BURTON
10.05am	X23	BURTON-SWADLINCOTE-LINTON-DONISTHORPE-MEASHAM ASHBY
11.00am	X23	ASHBY-MOIRA-SLACKY LANE-LINTON-SWADLINCOTE-BURTON
11.45am	X33	BURTON-LINTON-OVERSEAL
12.45pm	X33	OVERSEAL-LINTON-BURTON
1.05pm	X22	BURTON-SLACKY LANE-MOIRA-ASHBY-MEASHAM
2.02pm	X22	MEASHAM-DONISTHORPE-LINTON-SWADLINCOTE-BURTON
2.45pm	X33	BURTON-LINTON-OVERSEAL-ACRESFORD-NETHERSEAL
3.40pm	X33	NETHERSEAL-OVERSEAL-LINTON-BURTON
4.05pm	X23	BURTON-SWADLINCOTE-DONISTHORPE-MEASHAM-ASHBY
5.00pm	X23	ASHBY-MOIRA-SLACKY LANE-LINTON-SWADLINCOTE-BURTON
5.45pm	X23	BURTON-SWADLINCOTE-DONISTHORPE-MEASHAM-ASHBY
		Then return PRIVATE to depot.
		FINISH 7.00 pm 10 ³/₄ HRS

SHIFT D

REPORT GARAGE 12.15pm
Take van to SWADLINCOTE ALEXANDRA ROAD & take over A SHIFT bus at 12.29pm.   Then do the following service as per Company timetable.   (ALL TIMES TO BE OBSERVED)

DEP.TIME	ROUTE No.	ROUTE
12.29pm	X22	SWADLINCOTE-BURTON
12.45pm	X33	BURTON-LINTON-OVERSEAL-ACRESFORD-NETHERSEAL
1.40pm	X33	NETHERSEAL-OVERSEAL-LINTON-BURTON
2.05pm	X23	BURTON-SWADLINCOTE-LINTON-DONISTHORPE-MEASHAM-ASHBY
3.00pm	X23	ASHBY-MOIRA-SLACKY LANE-LINTON-SWADLINCOTE-BURTON
3.45pm	X22 (ONLY)	BURTON-SWADLINCOTE ALEXANDRA ROAD
		Then private to Pingle School
4.10pm	——	PINGLE SCHOOL TO LINTON RED LION (Contract No.3)
		Then private to Burton to do
4.45pm	X22	BURTON-SWADLINCOTE-LINTON-OVERSEAL
5.45pm	X33	OVERSEAL-LINTON-BURTON
6.05pm	X23	BURTON-SWADLINCOTE-LINTON-DONISTHORPE MEASHAM-ASHBY
		Then return PRIVATE to depot.
		FINISH 7.30pm 7¹/₄ HRS

SHIFT E
REPORT GARAGE – 2pm   (FRIDAYS ONLY)
Take van to Swadlincote Alexandra Road & take over Shift Bus at 2.24pm then do
the following as per Company timetable (ALL TIMES TO BE OBSERVED)

DEP.TIME	ROUTE No.	ROUTE
2.24pm	X23	SWADLINCOTE-LINTON-DONISTHORPE-MEASHAM-ASHBY
3.00pm	X23	ASHBY-MOIRA-SLACKY LANE-LINTON-SWADLINCOTE-BURTON
3.45pm	X22	BURTON-SWADLINCOTE-ALEXANDRA ROAD (ONLY)
		THEN PRIVATE TO PINGLE SCHOOL
4.10pm	—	PINGLE SCHOOL TO LINTON RED LION (Contract No.2)
		THEN PRIVATE TO BURTON TO DO
4.45pm	X22	BURTON-SWADLINCOTE-LINTON-OVERSEAL
5.45pm	X33	OVERSEAL-LINTON-BURTON
6.05pm	X23	BURTON-SWADLINCOTE-LINTON-DONISTHORPE-MEASHAM-ASHBY
7.00pm	X23	ASHBY-MOIRA-SLACKY LANE-LINTON-SWADLINCOTE-BURTON
8.05pm	X23	BURTON-SWADLINCOTE-LINTON-DONISTHORPE-MEASHAM-ASHBY
9.00pm	X23	ASHBY-MOIRA-SLACKY LANE-LINTON-SWADLINCOTE-BURTON
10.05pm	X22	BURTON-SWADLINCOTE-LINTON-SLACKY LANE-MOIRA-ASHBY
10.53pm	X22	ASHBY-MEASHAM-OAKTHORPE-DONISTHORPE MASONS ARMS-MOIRA TOLLGATE

Then PRIVATE to depot.
FINISH 11.30pm   9$\frac{1}{2}$ HOURS

SHIFT X
REPORT GARAGE 8.45am   FIT DESTINATION BOARDS TO COACH
Proceed direct to DONISTHORPE MASONS ARMS then do the following service
as per Company Timetable (ALL TIMES TO BE OBSERVED)

DEP.TIME	ROUTE No.	ROUTE
9,09am	X22	DONISTHORPE-ACRESFORD-NETHERSEAL-OVERSEAL-LINTON-SWADLINCOTE-BURTON
9.45am	X33	BURTON-LINTON-OVERSEAL
10.45am	X33	OVERSEAL-LINTON-BURTON
11.05am	X22	BURTON-SWADLINCOTE-LINTON-SLACKY LANE-MOIRA-ASHBY-MEASHAM
12.02pm	X22	MEASHAM-DONISTHORPE-LINTON-SWADLINCOTE-BURTON
12.45pm	X33	BURTON-LINTON-OVERSEAL-ACRESFORD-NETHERSEAL
1.40pm	X33	NETHERSEAL-OVERSEAL-LINTON-BURTON
2.05pm	X23	BURTON-SWADLINCOTE-LINTON-DONISTHORPE-MEASHAM-ASHBY
3.00pm	X23	ASHBY-MOIRA-SLACKY LANE-LINTON-SWADLINCOTE-BURTON
		BREAK IN BURTON 3.45PM TO 4.05PM
4.05pm	X23	BURTON-SWADLINCOTE-LINTON-DONISTHORPE-MEASHAM-ASHBY
5.00pm	X23	ASHBY-MOIRA-SLACKY LANE-LINTON-SWADLINCOTE-BURTON
5.45pm	X23	BURTON-SWADLINCOTE-LINTON-DONISTHORPE-MEASHAM-ASHBY

Then PRIVATE to depot
FINISH 7.00pm   10$\frac{1}{4}$ HRS

SHIFT Y
REPORT GARAGE 7.00am   FIT DESTINATION BOARDS TO COACH
Proceed direct to SWADLINCOTE ALEXANDRA ROAD then do the following
service as per Company timetable (ALL TIMES TO BE OBSERVED)

DEP.TIME	ROUTE No.	ROUTE
7.24am	X22	SWADLINCOTE-LINTON-SLACKY LANE-MOIRA-ASHBY-MEASHAM
8.02am	X22	MEASHAM-ACRESFORD-NETHERSEAL-OVERSEAL-LINTON-SWADLINCOTE-BARGATES-BURTON HIGH STREET
9.05am	X22	BURTON-SWADLINCOTE-LINTON-SLACKY LANE-MOIRA-ASHBY-MEASHAM
10.02am	X22	MEASHAM-DONISTHORPE-LINTON-SWADLINCOTE-BURTON
10.45am	X33	BURTON-LINTON-OVERSEAL-ACRESFORD-NETHERSEAL
11.40am	X33	NETHERSEAL-OVERSEAL-LINTON-BURTON
12.05pm	X23	BURTON-SWADLINCOTE-LINTON-DONISTHORPE-MEASHAM-ASHBY
1.00pm	X23	ASHBY-MOIRA-SLACKY LANE-LINTON-SWADLINCOTE-BURTON
1.45pm	X33	BURTON-LINTON-OVERSEAL
2.45pm	X33	OVERSEAL-LINTON-BURTON
3.05pm	X22	BURTON-SWADLINCOTE-SLACKY LANE-MOIRA-ASHBY-MEASHAM
4.02pm	X22	MEASHAM-DONISTHORPE-LINTON-SWADLINCOTE-BURTON
		Break in BURTON 4.45pm to 5.05pm
5.05pm	X22	BURTON-SWADLINCOTE-LINTON-SLACKY LANE-ASHBY-MEASHAM
6.02pm	X22	MEASHAM-DONISTHORPE-ACRESFORD-NETHERSEAL-LINTON-SWADLINCOTE

Then return PRIVATE to depot
FINISH   7.00pm   12 HOURS

SHIFT Z
REPORT GARAGE 8.30 am   FIT DESTINATION BOARDS TO COACH
Proceed direct to SWADLINCOTE ALEXANDRA ROAD then do the following
service as per Company timetable   (ALL TIMES TO BE OBSERVED).

DEP.TIME	ROUTE No.	ROUTE
8.54am	X23	SWADLINCOTE-LINTON-DONISTHORPE-MEASHAM-ASHBY
9.31am	X23	ASHBY-MOIRA-SLACKY LANE-LINTON-SWADLINCOTE-BURTON
10.05am	X23	BURTON-SWADLINCOTE-LINTON-DONISTHORPE-MEASHAM-ASHBY
11.00am	X23	ASHBY-MOIRA-SLACKY LANE-LINTON-SWADLINCOTE-BURTON
11.45am	X33	BURTON-LINTON-OVERSEAL
12.45am	X33	OVERSEAL-LINTON-BURTON
1.05pm	X22	BURTON-LINTON-SLACKY LANE-MOIRA-ASHBY-MEASHAM
2.02pm	X22	MEASHAM-DONISTHORPE-LINTON-SWADLINCOTE-BURTON
2.45pm	X33	BURTON-LINTON-OVERSEAL-ACRESFORD-NETHERSEAL
3.40pm	X33	NETHERSEAL-OVERSEAL-LINTON-BURTON
		Break at BURTON 4.05pm to 4.45pm
4.45pm	X22	BURTON-SWADLINCOTE-LINTON-OVERSEAL
5.45pm	X33	OVERSEAL-LINTON-BURTON
6.05pm	X23	BURTON-SWADLINCOTE-LINTON-DONISTHORPE- MEASHAM-ASHBY

Then PRIVATE to depot
FINISH 7.00pm   10$\frac{1}{2}$ HOURS

Note: The Driver Shift Patterns shown are those used by the Company during the early to mid-1980's. From time to time changes to services to meet the changing needs and travel patterns of passengers, inevitably required adjustments to both the scheduled timings and routes taken.

Six vehicles were required to operate Shifts A,B,C,X,Y,Z, each day, whilst the two other shifts – D & E – were for the early afternoon to late evening operations. One employee would operate Shifts D & E – D operated on Mon-Thurs, whilst Shift E was a Fridays only workming.

There is reference in the shift patterns shown to three School contracts for the Pingle School, Woodville (Derbyshire Contracts), and further contracts for the Bitham Lane School, Stretton; the Forest of Needwood High School, Rolleston-on-Dove; the Wulfric School, Rolleston-on-Dove; and for Anslow School (all Staffordshire Contracts). However, the School Contracts referred to were fore-runners of the sixteen School Contracts operated by Viking Motors in mid-1987.

E. M. SALES (trading as SALES BROTHERS) – 1921-1930
& VICTORIA MOTORWAYS LTD. – 1930-1987 – List of Vehicles

Mr. Mark Sales operated a taxi service soon after the end of the First World War, and later started a bus service between Measham and Burton upon Trent. This fleet information summary has been extracted from The PSV Circle's Fleet History publication, PD18, and the author wishes to place on record his thanks for the Circle's permission to include this tabulated data.

Vehicles listed in year of acquisition

Regn Number	Type	Body by:	Seating	New in:	To Sales	Date w/drawn	Pre-Victoria owners & disposal
1921 (no record of vehicles prior to 1921)							
R 3205	Renault	?	6	?	4/21	?	Original owners not traced, scrapped – date not known
FA 727	Ford T	?	B14	1/20	?	6/25	Original owners not traced. UK owner, Derbyshire 10/25
1927							
RA 3155	Overland	?	?	6/27	6/27	2/28	Ridgways, Maesteg, regn void 4/34
UT 1173	Reo	?	B—	6/27	6/27	4/31	Keighley, Armthorpe 12/31, Last licensed 1/37

Note: *The vehicle registration card records this vehicle as registered in the names of Sales and Lloyd 6/28*

Regn Number	Type	Body by:	Seating	New in:	To Sales	Date w/drawn	Pre-Victoria owners & disposal
1928							
UT 33	Chevrolet X model	?	B14	1/27	2/28	6/29	New to Wileman & Hart, Donisthorpe Unidentified owner, Southport 6/29 Converted to goods vehicle 1/31, W/d 3/36
UE 5643	Reo Pullman	Bracebridge	C26F	2/28	2/28	6/29	Lymm, Twogates 3/29, scrapped 9/36
UE 5951	Reo Pullman	"	C26	3/28	3/28	8/28	Burton, Nottingham 8/28, w/d 9/30

Note: *The vehicle registration card records this vehicle as registered in the names of Sales and Lloyd 6/28*

Regn Number	Type	Body by:	Seating	New in:	To Sales	Date w/drawn	Pre-Victoria owners & disposal
UE 1003	Reo Sprinter (or Speed Wagon)	?	B20	4/26	?/28	c8/28	New to J.C.Arnold, Dosthill *Evans Bros (De Luxe Buses, Atherstone ?/28*
UE 6904	Reo Sprinter	?	B20	7/28	7/28	3/36	Not traced
UE 6961	Maudsley ML3	?	C32	8/28	8/28	7/30	To Mann Whitwick 7/30, R'td to Victoria 11/34, Disp 12/38

Note: *The following Thornycroft & Reo buses were received from Barton in July 1929, in exchange for Barton acquiring Victoria's two Gilfords, UE 7865/6*

Regn Number	Type	Body by:	Seating	New in:	To Sales	Date w/drawn	Pre-Victoria owners & disposal
RA 5547	Thornycroft A2 Challand Ross		B20	4/28	7/29*	11/30	New to Barton To D. Williams, Carnswllt 11/30
??	REO	?	B14	?	7/29*	?	New to Barton
1929							
?	Maudsley ML4 Special	?	?	1/27	3/29	?/30	Demonstrator owned by Maudsley Motor Co.Ltd. Coventry Not owned by Sales
UE 7865	Gilford 166OT	?	C32F Re-seated to 26 by 9/29	3/29	3/29	7/29	Barton Transport, Chilwell 7/29, W/d 1936 Anderton, North Hykeham -/36, w/d 9/36
UE 7866	Gilford 166OT	?	C32F	3/29	3/29	7/29	Barton Transport, Chilwell 7/29, W/d 1936 No further operator

Note: The PSV Circle fleet listing (PD18), states: *"1921-1930 – It is known that a Reo, a Reo Pullman, and a Reo Sprinter, all with Bracebridge bodies, were operated* (during the period). *Some or all of these may be included in the above listing."* Unfortunately, no further information has been obtained on such vehicles, and if any reader can provide information and/or photographs of any of these vehicles, the author and The PSV Circle would be very pleased to hear from them.

VICTORIA MOTORWAYS LTD. (Company Incorporated 12th March 1930) – List of vehicles
Vehicles listed in year of acquisition

Regn Number	Type	Body by:	Seating	New in:	To Sales	Date w/drawn	Pre-Victoria owners & disposal
1930							
NR 8262	Guy BA	N.C.M.E.	B26	3/26	7/30	4/31	New to Mann, Whitwick Offered for sale 11/29, Crockett, Measham 4/31, w/d 9/33
1931							
UT 8190	Ford AA	?	B20-	1/31	4/31	10/36	New to Wileman & Hart, Moira, w/d no further operators
VT 2901	AEC Reliance	Dixon	B32F	5/29	4/31	?	New to Buckley, Basford, Stoke-on-Trent, then to Buckley Bros, then to Caswell, Tunstall 3/30 Then to Viking Motors, Burton c.1940
VT 6172	Commer Invader	?	C20F	4/31	4/31	6/37	w/d 6/37, no further operators

1933

Reg	Type	Body	Config				Notes
EK 6409	Bristol B	Bristol	B30D	7/28	6/33	?	New to Wigan Corpn, then Beech(dealer), w/d ? No further operators
RB 3764	Albion PKA26	Rushton & Wilson	C26F	3/31	12/33	7/34	New to Clamp & Bailey. To Victoria 12/33 To Miller, Eastleigh 12/34 Rowland & Graham, Carlisle 1/36 F. Welch, Carlisle 1/37 Hartness, Skelton Road End 1/38, LL 9.38

1934

Reg	Type	Body	Config				Notes
UE 6961	Maudsley ML3	?	C32	8/28	11/34	12/38	New to Sales (Netherseal), then to Mann, Whitwick 7/30, then to Victoria Motorways
BEH 401	Leyland LT5A	Burlingham	C34F	12/34	12/34	?/37	To Osborne & Sons, Tollesbury 10/37 w/d 6/44 then to Tye Bros, Mendlesham 11/44 then to Braybrooke, Mendlesham 6/49 w/d 10/52

Note: *This vehicle was ordered by J.Hawthorn, Stoke-on-Trent before he sold his business to Potteries Motor Traction Co.Ltd. in July, 1934. After completion of the sale, Mr. J. Hawthorn became a Director of Victoria Motorways Ltd. in late 1934, and BEH 401 joined the Victoria fleet in December 1934.*

1935

Reg	Type	Body	Config				Notes
GX 2743	TSM C60A7	?	C32F	5/32	10/35	7/37	New to Highways, London, W/d 10/33 to Cooke, Sandbach 7/37
MV 2669	Leyland TS4	?	C32F	5/32	c/35	6/38	New to Ealing Direct Motor Coaches, London then to Valliant Direct Coahes, London ?/33 to Mann's Superlux Coaches, Smethwick 6/38
FA 5840 (vehicle No.15 in the fleet)	Leyland TS7	Burlingham	FC31F	6/35	6/35	12/40	(Known as the 'Black Hawk') to Mann's Superlux Coaches, Smethwick 1/41 Last licensed 12/56

1936

Reg	Type	Body	Config				Notes
JD 4828	Ford WHB	?	B20-	12/34	c/36	?	New as lorry – bus body fitted c/36, disp.not traced
UT 7601	Chevrolet U	?	B20F	7/30	12/36	6/40	New to Crockett, Measham, then Horsfield, Overseal 9/34 W/d 6/40, no further operator

1937

Reg	Type	Body	Config				Notes
FA 6627	Bedford WTB	Duple	C25F	2/37	5/37	4/38	To Williams (Victoria Motorways), Treochy 5/38 Last licensed 3/50
FA 6656	" "	"	C25F	5/37	5/37	7/42	To Machin's, Ashby-de-la-Zouch 7/42, W/d 4/54, later derelict

1938

Reg	Type	Body	Config				Notes
FS 1762	Albion PV70	Alexander	B32F	12/31	1/38	5/49	New to Scottish Motor Traction, Edinburgh (originally to have been Alexander, Falkirk) To Bland, Cottesmore 5/49, w/d by 6/63
VT 8132	TSM B39A7	Lawton	B36F	6/32	c/38	?	New to Wilshaw, Cheadle, then Potteries M.T.Co. Stoke W/d 1938 , then to Brooks Bros. Castle Gresley then to Victoria Motorways c.1938 To Bilson (showman) Carlton by 8/46, LL 11/50

1940

Reg	Type	Body	Config				Notes
VT 7065	TSM C60A6	Lawton	C32F	11/31	c/40	12/49	New to Wilshaw, Cheadle, then to Potteries Motor Traction Co. Stoke, w/d 1937 then to Brooks Bros. Castle Gresley hen to Victoria Motorways ?/40 To Rhodes (dealer) Carlton, 12/49
FV 1689	Leyland TS2	Burlingham	C32F	3/31	c/40	?/44	New to Wood Bros, Blackpool, then to Standerwick, Blackpool 9/36, w/d ?/37 then to Broadhead (dealer) Bollington 3/38 then to J.C.Broadhead, Bollington rebodied by Harrington, then Victoria ?/40 then to Viking Motors, Burton ?/44

1941 (Fleet Nos. carried by TF 3172, ATE 77-79, were those of Darwen Corporation, sequence later continued by Victoria)

Reg	Type	Body	Config				Notes
TF 3172 No. 9	Leyland LT2	Leyland	B32F	10/30	9/41	1/49	New to Darwen Corp'n On hire from Darwen Corpn 9/41 until purchased by Victoria 9/44 W/d 1/49 – no further operators
ATE 77 No. 11	Leyland LT7	E.E.C.	B32R	2/36	9/41	by 1957	New to Darwen Corp'n On hire from Darwen Corpn 9/41 until purchased by Victoria 9/44 W/d by 1957 – no further operators

Reg / Fleet No	Chassis	Body	Seating				Notes
ATE 78 No.12	Leyland LT7	"	B32R	2/36	9/41	12/57	New to Darwen Corp'n On hire from Darwen Corpn 9/41 until purchased by Victoria 9/44 To Biggs, Swadlincote 7/60, LL 4/63
ATE 79 No.13	Leyland LT7	"	B32R	2/36	9/41	12/57	New to Darwen Corp'n On hire from Darwen Corpn 9/41 until purchased by Victoria 9/44 W/d 12/57 – no further operators
FA 3889	Guy C	Guy	B26F	1/30	12/41	?	New to Burton Corporation Acquired by Victoria, but stated not to have been operated by them, then to Walters & Co., Brinsley then to Earth, Boston 3/46 then to Ward, Oakham 8/46, but apparently not opt'd
FA 3893	Guy C	'	B26F	1/30	7/42	?	New to Burton Corporation To G. Hobson (showman), Salford 4/47, LL 6/47

1942

Reg / Fleet No	Chassis	Body	Seating				Notes
CK 4336 -	Leyland TS2	Spicer	C—F	3/30	c/42	c/54	New to Scout Motor Services, Preston then to Winfield, London 3/37 w/d 5/42 *To Thistle Services, Benfield as C33F by 5/54* *then to Measures, Skegness 6/55* *Last licensed 12/56, scrapped 10/57*
FA 3856 -	Guy BB	Guy	B26F	12/29	7/42	?	New to Burton Corporation Acquired by Victoria, but stated not to have been operated by them, and used for spares
FA 3890 No.14	Guy BB	"	B26F	1/30	7/42	?/44	New to Burton Corporation scrapped 1944
FA 3894 No.15	Guy BB	"	B26F	1/30	12/41	?/44	New to Burton Corporation scrapped 1944

Note: FA 3890 & 3894 appear not to have been operated by Victoria, yet received fleet numbers, perhaps in anticipation of return to service.

1943

Reg / Fleet No	Chassis	Body	Seating				Notes
ARA 172 No.10	Leyland LT5A	Burlingham	B36F	6/34	?/43	12/54	New to Blue Bus Services, Willington, W/d – no further operators
GG 4946	Albion PMB28	Cowieson	C29-	11/31	c/43	?	New to Baillie Bros, Dumbarton then to Central SMT Co., Motherwell 6/36 w/d by 1939, then to Victoria 1943, re-seated to 31 To Viking Motors, Burton -/44

1946

Reg / Fleet No	Chassis	Body	Seating				Notes
ADG 742	Albion PK115	?	C—R	1/36	c/46	?	New to Phillips Bros, Penrhiwceiber w/d 4/46 Victoria c/46, then to Hyams, London, w/d 3/55
OV 9147 No.14	Maudsley ML3E	Rushton & Wilson	C32F	4/32	c/46	?	New to Grimsley, Birmingham then to Brooks Bros, Castle Gresley by 3/44 Disposal not traced
FA 8167 No.16	AEC Regal	Burlingham	B34F	4/46	4/46	6/59	To Mudd & Sons Ltd. Grimsby by 9/59 Last licensed 12/63
FA 8224 No.17	AEC Regal	"	B34F	6/46	6/46	2/61	To International Combustion Ltd., Derby 8/61 Last licensed 9/62

1947

Reg / Fleet No	Chassis	Body	Seating				Notes
FA 8791 No.18	Daimler CVD6	"	B35F	9/47	9/47	10/60	To Int'l Combustion Ltd., Derby 10/60 last licensed 6/64 by their associated Co., Cheadle Plant Hire Ltd., Cheadle, Cheshire
FA 8792 No.19	Daimler CVD6	"	B35F	9/47	9/47	10/60	To Int'l Combustion Ltd., Derby 10/60 last licensed 9/64 by their associated Co. Cheadle Plant Hire Ltd., Cheadle, Cheshire
FA 8822 No.20	Daimler CVD6	"	B35F	10/47	10/47	10/60	To Int'l Combustion Ltd., Derby 10/60 Last licensed 12/64

1950

Reg / Fleet No	Chassis	Body	Seating				Notes
FA 9847 No.7	Daimler CVD6	"	DP35F	5/50	5/50	12/64	W/d – no further operators

1960

BJP 271 No.15	Leyland PSUC1/2	Alexander	C41F	4/55	?/60	10/63	New to Smith & Co., Wigan then to Viking Motors, Burton 9/57 then to Victoria Motorways To Prout, Port Isaac 10/63, w/d 7/72
BJP 387 No.14	Leyland PSUC1/2	"	C41F	5/55	?/60	10/63	New to Webster, Wigan then to Silver Grey, Morecambe 4/56 then to Viking Motors, Burton 9/57 then to Victoria Motorways To Happy Days, Woodseaves 11/63, w/d 12/72

1961

DFA 548 No.8	AEC Reliance	Willowbrook	DP41F	5/55	?/61	5/66	New to Viking Motors, Burton To Coleman, Leverington 12/66 To Sykes & Son, Appleton Roebuck 8/68
DFA 550 *No.10*	AEC Reliance	"	DP41F	5/55	?/61	6/66	New to Viking Motors, Burton To Creed, London

1962

HFA 3 No.2	Leyland PSUC1/2	"	C41F	5/58	5/62	10/72	New to Viking Motors, Burton To Hollis, Queensferry 1/73, w/d 5/74 and to unknown owner, Glasgow

1963

JFA 519 No.12	AEC Reliance	"	C41F	3/59	?/63	6/66	New to Viking Motors, Burton To Martin Baker Aircraft, Crumlin, Co.Antrim 7/66, Sold by 7/88

1966

EFA 497D No.7	Bedford VAM5	Strachan	B45F	5/66	5/66	6/67	To Monty Coaches, Nuneaton 7/67, w/d 7/70 To County Travel, Leicester 7/70 for spares
EFA 498D No.8	Bedford VAM5	"	B45F	5/66	5/66	6/67	To Monty Coaches, Nuneaton 7/67, w/d 3/74 To Osmond, Curry Rivel 4/74, w/d 1/88 No further operator
EFA 499D No.9	Bedford VAM5	"	B45F	5/66	5/66	6/67	To Monty Coaches, Nuneaton 7/67, w/d 3/74 To Osmond, Curry Rivel 4/74 To Leigh Sinton Farms, Leigh Sinton 6/87
EFA 500D No.10	Bedford VAM5	"	B45F	5/66	5/66	6/67	To York Bros, Northampton 8/67 To Errington (dealer) Leicester 3/72 To Lloyd & Son, Nuneaton 4/72, w/d 10/82, sold 10/83

1967

HFA 207E No.7	Bedford VAM5	"	B45F	6/67	6/67	3/70	To County Fermanagh Education Committee, Enniskillen, -/72 – Re-registered AIL 4202 then to Western Education & Library Board, Enniskillen, 10/73 then to Celbridge Transport, Celbridge by 4/85, derelict at depot 5/86
HFA 208E No.8	Bedford VAM5	"	B45F	6/67	6/67	6/68	To General Omnibus Services, Chester-le-Street 7/68 then to Derwent Coaches, Swalwell 11/70 then to McLeod, Cheadle Hulme 2/71
HFA 209E No.9	Bedford VAM5	"	B45F	6/67	6/67	3/70	To Whitworth Holdings, Irthlingborough, by 8/72, w/d 11/81
HFA 210E No.10	Bedford VAM5	"	B45F	6/67	6/67	3/70	To J.M.Smith, Amble 5/70, w/d 4/74

1970

OFA 917H No.7	Ford R192	Willowbrook	B45F	3/70	3/70	1/73	To Weetabix Ltd., Burton Latimer 3/73 w/d 9/78
OFA 918H No.8	Ford R192	"	B45F	3/70	3/70	1/73	To John White Footwear, Higham Ferrers 3/73, w/d by 6/81
OFA 919H No.9	Ford R192	"	B45F	3/70	3/70	1/73	To Weetabix Ltd., Burton Latimer 3/73 w/d ?/78, to un-ident'fd owner as a transporter

1972

EFA 494D No.4	Bedford VAL14	Duple	C49F	4/66	12/72	7/73	New to Viking Motors, Burton To Wood's Taxis, Barnsley 7/73 then to Magnet Taxis, Barnsley 12/74 then to Johnson, Hazel Grove 11/76

1973

DFA 125L No.8	Ford R192	Willowbrook	B47F	1/73	1/73	10/78	To Horton's Coaches, Ripley, Derbys, then to Jones, Mansfield by 3/87
DFA 126L No.9	Ford R192	"	B47F	1/73	1/73	?	Disposal not traced
DFA 127L No.10	Ford R192	"	B47F	1/73	1/73	10/78	To Walwyn's Coaches, Maidenhead 8/79 then to Wacton (dealer), Bromyard 7/84 then to Sykes (dealer), Carlton 8/84
UFA 517J No.17	Ford R226	Duple	C53F	6/71	12/73	1/76	New to Viking Motors, Burton To Wood, Pollington 1/76, w/d 1/77, then to Astill & Jordan, Ratby 3/77, then to Yeates (dealer), Loughborough 9/82 then to Clifton Banderleros Jazz Band, Clifton, by 2/83

1974

SFA 196M No.16	Bedford YRT	Plaxton	C53F	6/74	6/74	5/80	To March, Kirkby

1977

TDP 25R No.2	Ford R1014	Plaxton	C45F	7/77	7/77	10/87	To Stevensons of Uttoxeter on acquisition of Victoria
TRY 3S No.3	Ford R1114	"	C53F	8/77	8/77	10/87	To Stevensons of Uttoxeter on acquisition of Victoria

1987

DDM 33X No.9	Leyland PSU3F/4R	Willowbrook	C47F	3/82	7/87	10/87	New to Crosville Motor Serv. Chester passing to Crosville Wales Ltd., Llandudno Junction 9/86, w/d 4/87 To Johnson (dealer), Harthill 4/87 To Victoria Motorways 7/87 To Stevensons of Uttoxeter, on acquisition of Viking & Victoria 10/87
LOA 834X	"	"	C49F	6/82	7/87	10/87	New to Midland Red (Express), Birmingham as C53F, 1/83 To Midland Red Coaches, B'ham 5/85 re-seated to 49 for one man operation 6/86 To Midland Red (North), Cannock 10/86, W/d 4/87. To Johnson (dealer), Harthill 4/87 To Victoria Motorways 7/87 To Stevensons of Uttoxeter, on transfer of ownership of Viking & Victoria 10/87

The vehicles, services, and business of Victoria Motorways Ltd., <u>but not the Victoria Motorways Ltd. company name</u>, were sold to Stevensons of Uttoxeter, with completion on 31st October, 1987. Four Victoria vehicles were included in the sale.

PLATE 126
Although registered as a Victoria Vehicle, SFA 196M was frequently used on Viking express services and tours, including regular forays to Blackpool, where it is seen parked in Rigby Road coach park, alongside another Viking coach. The coach park was alongside the ex-LMS/BR Blackpool Central loco shed, an obvious attraction for those interested in trains and train spotting. The large number of excursions to Blackpool, particularly during the summer and illuminations period, brought many engines to the shed.

VIKING & VICTORIA EMPLOYEES....

The number of people employed by Regent, Viking & Victoria between 1919 & 1987, would probably run into the two or three hundred, the majority of whom there is no photographic record. The photographs in this section are either from the Company's file, or from relatives and friends who would like to see their relatives remembered in this publication. Names are given where these are known.

PLATE 127 (left)
The late Ronald Woods, conductor with Victoria, seen here in Netherseal in the mid 1930's alongside EK 6409, the only Bristol bus ever owned by Victoria, was purchased in June 1933, but date of disposal is not known. Victoria's Netherseal garage front is just visible beneath trees on the right.

Courtesy Miss R. Walton

PLATE 128 (right)
Whilst the Victoria name is above the driver's screen, and Don Newbold (R), the registration xxB 601 is not listed in the Victoria section in The PSV Circle Fleet publication PD18. The author would like to hear from any reader who can supply details of this vehicle.

PLATE 129 (left)
Ernest Elliott, joined Victoria as a conductor in 1954, later obtaining his PSV licence to drive both Victoria and Viking vehicles, regularly driving the summer Yarmouth express service. After becoming John Lloyd's personal assistant, he was appointed Assistant Manager of the Company, and by way of tribute, Mr Lloyd described him "... as highly respected by his colleagues, and very popular with customers - a fine man".

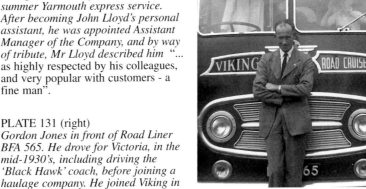

PLATE 131 (right)
Gordon Jones in front of Road Liner BFA 565. He drove for Victoria, in the mid-1930's, including driving the 'Black Hawk' coach, before joining a haulage company. He joined Viking in 1943, remaining with the Company until retirement.

Courtesy Mrs N. Jones

PLATE 130 (above)
Ernest Newbold in front of AEC No.FA 8167, in the traditional coach driver's white coat, on a short distance private hire trip.

PLATE 133
Don Leitch *Director*, flanked by coach drivers Alonso Staley and Ron Ratcliffe, seen in the Matlock Bath riverside gardens.

PLATE 132 (below) *L-R Ernest Newbold, Don Newbold, ? , Ray Price, Ernest Tipper, ? , on one of Blackpool's three piers.*

PLATE 134 (above)
1980's group of employees, pictured in 2003 during discussions for this book with John Lloyd - Malcolm Price, Brenda Veitch and Jane Musto.

PLATE 135 (above right) The Woodville team – L-R. Eric Nicholls, Sue Gardner *lady coach driver*, John Lloyd *director*, John Rowlands *coach driver*, Jayne Young *Travel clerk, Burton*, Graham Tomlinson, Margaret Doole *Mr.Lloyd's Secretary & Travel clerk*, – ? –, Evelyn Wileman *Travel clerk*, Roland King *Garage Superintendan* Margaret Lakin *Book-keeper*, George Paling *Garage hand and driver*, Alan Baxter *Garage mechanic*, Harry Jolle *Garage mechanic*, Eric Langley *Garage hand.*

PLATE 136 (left)
Jimmy Hassall was one of two fully trained mechanics to move from Maudsley Motors, Coventry, joining Viking as a driver and mechanical fitter in 1933. The other Maudsley trained man, Arthur Etherington, had joined Viking in 1932 as a mechanic, and he reportedly gained a reputation as 'being able to knit with fog' ... able to repair practically anything.

PLATE 137 (right)
Eric Nicholls, John Lloyd, John Holmes, Alan Baxter , Roland King, during a session with the author in 2002.

PLATE 138. *The Robin Hood Inn at Overseal Cross Roads, was the venue for a dinner for Viking & Victoria staff and their partners, see here in good form before commencing the meal. Those who can be identified are listed below:*

Facing line: L-R: *Mrs. Poultney – unfortunately the names of the line of ten ladies facing the camera cannot be recalled*
Centre line: L-R: *Colin Fairbrother, Joe Flint, George Poultney, Harold Shelley, Jack Stone, Jack Wykes, Albert Eames, Harry Tive Len Gilliver, George Paling, Ron Hallam, Don Leitch,*
Right hand group: L-R: *Stan Parkes, Ron Ratcliffe, Derek Law, Bill Bailey, Gordon Jones*

Gallery….more memories of Viking & Victoria….

PLATE 139
An excellent side profile of FA 9073, the first of three Daimler CVD6 with 33 seat Burlingham standard post-war style coach, delivered in June 1948. The rear half of this design and a front half with lower stepped waistrail, was first introduced by H.V. Burlingham in 1937. Note the badge, a black triangle with superimposed Viking head, with VIKING MOTORS along the lower edge.

PLATE 140
FA 9073 when new, and prior to receiving the name 'Viceroy'.

PLATE 141
The author with brother Graham at Sandringham, on one of mother's day trips to Hunstanton in 1948.

PLATE 142
FA 9073 after the original written style Viking *had been replaced by the block style. The 'Emergency Door' lettering has been re-positioned from the earlier bottom-of-door placing. The radiator sheeting has been painted black, making it less noticeable than that seen in Plate 140, and the radiator cap has been fitted with the miniature cast alloy Viking head.*

Courtesy R.Marshall

PLATE 143
The second of the three Daimlers, FA 9325 in standard livery, with block 'Viking' beneath windscreen, and the Viking radiator cap. The 1948-9 Burlingham half-cab coaches had – in the author's opinion – a very stately look about them and were very comfortable to ride in.

Courtesy R.H.G.Simpson

PLATE 144
Another picture of FA 9073, with Viking 'Viceroy' name and cut-out Viking badge on the side, but this time in the ownership of 'Says Luxury Coaches', Gloucester. It was sold by Says in February 1961, and exported to the Canary Isles.

Courtesy D. Fleming

PLATE 146 (below)
The second Burlingham Seagull AFA 953, on the return leg of the Yarmouth express service in 1952. It carries the original style gold-shaded-black Road Liner lettering – the apparent darker side panels are due to the type of film used to take the photograph.

PLATE 145 (right)
Two Viking AEC Burlingham's parked up at Doncaster Races c.1950, with driver Ron Ratcliffe waiting for the photographer.
Courtesy A.Prince

PLATE 147
This picture of AFA 953 taken on 15 March 1958, shows the un-shaded Road Liner lettering. The 'Valkyrie' name is seen nearside front.
Courtesy K.West

Viking's four Plaxton Venturers....

PLATE 148
The arrival of BFA 565 in April 1953 heralded the presence in the Viking fleet of a body builder previously un-used by the company. The full-front 41 seat Plaxton Venturer body, on AEC Regal IV chassis, was rather more imposing than the two Burlingham Seagull bodied coaches in 1951-2, and they were ideal for use on the long distance routes. BFA 565 was bestowed with the Vanguard name, which it retained after repainting into the two-tone grey livery in 1958. It is seen loading in Derby Bus Station on 11 August 1962, for the Friday overnight service to Torquay. The '4' in the front window suggests four vehicles on the Torquay service that evening.

Copyright Philip Thomas

PLATE 149 (left)
Sister vehicle, BFA 566, was delivered in May 1953, whereupon it was named Venturer. The only slight differences in appearance from it's sister (in the two photographs), is (1) the absence of a semi-circle above the AEC badge, and the higher placing of the AEC badge beneath the windscreen, and (2) BFA 566 has recessed indicator arms, whilst those on BFA 565 are flashing light pods. However, it is probable they both arrived with recessed indicator arms, and converted to the flashing pods.

PLATE 150 (middle)
RMB 159 was one of two Plaxton Venturers purchased secondhand from Altrincham Coachways Ltd., Altrincham. Cheshire in March 1954. They were new to A.C. in July 1953, and were fitted with four x 1/3rd wind down windows, not the four horizontal sliding windows on the two BFA series. RMB 159 is seen on 1st February 1964, after repainting in two-tone grey livery, having retained its Viscount name, albeit slightly higher placed than previously. The two destination panels are now above the windscreen, rather than below, as on the two earlier Venturers.

Copyright Philip Thomas

PLATE 151 (bottom left)
What could be a more appropriate name for a motor coach than the Voyager name on RMB 240, seen here parked in London.

PLATE 152 (bottom right)
Photographs of the rear end of coaches are generally few and far between, and when RMB 240 turned up at Crich Tramway Museum a few summers ago, the opportunity to capture this rear-end view was one which could not be missed. RMB 240 is believed to be the only ex-Viking vehicle in preservation, and it was in very good condition when it visited Crich. A preserved vehicle to look out for at bus rallies.

PLATE 153
DFA 550 as delivered in Viking livery in May 1955, with the cut-out Viking head badge. Whilst the box shape was the start of a new simplified psv body style, and replaced the earlier plethora of half-cab types, this Willowbrook dual purpose designated body was a less stylish simple box, than some of the later designs.
Courtesy P. Yeomans per J. Bennett

PLATE 154
In the two years following the arrival of the first two Willowbrook DP types DFA 548/550, with Viking, improvements to the styling of the basic box type were available, as seen on FFA 811, after arrival in June 1957. The chrome coach lines and destination panels below the front screen, make for a more purposeful and stylish appearance. FFA 811 remained a Viking vehicle until disposal in March 1966.

PLATE 155
An ex-work publicity illustration of HFA 3 prior to delivery from the Willowbrook factory in Loughborough. The livery is the short-lived light buff with red wheels and safety panel between the wheels, whilst the chrome trim serves to emphasise the late 1950's modern coaching style rather than the earlier bus appearance of the 1955 Willowbrook deliveries.

PLATE 156
A September 1960 view of HFA 3 parked in Nottingham in the light buff livery, with the addition of the Viceroy II name, which it retained after transfer to Victoria in May 1962, for stage carriage services. Courtesy K. West

PLATE 157
BJP 387 was one of two Alexander bodied coaches bought second hand by Viking in May 1955. Both arrived in a light buff and red livery, which contrasted with the Antique Red and Tan carried by Viking vehicles since the 1930's. This vehicle named Valorous II, *is parked alongside FFA 811.*
Courtesy P. Yeomans per J.Bennett

PLATE 158
The 'un-named' Alexander bodied Leyland, BJP 271, seen leaving Olympia London. Both BJP's were transferred to Victoria Motorways for bus work in 1960, before being sold in October 1963. Whilst the two were virtually identical, and both new to different Wigan operators, '271' was bought from J.Smith & Co. (Wigan) Ltd., and '387', new to Webster Bros. (Wigan) Ltd., passed to Morecambe Motors (Silver Grey) Ltd., before arriving with Viking.

PLATE 159
This March 1959 Willowbrook bodied AEC Reliance, JFA 519, received the name Vamoose *in a smaller different style of inclined block letters. Another vehicle which looked well in the light buff and red livery, and whilst the basic body style was very close to that of HFA 3, the greater area of red gave it a somewhat more striking appearance.*

PLATE 160
JFA 798 was the second Duple bodied Bedford to be purchased by Viking, arriving in June 1959. It was named Vampire, *and after eight years service it was purchased by an unidentified operator in Gwynedd, North Wales.*
Courtesy P. Yeomans per J.Bennett

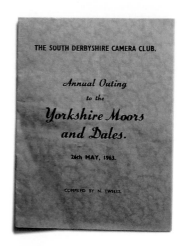

THE SOUTH DERBYSHIRE CAMERA CLUB.

Annual Outing
to the

Yorkshire Moors
and Dales.

26th MAY, 1963.

COMPILED BY N. TWELLS.

PLATE 161 (above)
NFA 317 is seen with a party of South Derbyshire Camera Club members enjoying a leg-stretch on the old A1 trunk road just north of Wetherby, on 26th May 1963. Well known local printer, Roy Till is seen with other members.

PLATE 162 (above right)
Brochure for the day trip to the Yorkshire Moors & Dales.

PLATE 163 (right)
The March 1960 arrival, Bedford SB3, LFA 153, was the second coach to carry the Valiant name, the first being the last Burlingham AEC FA 9354. LFA 153 is seen on the approach to Trent Bridge, Burton, having just crossed the Bargates junction.

Copyright P.Thomas

PLATE 164 (above)
PFA 438, the first coach in April 1962, to receive the two-tone grey livery from new, specially posed in the Woodville Brewery Yard depot premises.

PLATE 165 (right)
Something of a problem on the Coniston-Greenodd road, with NFA 316 unable to get past this Bedford SB3. Local tailor, Jack Bancroft is ready to take measurements, but the narrowness of the road at this point required a lengthy reverse manoeuvre by the Bedford to ensure safe passage for the Viking.

PLATE 166(left)
PFA 439 seen here in Derby Bus Station on 8th September 1962, ready to start the long overnight service to Torquay. Copyright P.Thomas

PLATE 167 & 168 (middle)
The two new 1964 arrivals, UFA 593 & AFA 134B, with identical Plaxton bodies, parked side by side at an unknown location.
Both Courtesy K.Lane

PLATE 169 (bottom)
This superb illustration shows not only the Bedford VAL14, CFA 646C, but also the Burton Enquiry Office and Garage frontage in Union Street, Burton upon Trent.

PLATE 172 (above)
July 1969 arrival, NFA 548G, together with sister vehicle, NFA 547G, were Ford R226 chassis with 53 seat Duple Viceroy bodies, and they had a more 'razor-cut' type of body than the customary Plaxton types used extensively by Viking throughout the 1960's.
Courtesy T.W.W.Knowles

PLATE 170 (top left)
Plaxton bodied Bedford VAL14, GFA 601E, seen parked in Derby, is believed to have been the last coach to carry the cut-out Viking badge.
Courtesy P. Yeomans per J.Bennett

PLATE 171(above)
One of two new Plaxton/ Bedford VAL70's in May 1968, KFA 776F appears to have had all Viking identification removed, and may be parked after disposal by Viking after only one year in the Viking fleet.
Courtesy P. Yeomans per J.Bennett

PLATE 173 (below)
Two further Duple Viceroy 53 seat coaches were delivered in early 1971, TFA 225J in February and TFA 226J in April. Both were on the Ford R226 chassis, and here the pair are seen in the Woodville garage yard, probably when the second had just been delivered.

PLATE 174 (above) *All that identifies this coach is the No.4 fleet number, with the photograph probably taken when the Plaxton Elite III type bodied Ford was new in mid-1973. The registration has been identified as GFA 480L. A further illustration of this coach during a London tour, is seen at Plate 40.*

PLATE 175 (left) *The Plaxton Elite III body style was adapted to produce the early 'Supreme' style c.1976. Whilst the basic body style remained largely unchanged, a new style of front panel was fitted. A deeper windscreen, lower destination window, and re-styled grill were the key changes, as seen here on OUT 353R.*
Courtesy Policy Transport Photos

PLATE 176 (below) *"another by PLAXTONS"*, reads the poster in the side window of this new Supreme IV, GJF 400V. Note the Viking head badge between the split trim levels, and new style of Viking name.

PLATE 177
Plaxton Supreme IV, EBC 672T, new in June 1979, is seen in Moreton-in-the-Marsh on 20th March 1983, whilst the passengers are away enjoying the ambience of this Cotswold town.

Courtesy K.West

PLATE 178
This side view of Duple bodied Leyland, LFO 800Y, in Station Street, Burton, shows the large advertising panel -"VIKING COACH TOURS & TRAVEL AGENCY" with Viking badge transfer, to good effect.

Courtesy R.Marshall

PLATE 179
The last new coach purchased by Viking was the dynamic looking Plaxton Paramount 3200 on D.A.F. chassis, delivered in June 1983, and registered as JGL 53, J.G. Lloyd's personal number plate. Mr. Lloyd is seen attending to alighting passengers, whilst there can be little mistaking the Viking name and 'king size' Viking head on the sides.
Whilst the vehicle passed to Stevensons in October 1987, the personalised numberplate was retained by Mr. Lloyd.

…..and more of Victoria Motorways….

PLATE 180 (above)
Whilst we believe this bus is the 32 seat TSM C60A7 type (Tilling Stevens Motors) bus, No. GX 2743, we have yet to identify the location. The driver is Stan Parkes, but the conductor has not been identified.

PLATE 181 (left)
FA 9847 is seen unloading at the end of Burton's Wetmore Bridge, and the Viking head badge on black triangle is clearly visible, despite the fact that it was registered as a Victoria vehicle. It remained in service until December 1964, when it was withdrawn. It served no further operators.
Courtesy K.West

PLATE 182
A rare nearside view of one of the postwar Burlingham buses. FA 8822 is seen at the Masons Arms Inn, Donisthorpe loading ready for re-tracing its steps into Burton. It was owned and operated by Victoria for 13 years, before being sold in October 1960 to International Combustion Co.Ltd. of Derby, for use as staff transport.
Courtesy M.Sutcliffe MBE

PLATE 183
The more common off-side front view of FA 8822 parked in Burton Wetmore Park, loading for its next trip to Donisthorpe. The large gold-edged black fleet No.20 is more evident than the 'Staffordshire Knot' emblem used as a badge on postwar Victoria vehicles, which is just seen on the panel in front of the wheel arch.
Courtesy P. Yeomans per J.Bennett

PLATE 184
No.19, Daimler FA 8792 parked in Burton Wetmore Park in between duties. It seems somewhat odd that whilst collecting material for this book, it has become evident that there were fewer pictures taken of the nearside than the offside, and I have yet to find one showing the back end. This may have something to do with the fleet number being placed only on the cabside.
Courtesy R.Marshall

PLATE 185
FA 8167 after repainting into the antique red & tan livery, as No.16 in the Victoria fleet, soon to set off on the Donisthorpe service, serving Stanton, Castle Gresley, Rickmans Corner, Overseal and Donisthorpe.
Courtesy P. Yeomans per J.Bennett

PLATE 186
The number of photographs of Victoria buses taken in Wetmore Bus Park, Burton, far out number those taken in other locations and along the routes to Donisthorpe and Measham. It may have been due to the fact that Wetmore Park was an interchange between Victoria, Midland Red, Stevensons, Blue Bus and Trent, and photographers had little time to get out on the various services. FA 8791, No.18, on the Measham service on 18th August 1957.
Courtesy K.West

PLATE 191
The Viking badges have been removed and HFA 3 is now in the two-tone grey livery. It has retained the Viceroy II name and although the illustration is undated it may have been taken after the registration was transferred to Victoria in May 1962.

PLATE 193 (below)
A simplified route diagram for the three 'X' services, showing the one-way only direction permitted by the licence through Burton town centre.

PLATE 192 (above)
A shining Strachan bodied Bedford VAM5 type, EFA 500D, taking on passengers for the Burton to Measham route. The two-tone grey livery and simplified 'VICTORIA' fleet names, give this box shaped body a very smart appearance. Four of these were purchased in May 1966, but the group were sold in June 1967 to Monty Coaches of Nuneaton.

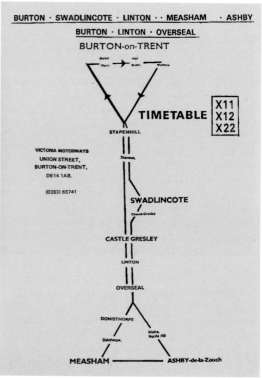

BURTON · SWADLINCOTE · LINTON · · MEASHAM · ASHBY
BURTON · LINTON · OVERSEAL
BURTON-on-TRENT

TIMETABLE   X11 X12 X22

VICTORIA MOTORWAYS
UNION STREET,
BURTON-ON-TRENT,
DE14 1AB.

(0283) 65741

STAPENHILL
SWADLINCOTE
CASTLE GRESLEY
LINTON
OVERSEAL
DONISTHORPE
MEASHAM ——— ASHBY-de-la-Zouch

PLATE 194
En-route to Donisthorpe through some delightfully rural countryside. The Willowbrook badge is a prominent addition to the grill on DFA 125L, the first of the three Ford R192's purchased in January 1973.
Courtesy R.Marshall

PLATE 195
*DFA 127L, another of the January 1973
arrivals, seen loading opposite the Co-op store
in Castle Gresley. The Willowbrook badges
were removed from the front panel before they
were sold in October 1978.*
Courtesy R.Marshall

PLATE 196
*The last of the three 1973 Willowbrook Ford R192 buses
to remain in use with Victoria. This view on 17 August
1985, was taken as DFA 126L travelled along Station
Street, from the direction of Burton Station, towards the
town centre, and some seven years after the two other
DFA's had been sold. The Willowbrook badge and the
'Victoria Motorways' lettering have been removed from
the front of the bus. There is no information on its
eventual disposal.*
Courtesy P.Swift

PLATE 197
*When Viking Motors secured several School Contracts in 1984, they
purchased two of these 76 seat Northern Counties bodied Daimlers,
which had already had 12½ years service with West Riding
Automobile of Wakefield. They arrived in August and were re-
furbished in time for the start of the new school year in September.
When not in use on school services, they were used on the X22
Burton-Linton-Gresley-Swadlincote service.*
Courtesy J.Bennett

PLATE 198
*LOA 834X, a 1982 Willowbrook bodied
Leyland had seen much use with various
Midland Red group companies, before it came
into Victoria ownership in July 1987. It
received an immediate repaint into two-tone
grey, and large lettering front and back, as
seen in this 5th September 1987 view taken
whilst loading in Station Street, Burton, for the
Linton-Gresley-Swadlincote route.*
Courtesy K.West

VEHICLE LIVERIES – General summary….

The only certainty in identifying vehicle liveries, is of course, either having seen the vehicles in real life, or good colour photographs. Since very few colour photographs were taken before the late-1950's, much reliance for livery has therefore to be placed on company records where these exist, the recollections of former employees, and those who can provide a general recollection from their own experiences of the company. All these sources have been used to compile the following summary of the three company's painting styles.

REGENT MOTOR SERVICES – 1919-1928
Red & Cream (or Light Buff) throughout the Company's existence, and the vehicles seen in Plate No 10 are in an overall light colour, with darker stripe below the windows.

VIKING - 1927-1957 – ANTIQUE RED & TAN
The first livery seen on RA 2838 (Plate 11) is believed to have been Antique Red & Tan. The side panels appear to be red, with 'tan' around the windows, mudguards and underside. This livery is seen to better effect on the Burlingham bodied AEC Regal coach No. FA 6199, Plate No.19 when new in March 1936. The last vehicle to be delivered in this livery was FFA 811(Plate 154). Lettering in gold edged black.

VIKING – 1957-1962 – LIGHT BUFF (Copper Fawn) & ANTIQUE RED
The arrival of two second-hand coaches in September 1957 (BJP 271 & BJP 387) in light buff with red around the side windows, were the first to carry this livery in Viking ownership. Five of the next six new coaches delivered to Viking were in these colours, albeit with various adaptations, eg. JFA 519 (Plate 159), NFA 317 (Plate 161). Lettering in gold edged black. NFA 316 & 317 were the only vehicles to carry polished aluminium strips along the red side panels.

VIKING – 1962-1987 – TWO-TONE GREY (Phantom Grey & Farina Grey)
This livery derives from being seen on a 1960's Rover 75 car at Chatsworth. The directors were looking for a new livery style, and the two-tone grey with chrome strip, met the requirement. Lettering in gold edged black. The first coaches to appear in this livery were PFA 438 & 439 April/May 1962. All subsequent vehicles, except the two double deckers purchased in 1984, were finished in slight derivations of this two-tone grey livery. The oldest vehicles to receive the two-tone grey livery, were the two 1953 Plaxton bodied AEC Regals, RMB 159 & 240 (Plate 228).

VIKING – 1984-1987 – DARK BLUE, WHITE & LIGHT BLUE ROOF
Two ex-Bradford double deck vehicles purchased in 1984, were the only vehicles to carry this livery.

VIKING – Viking's head Radiator cap
A cast aluminium Viking's head was fitted to the radiator cap, with FA 8882 appearing to be the first to carry this adornment. The six additional postwar half cab coaches also carried this radiator cap. The last new vehicle to be photographed with it, was FA 9847 on 15 June 1963 (Plate 225).

VIKING – Badges on side panels
1927 - Mr. Lloyd's first coach, RA 2838 (Plate 11), has lettering within an oval garter emblem – 'Viking' can just be made out within the top of the emblem.

1928 – The second vehicle in Viking livery, FA 3271(Plate 13), had 'The Viking Coaches' lettering within a garter circle on both sides and probably rear panel also.

1936 – 1949 – A full colour hand painted Viking warrior head superimposed on a black triangle, was carried on both sides. FA 6199, new in March 1936, is the earliest coach photographed with this badge. The last Viking coach to carry the hand-painted badge appears to have been FA 9354, a March 1949 arrival. However, the last vehicle to have the painted badge was FA 9847, a half-cab Daimler bus with coach seating, registered in the name of Victoria Motorways in May 1950, and carried until at least April 1952.

1949-1962 – A cut-out plastic Viking's head, with 'Viking Motors' along the bottom, first appeared on the sides of Burlingham Seagull AFA 499 in June 1951, held in place by six screws. The last new vehicle to carry this badge appears to have been GFA 601E, new in March 1967. However, FA 9073, 9325/6 are known to have had the transfer replaced by the cut-out plastic version. In the late 1960's, it became apparent that vehicles were returning to Woodville minus one or both plastic badges, and the decision was taken to remove all remaining badges.

VIKING – Viking head and name on side panels
VIKING in large letters, with or without Viking badge, appeared on the side of coaches in the late 1970's. The badge appears to have been in three distinct sizes, viz Plates 39, 176, 178, 179, and Plate 176 also shows a small Viking badge between the split level side trim.

Small Viking head between trim lines
Three Plaxton Supreme IV coaches, GJF 400V, LJF 735V, RJU 383W, had a small Viking head badge between a break in the horizontal side trim.

VIKING – Names applied to vehicles
Names beginning with **V** were given to a number of coaches, with the first of the Burlingham bodied half-cab AEC Regals, FA 8882, receiving the name *'Valorous'*. Mr. W. J. Lloyd's own list of names (Plate 201) includes those which were not applied. The lettering was gold edged black. The last new coach to receive a name appears to have been LFA 153 *'Valiant'*, delivered May 1960.
HFA 3 retained its name *'Viceroy II'* after transfer to the Victoria fleet, thus believed to be the last vehicle to carry a name.

VIKING & VICTORIA – Combined fleet number sequence:
FA 8882 was the first Viking coach to receive a fleet number in 1948 - No.22.   The first Victoria bus to carry a fleet number – No. 9 - was Leyland No. TF 3172 , and this vehicle was one of four to come to Victoria on loan from Darwen Corporation in September 1941. It was No. 9 in the Darwen fleet.   The other three loan vehicles were numbered 11,12 & 13. Two 1942 acquistions from Burton Corporation in July 1942, were the next to be given fleet numbers, 14 (FA 3890) & 15 (FA 3894).   They had previously been No's 37 & 41 in the Burton fleet.

VICTORIA MOTORWAYS (Sales Brothers) 1921- ? - *based on interpretation of photographic evidence*

1921 – R 3205 - the first Victoria vehicle in April 1921, a six seat Renault, is seen in Plate 94.   The livery appears to be:
WHITE ROOF, BLACK OR OTHER DARK COLOUR around the windows, possibly LIGHT BUFF lower panels, with CREAM between the window and lower panel.

1928 – UE 5643 - Reo Pullman vehicle new to Victoria in February 1928.   May have been BLACK WITH GREY ROOF.   It is interesting to note the 'Safety Coach' lettering below the winged badge, which may have been 'adopted' from the 'Safety Coach' addition on the sides of Regent Motor Service vehicles.

1934 – BEH 401 - Leyland 34 seat coach. The livery of this vehicle, brought to Victoria in December 1934 by a Mr. J. Hawthorn of Stoke on Trent, who had originally ordered it for his own coach company, is not known.   Mr. Hawthorn became a director of Victoria Motorways.   The livery could have been red and black or brown, similar in fact to Viking Antique Red & Tan.

1935 – GX 2743 - Tilling Stevens 32 seat bus (Plate 99) – this vehicle appears to have a GREY ROOF WITH BLACK AROUND THE WINDOWS AND BLACK MUDGUARDS.   This vehicle, new to Highways Ltd., London, in May 1932 , was purchased by Victoria in 1935, and Victoria may have put the vehicle into service without a full repaint, with only 'Victoria Motorways' fleet names being added to the sides, front and rear panels.

1935 - FA 5840 - Leyland coach (Plate 100/1).   New to Victoria in June 1935, it was known as 'The Black Hawk'.   Overall livery was BLACK with CREAM SIDE FLASHES, and a diving hawk as the side badge, presumably to give the impression of being a fast mover.

1941 – ATE 77 - Ex-Darwen Corporation vehicle (Plate 107).   The four vehicles received on loan from Darwen Corporation, arrived in September 1941, and retained the RED & CREAM Darwen livery.   The Darwen fleet No's 9, 11-13, were retained, and it is believed these fleet numbers were the precursor for the Victoria and Viking fleet numbering sequence.

VICTORIA MOTORWAYS – Lloyd, Leitch & Atkins (acquired 1943)

– RED & CREAM
The 1943 acquisition, ex-Blue Bus Services Leyland bus ARA 172, was repainted red and cream as standard Victoria livery.

Last Victoria bus to carry Red & Cream from new, is believed to have been FA8167, an AEC new in April 1946 (see Plate No. 113).

1946-1966 – ANTIQUE RED & TAN
No photographic evidence of the other four 1946-7 Burlingham bodied acquisitions (FA 8224/8791/2/8822) has been found, and it is assumed therefore, they were delivered in the Antique Red & Tan livery.   The last two in this livery were No's DFA 548 & 550, which were sold in 1966.

1960-1963 – LIGHT BUFF (Copper Fawn) & ANTIQUE RED
Three vehicles transferred from Viking Motors, BJP 271/387, JFA 519, retained this livery until sold by Victoria.

1966-1987 – TWO-TONE GREY (Phantom Grey & Farina Grey)
All services buses new to Victoria from 1966 onwards, were delivered in this livery. HFA 3, transferred from Viking in May 1962, received the two-tone grey livery in 1966.   The two July 1987 acquisitions, DDM 33X & LOA 834X, had received this livery by mid-August, 1987.

1987 – LIGHT GREY bottom panel, ROYAL BLUE centre panel applied to TFP 25R & TRY 3S – TFP 25R with LIGHT BLUE window surrounds – TRY 3S with DARK GREY window surrounds – both with route lettering on side panels.

VICTORIA – Winged emblem, with V in centre circle
c.1928 – UT 5643 (Plate 95) - a Reo bus new in June 1927, with REO 'winged' badge above the Victoria name.

1934 - BEH 401 (Plate 97) – a 'winged emblem' seen on the coach brought to Victoria by Mr. J. Hawthorn of Stoke-on-Trent.

VICTORIA – 'Staffordshire Knot' badge - 1946-1962
A large rope emblem in the form of the 'Staffordshire Knot', in gold shaded black, with a 'V' superimposed above 'M', with the bottom of the 'V' nestling in the mid-V of the 'M'.   The four ex-Darwen vehicles, and ex-Blue Bus (ARA 172), all carried the badge.   The 'Knot' badge was introduced with the Red & Cream livery, and applied to new vehicles and repaints into the 'Antique Red & Tan' livery.

Names applied to Viking coaches

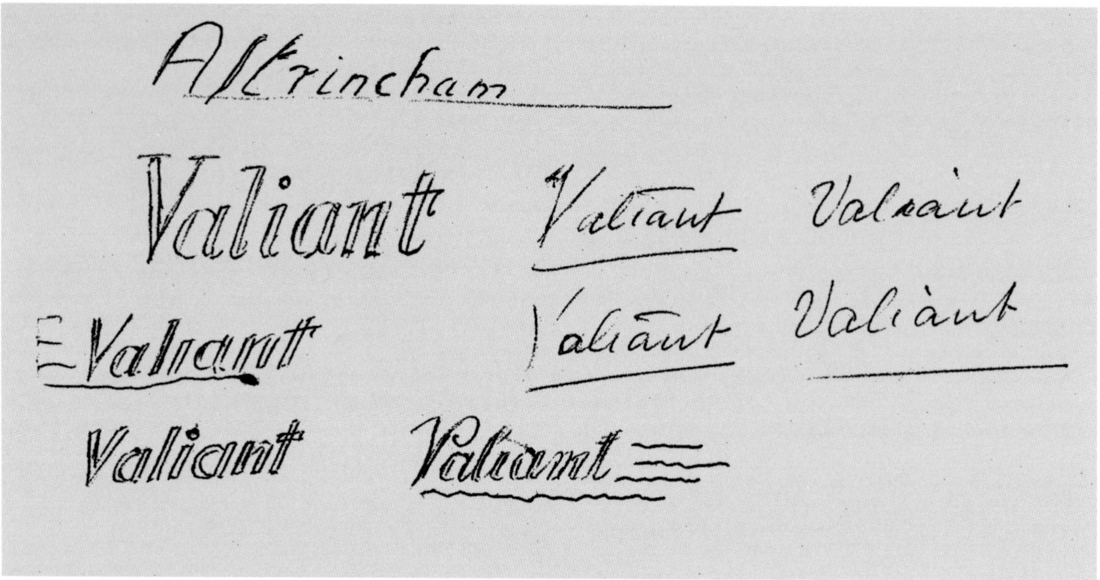

PLATE 199
When Mr.W.J.Lloyd deci
to add names to the 1
Burlingham coaches,
experimented with seve
different styles as shown
his original artwork.
bottom centre exam
appears to have b
nearest match to the st
which was used.

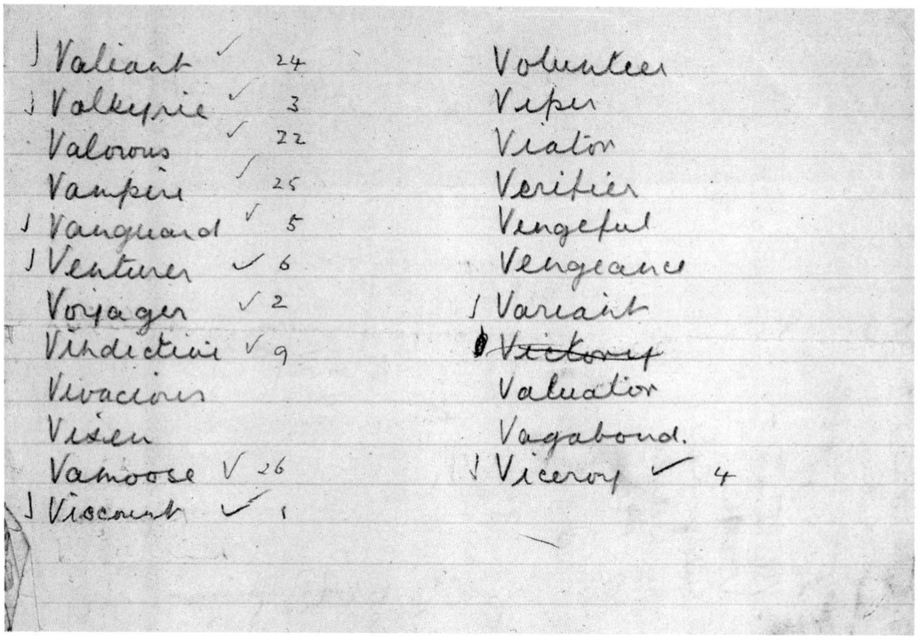

Valiant 24
Valkyrie 3
Valorous 22
Vampire 25
Vanguard 5
Venturer 6
Voyager 2
Vindictive 9
Vivacious
Vixen
Vamoose 26
Viscount 1

Volunteer
Viper
Viator
Verifier
Vengeful
Vengeance
Variant
~~Victory~~
Valuator
Vagabond.
Viceroy 4

PLATE 200 (left)
The original list of names. Sixteen coache were named, with Vamoose, Vampire *an* Valiant *being used twice.*

PLATE 201 (bottom left)
Mr. Lloyd's list of names applied, with flee and registration numbers.

PLATE 202 (bottom right)
Full list of coaches which received names, an the unused names.

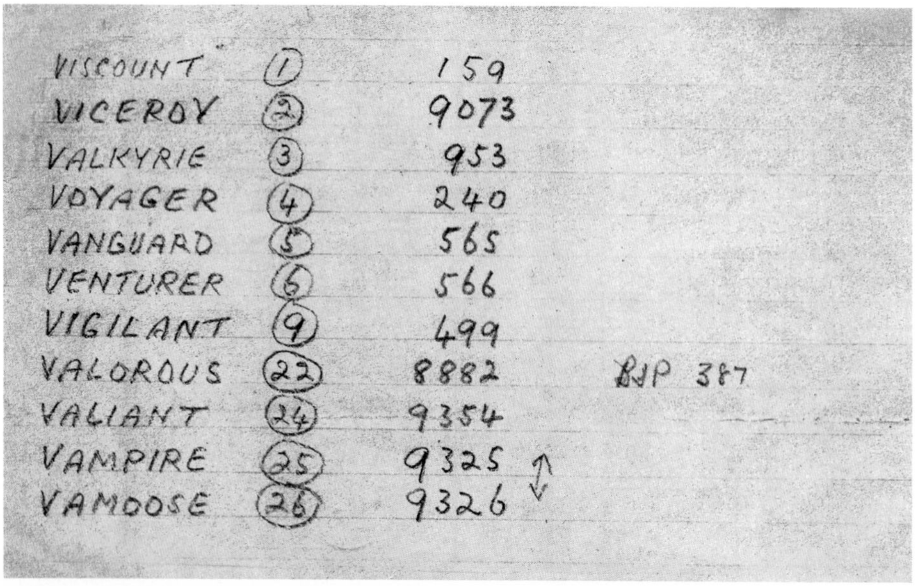

VISCOUNT	1	159
VICEROY	2	9073
VALKYRIE	3	953
VOYAGER	4	240
VANGUARD	5	565
VENTURER	6	566
VIGILANT	9	499
VALOROUS	22	8882 BJP 387
VALIANT	24	9354
VAMPIRE	25	9325
VAMOOSE	26	9326

VIKING MOTORS

Names given to Coaches

FA 8882		VALOROUS
FA 9073		VICEROY
FA 9325		VAMOOSE
FA 9326	JFA 798	VAMPIRE
FA 9354	LFA 153	VALIANT
AFA 499		VIGILANT
AFA 953		VALKYRIE
BFA 565		VANGUARD
BFA 566		VENTURER
RMB 159		VISCOUNT
RMB 240		VOYAGER
HFA 3		VICEROY II
JFA 519		VAMOOSE
BJP 387		VALOROUS II

Other names listed – no evidence to show they were applied to vehicles

VINDICTIVE	VENGEFUL
VIVACIOUS	VENGEANCE
VIXEN	VARIANT
VOLUNTEER	VICTORY
VIPER	VALUATOR
VIATOR	VAGABOND
VERIFIER	

Victoria & Viking in colour….

PLATE 203

This magnificent picture of the last of Victoria's half-cab buses in the antique red & tan livery, in Burton Wetmore Park on 15 June 1953. The Staffordshire Knot badge has replaced the original Viking badge seen in Plate 181.

It was withdrawn in December 1964 and initially stored with a view to preservation, but was later disposed of.

Copyright P.Thomas

PLATE 204

This former Viking dual purpose coach has had the Viking badge replaced by Victoria's Knot, and fleet number added. The mesh grill has been added to improve air supply to the under-floor engine, and advertising panels on both sides of the roof became an additional source of revenue. The building on the right was the Midland Red staff canteen in the Wetmore Park bus station, but bus crews from Victoria, Blue Bus, Trent and Stevensons were able to use the facility.

Courtesy K.West

PLATE 205

HFA 3 at one of Victoria's stands in the re-arranged Wetmore Park, in a well weathered condition. With the entrance alongside the driver, it was suitable for one-man operation and it was transferred from the Viking fleet to Victoria in May 1962, before finally being sold in October 1972.

PLATE 206
Whilst FFA 811 was never transferred to the Victoria fleet, it was used on Victoria services quite extensively in the last few years with Viking. This Burton Wetmore Park view was taken before its departure on the Donisthorpe service on a murky wet day. The Viking badges have been removed and whilst this picture is undated, it was probably taken in late 1965.

PLATE 207
EFA 498D, a May 1966 arrival, received one of seven consecutive number plates (EFA 494D-500D) issued to Viking/Victoria for new vehicles in 1966. The two-tone grey livery and simple VICTORIA name suits the Strachan body type.

Courtesy Policy Transport
Photographs

PLATE 208
One of the four Strachan bodied Bedford VAM5's purchased in June 1967, as replacements for the 1966 batch sold after just twelve months service. The main design changes were deeper side windows, less pronounced front panel and lower side strips, whilst the full VICTORIA MOTORWAYS name on the front and sloping VICTORIA above the front wheels in red edged gold lettering, are seen on HFA 208E.

PLATE 209
The 1970 batch of three services buses were Ford R192 chassis with Willowbrook bodies, and OFA 919H was the third arrival in March 1970. They were finished in a darker shade of grey than previous batches.

PLATE 210
The 1973 new service buses were also Willowbrook R192's, but with a lighter shade of main colour grey. The front grill extended across the width of the panel, with the prominent Willowbrook badge fitted. The full fleet name was retained, and DFA 125L is seen soon after delivery, and before advertising panels had been added.

Courtesy K.West

PLATE 211
This Plaxton Panorama Elite II bodied Bedford YRT, No. SFA 196M, was registered as a Victoria vehicle from new, it was regularly used for the full range of Viking express services and day trips, as some of the photographs in this volume will show. It is seen here on stage carriage work, at one of the newly placed stops which was part of the first re-organisation of Wetmore Park in the late 1970's.

PLATE 212 (above)
TRY 3S, with the Plaxton Supreme body introduced in the mid-1970's. The principal changes were re-styled panel below the windscreen and bolder grill, with simplified trim lines on the sides, compared with SFA 196M above.

PLATE 213
TRY 3S again, but the darker grey of the two-tone grey livery has been replaced with a royal blue panel, on which the principal route towns are shown. The panel around the windows is now sky blue. It is seen loading in Bank Square, Burton on 19 April 1986.

Courtesy K.West

PLATE 214
TFP 25R is another Plaxton Supreme, delivered in two-tone grey in July 1977, and like TRY 3S, Victoria's standard livery has been replaced with the royal blue and light blue panels in this 30 March 1987 illustration. The ASHBY name seen on TRY 3S had been removed when the service stopped running through to the Leicestershire town.

Courtesy K.West

PLATE 215 & 216 (below left and right)
In July 1987, a Leyland with Willowbrook 47 seat body, No. DDM 33X, was purchased secondhand after service with Crosville of Chester. It arrived in white with blue and red lines and black around the windows and the roof, but was quickly adorned with Victoria names and Viking badge added to the black grill before entering service. It is seen loading in Station Street, Burton, soon after arrival.

Both Courtesy K.West

PLATE 217
On the 15 August 1987, DDX 33X is back in Station St., in medium grey relieved by light blue panels, yet another livery variation for Victoria in the last few months of 1987.

PLATE 218
This forlorn looking DFA 126L is still in operation on 20 December 1986. De-frocked of all identity except the statutory ownership details in small print behind the front wheel, it is seen parked on the forecourt of the company's Union Street garage. It has the Linton-Burton destination blind showing and was probably waiting for its next journey to Linton.

Courtesy K.West

PLATE 219 *A selection of the types of ticket used by Victoria.*
Courtesy A.Condie

PLATES 220 & 221 *Victoria share certificates dated 1933 and 1942.*

COACHES & TRAVEL AGENCY

VIKING MOTORS (BURTON) LTD

Central Garage, Union Street, Burton-on-Trent. Telephone 5741 REGISTERED OFFICE
DE14 1AB

Branches: High Street, Woodville. Tel. Swadlincote 7012/3 · 70 Osmaston Road, Derby. Tel. 44634
DE11 7EA   DE1 2HZ

Please reply to:

61521

PLATE 222
A Viking letterhead overprinted with the Post Codes.

PLATE 223
'An Invitation' with ribbon, an enterprising venture designed to attract American visitors to Viking and the UK in the early 1980's.

PLATE 225 (above)
The aluminium 'Viking' head which was fitted to the radiator cap of one of the 1948 AEC Burlingham coaches, made into an ash tray.

PLATE 224
The cover and sample pages from the brochure circulated in America. The illustations were adapted from photographs with some artist's licence as regards the Boeing 707 in British Midland livery. The five coaches used for the line-up are the latest Plaxton Supreme IV type, and the coach side illustrations make for a smart and efficient image.

PLATE 226
An after-life for a Viking coach ! Something of a change of duties for BFA 565, seen here parked on the outskirts of Newport Pagnell in September 1965, after purchase with BFA 566 by Wilson Contractors of Northampton. The pair provided luxurious transportation for building workers from the Buckinghamshire area to building sites in the Luton area each day.

PLATE 227
Another annual outing of South Derbyshire Camera Club members, enjoying a picnic lunch in picturesque Wales against the backdrop of RMB 240 Voyager in 1961 – what better colour scheme than this on a bright sunny day!

PLATE 228
The two ex-Altrincham Coachways Plaxton's received the new two-tone grey livery and retained their names. RMB 240 is seen loading for an afternoon tour on the forecourt of Viking's Burton coach station and garage in Union Street. A grey RMB 159 is seen in Plate 150. The red wheels add to the overall excellent appearance.

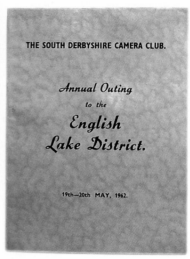

PLATE 230
H.J.Till, Printers, Swadlincote, printed the outing brochure.

PLATE 229 (above)
The light buff and red livery was adopted from the two secondhand Alexander BJP registered coaches which had arrived with Viking in 1957. NFA 316, with driver Norman Binns in conversation with the car park attendant, before parking for a short stay at Bowness on Windermere, during the South Derbyhire Camera Club weekend tour of the Lake District, 19-20 May 1962.

PLATE 231 (right)
NFA 316 is parked outside the Prince of Wales Hotel, Grasmere, where the group were accommodated, and took advantage of the long May daylight hours to photograph the local scenery.

PLATE 232
The author was Hon.Secretary of the South Derbyshire Camera Club in the early 1960's and the various photographic trips were always very popular. Amongst the group on the 1962 Lakes tour, are many recognisable faces – your author on the right !

PLATE 233
This sight of three Viking coaches parked in Torquay Coach Station in August 1964, greeted the author as he and family arrived for the return journey to Burton at the end of their holiday. The three had arrived after the usual overnight journey from Derby and Burton, and they just had to be photographed. UFA 593, NFA 317 and A134B were unquestionably – to the author - the smartest coaches around, and on a dull Torquay day without sunshine, NFA 317 looks even more pristine than its twin-grey sisters.

PLATE 234 (left)
PFA 438, the Leyland bodied Plaxton Panorama of 1962, is seen parked in the village of Crich, close to the site of the National Tramway Museum.

PLATE 235
The twin-grey livery suited the long sleek lines of the Plaxton Panorama body. UFA 593 is seen loading in Torquay's Lymington Coach Station in August 1965. Torquay was a hugely popular resort in the 1960's with the overnight journey serving to emphasise the 240+ miles from Burton, and Viking often required 2 and 3 coaches for this service during the peak period.

PLATE 236
The tartan upholstery in EFA 494D can be seen in this view, whilst the three axle Duple bodied Bedford VAL 14 is parked at the Crich Tramway Museum. The bright sunshine highlights the simple body trim.

PLATE 238
Another Viking parked in the Crich Tramway Museum car park. The Plaxton Panorama Elite II bodied Leyland, PHA 791H, was the only new coach for Viking in 1970.

PLATE 237
A ceramic ash tray with cigarette rest, produced as a promotional aid.

PLATE 239
Another Plaxton Panorama Elite coach standing in the Company's Woodville garage yard. Delivered new in August 1972 with gold shaded red TRAVEL VIKING transfers, BFA 435L is believed to be the only Viking coach to have received the colour matched lettering EUROPEAN & EXECUTIVE TRAVEL on the front panel as seen here.

PLATE 240 (above)
Plastic coasters are still a very cheap and popular promotional aid, and the 'punch-line' on this example produced for Viking, COACH HIRE FOR EVERY OCCASION encapsulates the raison d'être of the Company.

PLATE 241
The sleek lines of SFA 196M are evident in this view of the June 1974 new arrival, registered in the name of Victoria Motorways, rather than Viking, probably due to vagaries of tax allowances and the like.   It was a regular carrier of Viking tour passengers.

PLATE 242
The arrival of two double deckers opened a new era for Viking.   They were purchased second-hand and speedily repainted into a new two-tone blue and white livery, and emblazoned with Viking Travel adverts.   Much has been written about these two buses elsewhere in this volume, but there could be no mistaking their presence on the open road.   The newly liveried pair await their next School Contract turn in December 1984, the purpose for which they were bought. Courtesy K.West

PLATE 243
The addition of Viking posters to the lower deck panel add a carnival appearance to BHL 625K. The Viking head has been moved to the rear end of the upper-deck advertising panel, with the ABTA (Association of British Travel Agents) logo on the front side panel.   A Burton-Measham-Linton board is in the front window, whilst the top deck destination panel shows the Burton Office telephone number – BOT 65741. Courtesy K.West

PLATE 244
BHL 621K waits outside the Union Street, Burton Enquiry Office and Garage on 26 September 1987.   Note the repainted garage nameboard to match the 1980's Viking style. Courtesy K.West

PLATE 245
The wide open countryside to the North of the Woodville depot can be seen behind GJU 686N.

PLATE 246 top R
When the two-tone livery was first introduced, the boot door was finished in light grey, as seen here, with driver Joe Warren in the picture.   Courtesy Mrs.P.Warren

PLATE 247 (above)
However, in foggy conditions the all-grey back end was not as visible as it should have been, and door panels were changed to a more visible bright yellow, a change which improved Viking's identity not only on the road.   After the change, the company noticed a greater number of enquiries being received from across a much wider geographic area.

PLATE 249 below L
At peak times coaches would be used on Victoria services, as seen here with GUT 795N loading in Burton Wetmore Park on 22 December 1980.   Courtesy K.West

PLATE 250 below R
Plaxton Supreme IV EBC 672T X is on Old Christchurch Road, Boscombe, about to pick-up passengers for the Saturday afternoon return journey to Burton.

PLATE 248 (above)
A more startling Viking back end on the last ne coach purchased, but there are no telephone number
Courtesy A. Prin

VIKING
UNION STREET BURTON
HIGH STREET WOODVILLE
70, OSMASTON ROAD DERBY

WALES
SCOTLAND
BLACKPOOL
CORNWALL
ISLE OF WIGHT
DEVON

COACH HOLIDAYS IN BRITAIN — 1980

PLATE 251/4/5
A selection of the colourful holiday, tour and coach hire brochures produced by Viking.

PLATE 252 (above)
Original registration when new in July 1980, was LJF 735V. This Plaxton Supreme IV was re-registered as OFA 10 in 1985. This was one of three Supreme IV's to have the small Viking head between the split level trim (see plates 176 & 254/255).
Courtesy K.West

VIKING coach tours
of beautiful and
historic Britain

VIKING COACHES

PLATE 253
...from a Compliments Slip.

Registered Office:
**Union Street, Burton-on-Trent,
DE14 1AB.
Tel: Burton 65741.**

VIKING COACHES

High Street, Woodville,
DE11 7EA.
Tel: Burton 217012/3

Registered Office
Union Street, Burton-on-Trent,
DE14 1AB.
Tel: Burton 65741.

70 Osmaston Road, Derby,
DE1 2HZ.
Tel: Derby 44634.

VIKING travel
Coach Hire and Travel Agency Service

PLATE 256
A ticket booked in the name of Derek Kinsey, for the trip to see the 1950's entertainer, Frankie Lane, at the De Montfort Halls, Leicester on 11 October 1954.
Courtesy D.Kinsey

CONDITIONS : THE COMPANY RESERVE THE RIGHT TO CANCEL ANY ADVERTISED TRIP
ALL LUGGAGE IS CARRIED AT PASSENGER'S OWN RISK
AND MUST BE PROPERLY LABELLED ON BOTH OUTWARD
AND RETURN JOURNEYS.
PASSENGERS ARE REQUESTED TO COMPLY WITH TIMES
AND OTHER INSTRUCTIONS GIVEN BY OUR DRIVERS
THE COMPANY WILL NOT BE RESPONSIBLE FOR
PASSENGERS WHO DO NOT REJOIN THEIR COACHES AT
THE SPECIFIED TIME AFTER REFRESHMENT STOPS.

VIKING MOTORS (BURTON) LTD

TELEPHONES :
BURTON-ON-TRENT 3625 AND 3681, SWADLINCOTE 7212

M	Kinsey	DATE OF JOURNEY 11 10 1954
TO	Frankie Lane	TIME 4-0 P.M.
BOARD COACH	Union Street	

NUMBER		RATE	£		D.
3	ADULTS	7		1	7	—
	CHILDREN (UNDER 14 YEARS)				
RETURN JOURNEY - PICK UP AT			£	1	7

C09705
ISSUED BY | DATE OF ISSUE 6 9 1954

113

PLATE 257
This Plaxton Supreme IV was delivered a.
NAY 79W in 1980 (as seen here), but the
registration was cancelled, and it was re
registered as RJU 383W in 1981.   It is
carrying a school party

PLATE 258
The re-registered RJU 383W awaitin.
passengers at a motorway services area.
Courtesy P.D.Scot

PLATE 259 (left)
The popular tours programme was advertised under the Going Places *banner, and this 4*
page list of tours was produced monthly throughout the year.   Generally there is a choice
of five destinations each day and on Sundays an increased programme.   Sections on the
4th page included 'Route Code Letters' showing pick-up points, list of Booking Agents
general information on child and group fares, smoking, and a reminder of the specia.
'Norseman's Club' member fares.   An
Escape! *list of one or two night breaks*
between September and January, rounds of
this informative brochure.

PLATE 260
An impressive side view of JGL 53, the las.
new coach to be delivered from Plaxton in
June 1983.

The day the Vikings came to town....

Saturday 20 May 1978, was unquestionably a day for the crowds to take to the streets of the County Borough of Burton upon Trent, as Burton's Centenary Charter celebrations were marked with one of the most spectacular and best supported events the town has ever seen.   As the Burton Daily Mail reported *"...almost every major employer in the town was anxious to get in on the act and there was clearly plenty of competition for the best-dressed float award."*   The newly-installed Mayor, Councillor Peter Haynes, received the ceremonial robe and chain of office in a time-honoured ceremony on the evening prior to the Charter Day celebrations, and for the parade, he had pride of place in a veteran Rolls Royce, at the head of a 1½ mile long procession of more than 80 decorated floats through the town.

One of the most striking exhibits was Viking's coach decorated as a Viking galleon.

PLATE 261
The Viking's head was an all-in-one paper-mache piece, made by David Kite, Art Master at Granville School, with the wood effect bow front and side panels made of heavy paper.   The effective colourful shields were made by Granville pupils.

PLATE 262
The be-decked coach, OUT 352R, ready to leave Viking's Woodville depot.

PLATE 263
A smiling Joe Warren, honoured at being invited to 'drive' the galleon.

PLATE 264
The full effect of the decorations, ready for the procession.

PLATE 265 top L
Rear door understandably clear, ensuring maximum public value for Viking Motors.

PLATE 266 (above)
The float passing along a crowded High Street

PLATE 267 (left)
Seven Viking coaches line up for a publicity photo shoot Foremarke Reservoir c.1982.

PLATE 268
OUT 352R with number plates removed for photography.

Fine Coaches • Reliable Drivers • Experienced Staff
Cars de Luxe • Chauffeurs Dignes de Confiance • Personnel Expérimenté
Luxus-Reisebusse • Zuverlässige Fahrer • Erfahrenes Personal

VIKING MOTORS (BURTON) LTD
Woodville
Burton-on-Trent
England
Telephone Burton-on-Trent 217012